Key Concepts in
Drugs and Society

The SAGE Key Concepts series provides students with accessible and authoritative knowledge of the essential topics in a variety of disciplines. Cross-referenced throughout, the format encourages critical evaluation through understanding. Written by experienced and respected academics, the books are indispensable study aids and guides to comprehension.

Key Concepts in
Drugs and Society

ROSS COOMBER, KAREN McELRATH, FIONA MEASHAM AND KARENZA MOORE

Los Angeles | London | New Delhi
Singapore | Washington DC

Los Angeles | London | New Delhi
Singapore | Washington DC

SAGE Publications Ltd
1 Oliver's Yard
55 City Road
London EC1Y 1SP

SAGE Publications Inc.
2455 Teller Road
Thousand Oaks, California 91320

SAGE Publications India Pvt Ltd
B 1/I 1 Mohan Cooperative Industrial Area
Mathura Road
New Delhi 110 044

SAGE Publications Asia-Pacific Pte Ltd
3 Church Street
#10-04 Samsung Hub
Singapore 049483

© Ross Coomber, Karen McElrath, Fiona Measham and Karenza Moore 2013

First published 2013, Reprinted 2017

Editor: Chris Rojek
Editorial assistant: Martine Jonsrud
Production editor: Katherine Haw
Copyeditor: Jeremy Toynbee
Proofreader: Jacque Woolley
Marketing manager: Michael Ainsley
Cover design: Wendy Scott
Typeset by: C&M Digitals (P) Ltd, Chennai, India
Printed and bound by Henry Ling Limited, at the Dorset Press, Dorchester, DT1 1HD

Library of Congress Control Number: 2012945625

British Library Cataloguing in Publication data

A catalogue record for this book is available from the British Library

ISBN 978–1-84787–484–9
ISBN 978–1-84787–485–6 (pbk)

contents

key concepts in
drugs and society

about the authors

Ross Coomber, PhD, is Professor of Sociology and Director of the Drug and Alcohol Research Unit at Plymouth University, UK. He has been involved in researching a wide range of issues relating to drug use, drug supply and formal and informal interventions in many societies around the world for over 25 years. He has published extensively within the drug field and is the author of *Pusher Myths: Re-Situating the Drug Dealer* (2006) and co-editor of *Drug Use and Cultural Contexts 'Beyond the West'* (2004) (both Free Association Books) among others.

Karen McElrath, PhD, is a Reader in Criminology at Queen's University, Belfast, UK. Her current research interests focus on: (1) new psychoactive stimulants; (2) methadone maintenance as social control; and (3) changing patterns of crime in the context of political conflict. Her research is often 'user-led' and she has been actively involved with various drug services and governmental bodies in an advisory capacity. She is the author/editor of three books, over thirty journal articles and book chapters and of numerous reports to government bodies.

Fiona Measham, PhD, is Professor of Criminology at Durham University, UK, and is an internationally renowned researcher with 20 years' experience in the field of drug and alcohol studies, gender, licensed leisure and the night-time economy. She is co-author of *Illegal Leisure* (Routledge, 1998), *Dancing on Drugs* (Free Association Books, 2001) and *Illegal Leisure Revisited* (Routledge, 2010), based on large-scale studies of young people's drug and alcohol use, and co-editor of *Swimming with Crocodiles* (Routledge, 2008), a cross cultural comparison of young people's 'extreme drinking'. Fiona is a member of the Advisory Council on the Misuse of Drugs, a member of the editorial boards of the British Journal of Criminology, Contemporary Drug Problems, Drugs and Alcohol Today and Alcohol and Culture, as well as regular referee for a wide range of academic journals. In recognition of her expertise, she has acted as expert witness in major trials and as consultant to the media.

Karenza Moore, PhD, is Lecturer in Criminology in the Department of Applied Social Science, Lancaster University, UK. She has published widely on illicit drug use, particularly the relationship between drug policy, law enforcement practices and prevalence and patterns of drug use in leisure settings. Karenza has also published on electronic dance music (EDM) cultures and on social aspects of new media technologies.

acknowledgements

We are thankful for and would like to acknowledge the help and/or support of Eddie Scouller, Joan Gavin, Ellie Coomber-Moore and Dr Jonathan Chippindall at different times in the course of this project.

key concepts in
drugs and society

viii

preface

When Sage Publications initially approached us to undertake this project there was a mixture of excitement and trepidation mixed with a healthy dose of scepticism. On the one hand, we firmly agreed with the idea itself and believed the 'drug field' to be in need of a text that effectively bridges the gaps between the kinds of texts commonly available to those new to engaging with substance-related issues, but on the other were unsure as to how successful this might be in practice. Commonly, standard textbooks dealing with drugs that are not simply introductory texts will focus in on a specific area (for example, crime; treatment; drug policy) and deal with that in some detail. Alternatively, most introductory texts that cover a greater breadth of material and issues often struggle to provide a sufficiently critical stance on the topics dealt with and provide little more than a basic overview of the areas and also seek to cover almost everything about drug-related issues they can. In some examples this results in huge, very expensive encyclopedias too big to easily 'dip' into and too costly for anything but the most well-endowed libraries. The challenge we accepted then was to provide insight into around 50 areas of interest that relate to substance use in society that we considered to be of the greatest relevance for informing an open-minded audience about the use of drugs in society. Not everything that could have been in the book is in it and the book could easily have been twice as big either in terms of having an extra 50, or more, concepts or by spending twice the length of time on each concept we have included, or both. In the end we have worked within the parameters set by the publisher with one agreeable eye on the laudable aim set by those parameters: to provide accessible, critical insight into important key concepts related to drug use in society that is affordable and portable. The other key difference between this text and nearly all others on the market dealing with drug-related issues is the way that many of the issues are contextualised by reference to a genuinely international perspective. Insight is provided that locates many concepts outside of a simple European or North American context and provides reference where possible to broader relevant geographical examples. In this sense the concepts are all approached with an attempt to provide the reader with a sense of drug use around the world and beyond their own shores. What this does quite clearly in numerous concepts is to provide the reader with an awareness of how, for example, patterns of drug use or risk-taking behaviour, cultures of drug use, approaches to treatment and/or drug control and how drug problems are understood differ from what they may have previously assumed or experienced in their own locality as universal views or practice.

Specific examples of how the concepts and issues are located differently across borders can be seen when looking at, in Section I of the text which has a focus on Types of Drugs and Patterns of Use, **prevalence and trends in illicit drug use** generally but also specifically **addiction; legal drugs; binge drinking, and raves and circuit parties; dance drugs/club drugs** and most especially in **cross-cultural and traditional**

drug use. An international perspective is also valuable in Section II, which considers specific issues relating to drug effects. In this section it is valuable to appreciate the differences around the world in relation to **drug effects: drug, set and setting; medical marijuana and other therapeutic uses of illicit drugs; novel psychoactive substances; drug-related violence; HIV/AIDS and other blood-borne viruses**, as well as the conceptual differences that can be found in relation to concepts such as **the gateway hypothesis/stepping stone theory**. In Section III where there is a focus on drug policy, treatment and perceptions of the drug problem we find that an international or comparative perspective is particularly valuable when considering **drug treatment and quasi-compulsory treatment (QCT); the new recovery approach; international drug control history/prohibition; drug markets – difference and diversity; drug trafficking; crop eradication, crop substitution and legal cultivation;** the **war on drugs; drug testing in schools and workplaces; drug courts; decriminalisation, legalisation and legal regulation; liberalisation**.

The 'issue' of drug use in society is not a simple one. Much that is commonly thought about drugs is misconceived and much so-called commonsense understanding is unproven or simply false. Because of this a further aim of the book was to provide – wherever possible – readers with an opportunity to gain fruitful knowledge about drug use related issues that would stretch their current understanding and beliefs and expose them to ideas and concepts that encourage them to push the boundaries of how they conceptualise drugs, drug use and drug-related problems. There are numerous examples in the text where normative judgements and beliefs around these issues are confronted. Not all drugs do the things to people they are commonly thought to do (see, for example, **drug effects: drug, set and setting; addiction; drug-related violence; medical marijuana and other therapeutic uses of illicit drugs**) nor do drugs always represent a threat to individuals, communities and society (see **cross-cultural and traditional drug use**) or perhaps in quite the ways suggested (see **drug scares and moral panics; new psychoactive substances/'legal highs'**). How drug use should be understood and approached and dealt with is also highly contested and Sections II and III of the book deal with many of the issues in some depth and variety.

By way of how to read the book: it can be both 'dipped' into for insight into specific topic areas or it can be read as whole. In terms of the latter, the reader would gain cumulative knowledge about drug use and supply and the impacts of drug use on individuals and society as well as how society has viewed and responded to drug use historically and in the present day and some of the options it has beyond a simple approach mostly encapsulated by criminalisation and prohibition.

Ross Coomber, Karen McElrath, Fiona Measham and Karenza Moore

key concepts in
drugs and society

Section I
Types of Drugs and Patterns of Use

1
What Is a Drug/Medicine?

> A drug is any psychoactive substance that can alter the way the mind or body works, regardless of legal status or medical approval. It can be synthetic or produced from natural sources and can be used for a variety of reasons including medicinal, recreational and spiritual.

The perceived benefits of natural botanical substances have led almost all societies throughout history to extract the desired active ingredients from plants, minerals and fungi for their perceived curative, preventative, therapeutic or spiritual properties. Along with these drugs extracted from the natural world, drugs can also be synthesised in laboratories and produced within the human body. The effects of psychoactive substances vary greatly and can alter the way a person thinks, feels or behaves, along with changes in a person's perception of themselves and the world around them.

There are two main ways to define drugs. First, a distinction may be drawn between medicines, which are medically sanctioned psychoactive substances used for clinical purposes, and drugs, which are controlled substances whose use is not sanctioned either by law or by medical practitioners. Second, drugs can be classified according to their pharmacological make up and attributed psychoactive effects. However, the definition of what is a drug, and the distinctions between drugs, substances and medicines are disputed.

MEDICO-LEGAL DEFINITIONS OF DRUGS

First, in terms of the medico-legal definition, drugs can refer to psychoactive substances with a range of different legal statuses, including legal, illegal and quasi-legal drugs:

1 *Legal* drugs are those that can be legally sold, possessed and used, albeit often with certain restrictions. They include tobacco, alcohol, caffeine, volatile substances, and over-the-counter and prescription medicines.
2 *Illegal* or *controlled* drugs are those whose sale, possession or use constitutes an offence under the Misuse of Drugs Act 1971 in the UK, the Comprehensive Drug Abuse Prevention and Control Act 1970 in the USA and equivalent legislation in other countries. In the UK, illegal use of controlled drugs is defined as the 'non-medical usage of the drugs controlled under the Misuse of Drugs Act'. Furthermore, legal sanction of specific drugs can also relate to their

physical state, so that in the UK prior to 2005 possession of psychedelic or 'magic' mushrooms containing psilocin in their fresh state was legal, but if prepared for consumption in any way (such as dried or boiled), possession was illegal and the drug was classified in the most harmful category (Class A) under the Misuse of Drugs Act 1971, prior to the Drugs Act 2005 which extended control to psilocin in all forms.

3 *Illicit* or *quasi-legal* drugs is a less clearly defined term, which includes the 'grey area' between legal and illegal drugs such as those drugs that are not legally controlled but may face certain formal or informal restrictions on their preparation, sale or use. Three British examples are given here. First, in terms of *preparation*, in the UK before the Drugs Act 2005 brought all forms of psilocin under control, it was the preparation of psilocin or 'magic mushrooms' for consumption that made it illegal but it was not controlled in its freshly picked form. Second, the *sale* of solvents is restricted to over 16s and tobacco to over 18s in the UK. Third, its is illegal to possess GBL (gamma-butyrolactone) if intended for human consumption but not for *use* as an industrial cleaner. Certain drugs may be available on prescription but can also be purchased illicitly and without a prescription (for example, on the Internet), but are not socially sanctioned if used other than for their intended purpose, such as the 'misuse' of prescription medicines for 'recreational' purposes for example, the erectile dysfunction medication Viagra (sildenafil) (see **8 typologies of drug use**). Most recently, some novel psychoactive substances (see **novel 18 psychoactive substances**) could be considered illicit in that they are not formally controlled by legislation, at least when they first appear, but their use is not legally or socially sanctioned and therefore it would be unacceptable to ingest 'legal highs' in many social situations.

Some countries have formalised this quasi-legal status. In New Zealand, for example, an amendment in 2005 to the Misuse of Drugs Act 1975 added Class D to the three pre-existing classifications (A-C), creating a category of drugs for which there were regulations surrounding minimum purchase age, manufacture, sale, supply and advertising. Benzylpiperazine (BZP or 'party pills') was the first drug to be (briefly) placed in this new category although subsequently banned.

In the UK, the Medicines Act 1968 covers the *medical* use of drugs, (prescription, pharmacy and general sales), whereas the Misuse of Drugs Act 1971 covers the *non-medical* use of drugs, criminalising the possession and trafficking (supply, intent to supply, import/export, production) of controlled drugs. These drugs are classified into classes A-C in accordance with perceived levels of harm, and schedules 1–5 in accordance with ease of access. Other jurisdictions have similar classification systems. Recently these classifications have been subject to dispute (Nutt et al., 2010), raising concerns about the relative arbitrariness of such supposedly 'objective' measures of harm which form the basis for legal classification of 'drugs'.

PHYSICAL/PSYCHOACTIVE DEFINITIONS OF DRUGS

Second, in terms of defining drugs by their attributed physical or psychoactive effects, there are four broad pharmacological categories of drugs:

1 *Stimulants* ('uppers') are drugs that speed up the central nervous system, make the user feel more alert and energetic, causing people to stay awake for long periods of time, decrease appetite and make the user feel euphoric. For example, cocaine, amphetamines, nicotine, caffeine.
2 *Depressants* ('downers') are drugs that slow down the functions of the central nervous system and make the user less aware of the events around them. For example, alcohol, opiates (painkillers, for example, opium, morphine, heroin, codeine, methadone, Demerol, Percodan), sedatives/hypnotics (for example, barbiturates, such as Seconal, sleeping medications, tranquilisers such as Valium, Librium and diazepam).
3 *Hallucinogens* (psychedelics) are drugs that distort the senses and one's awareness or perception of people and events, possibly resulting in hallucinations (seeing or hearing things that do not exist). For example, LSD, PCP (angel dust), mescaline (buttons), psilocin (contained in 'magic' mushrooms).
4 *Deliriants* is a fourth category, sometimes submerged into depressants, which includes drugs that result in a dissociative effect between the mind and body, or 'out-of-body' experience. This has led some drugs in this category to be used as anaesthetics with humans and animals, for example, with children and on the battlefield, when traditional general anaesthetics may be considered to be either impractical or too risky for the patient. For example, solvents, ketamine.

It should be noted, however, that the above categories based on psychoactive effect can be modified by overlapping effects as some drugs fall into more than one category depending on the dosage, the individual user and other variables. So for example, cannabis, ketamine and alcohol are all perceived to have some stimulant properties at lower doses, but become predominantly sedative at higher doses. Furthermore, although the specific drug and strength of dosage is important, the existence and amount of other additives or adulterants, simultaneous use (see **6 polydrug use**), the physical and psychological characteristics of the individual user and the wider environment can also influence the psychoactive effects that a drug can have upon the user.

Other typologies of drugs include a distinction favoured in mainland European and Nordic countries between 'hard' drugs and 'soft' drugs (see **8 typologies of drug use**). 'Hard' drugs usually include those drugs which are seen as more likely to result in 'addiction' (see **4 addiction**), daily or problem use of drugs such as heroin and crack cocaine. A 'soft' drug primarily relates to cannabis but may also include other drugs such as those which are used occasionally and/or 'recreationally' and may also include hallucinogens and MDMA. In the Netherlands the distinction between 'hard' and 'soft' drugs is integral to their drug policy, with an official tolerance of the sale and use of small amounts of cannabis by Dutch residents in designated 'cannabis cafes' or coffee shops in order that cannabis users may access their drugs without making contact with networks of 'hard' drug suppliers (see **19 the gateway hypothesis**).

Drugs are not necessarily external substances. Within the body too, naturally occurring substances alter the way the mind and body works. Dopamine, serotonin and creatine, for example, are all naturally occurring substances that alter mood and performance, regulated by the body as well as potentially stimulated by psychoactive drugs. Given sugar and chocolate's effects on the body, they too have been described as drugs, although this expansion of the term to include such substances has been contested leading to a questioning of the term itself.

CRITIQUES OF THE TERM 'DRUG'

The debate between 'drug' and 'medicine'

The term 'drug' is both socially contested and culturally context-specific. Some countries (for example, the UK) distinguish between substances that are medically and legally sanctioned known as 'medicines', and substances that are disapproved of in some way and known as 'drugs'. By contrast countries such as the USA term all psychoactive substances regardless of legal status or medical sanction as 'drugs', as epitomised in the term 'drug store' rather than pharmacy. Other countries do not have a word for 'drugs' and do not make a distinction between socially sanctioned 'medicines' and socially disapproved or illicit 'drugs'.

For many researchers and commentators, particularly in Western societies, the distinction between a drug and a medicine is the difference in its formal or informal acceptability. As Mary Douglas (1978) expressed it, 'a drug is a chemical which is in the wrong place at the wrong time'. It has been argued that the distinction between 'drugs' and 'medicines' relates less to their relative physical or social harm and more to issues of regulation and social control (Ruggiero, 1999; Blackman, 2004). As Derrida famously noted, 'there are no drugs in "nature" ... the concept of drugs is not a scientific concept, but is rather instituted on the basis of moral or political evaluations' (1993, in Fraser and Moore, 2011: 10). Thus the concept of drugs, like the concept of addiction, can be considered to be socially constructed and based on historical and cultural context, value judgements and norms.

A distinction is sometimes drawn between legitimate drug 'use' and drug 'misuse' where the drug taking is judged to be inappropriate, dangerous and addictive (see **8 typologies of drug use**). Indeed Fraser and Moore have suggested that 'the category of drugs is an entirely political one ... it contains all substances society disapproves of at a given time, and which society says normal people should avoid, and want to avoid ... the terms "addiction" and "drugs" need therefore to be seen as social, cultural and political categories' (2011: 11). Additionally, MacGregor has noted that some cultures do not have a word to describe the concept of addiction.

The debate between 'drug' and 'substance'

There is also a debate between the terms 'drug' and 'substance'. The 1992 World Health Organisation expert committee included both legal and illegal psychoactive substances within its definition of the word drug – including alcohol and tobacco. By contrast the 1997 World Drug Report made a distinction between substances (which includes alcohol and tobacco) and 'the unauthorised or non-medical use of drugs which, because of their potential for causing dependence, have been brought under international control' (UNDCP, 1997: 10).

Given the contested nature of the term 'drug', some researchers have argued for the use of a more neutral term such as 'substance use' rather than 'drug use'. In making the case, Ettorre defines substance use as:

> Any substance, chemical or otherwise, that alters mood, perception or consciousness and/or is seen to be misused to the apparent detriment of society and the individual. By replacing 'drug use' with 'substance use' we are explicitly including new discourses on bodily management and regulation … from the viewpoint of women, 'substance use' is a more illuminating notion. (1992: 7)

SUMMARY

A 'drug' is usually understood as a psychoactive substance which alters the way that the mind or body works, and can be extracted from nature, synthesised in laboratories or produced within the human body. However, what counts as a 'drug' varies between historical and cultural contexts and the term can be seen as politically and morally value-laden in terms of which substances are legally and medically sanctioned or socially disapproved of, rather than related to the intrinsic qualities of the substance itself and its effects on the user.

REFERENCES

Blackman, S. (2004) *Chilling Out: The Cultural Politics of Substance Consumption, Youth and Drug Policy*. Maidenhead: Open University Press.

Douglas, M. (1978) *Purity and Danger: An Analysis of Concepts of Pollution and Taboo*. London: Routledge and Kegan Paul.

Ettorre, E. (1992) *Women and Substance Use*. Basingstoke: Macmillan.

Fraser, S. and Moore, D. (2011) *The Drug Effect: Health, Crime and Society*. Melbourne: Cambridge University Press.

Nutt, D., King, L. and Phillips, L. (2010) 'Drug harms in the UK: a multicriteria decision analysis', *The Lancet*, 376 (9752): 1558–65.

Ruggiero, V. (1999) 'Drugs as a password and the law as a drug: discussing the legalisation of illicit substances', in N. South (ed.), *Drugs: Cultures, Controls and Everyday Life*. London: Sage.

United Nations Office on Drugs and Crime (1997) *World Drug Report*. Vienna: UNODC.

Prevalence and Trends in Illicit Drug Use

*In behavioural or medical terms **prevalence** refers to the extent to which some-thing, like a disease or in this case drug use, occurs within a given population. For the purpose of this chapter the populations under consideration will be both world-wide and national with a focus on illicit substances. **Trends** are patterns that take place over time. When we look at drug use prevalence and trends we can see how much drug use is taking place, what changes in drug use have occurred and are occurring, where these changes are occurring and in relation to which substances.*

HISTORICAL CONTEXT

Drug use for recreational pleasure involving products from a multitude of naturally occurring substances (for example, plants, reptile venom/secretion, fungus, among others) has been a feature of nearly all societies for thousands of years. Depending on the particular moment in history and the particular group, we can see that drug use has been both extensive, and 'everyday' (like the current use of tea and coffee) in its usage, or that it has been highly ritualised, restricted and used for specific reasons such as religious ceremonies or something in between. Different drugs can be seen to have had different uses and meaning to different groups and for these to have shifted over time. In other words, a drug or substance does not carry with it a pre-determined or inherent way of being used, of being understood or a quality that means that society will react to it, or use it, in a particular way.

In terms of prevalence and trends we have no explicit data for the pre-modern and traditional worlds but we do know that specific forms of drug use used to correspond with the local availability of the substances. So Amazonian tribes would use hallucinogens available from vines and plant growth local to them and Asian communities found that local poppy and hemp plants provided opium and cannabis respectively. Patterns of use were influenced by culture and acceptability but sometimes also need. In England in the 17th century for example, beer (from local wheat or barley) was consumed as a main part of the diet for most ordinary people from breakfast through to evening (Schivelbusch, 1993).

In the end, exploration, trade, war and curiosity meant that many substances were increasingly exposed to other places throughout the world. Science has of course also added to the list through the production of numerous new drugs and in our increasingly globalised age both drugs and the cultures of use that surround them are more easily transported around the globe than ever before.

Much traditional drug use was highly integrated into everyday life as well as specialised activities of the societies in question and (see also **12 cross-cultural and traditional drug use**), contrary to contemporary views, often was not seen in terms of being a 'problem'.

MODERN CONTEXT

Drug use in modern societies is viewed (by most dominant voices, such as governments, the police and the media) quite differently. The non-medical use of substances that do not have a traditional place in those societies is now seen as essentially problematic and is often prohibited in law. The monitoring of prevalence and trends is seen as an important part of the effort to control such use, use that is deemed as fundamentally damaging to society.

PROBLEMS WITH MEASURING PREVALENCE AND OTHER TRENDS

Measuring prevalence and drug trends is an inexact science. Drug use and other 'deviant' behaviours are hidden and those involved may be less likely to declare involvement in surveys of the kind used to collect prevalence data. Moreover, although some of the prevalence data gives an indication of trends, for example, the proportions reporting having used in the last month, they tend to not to be able to disaggregate those that used once, twice or 20 times. Similarly 'lifetime use' prevalence statistics provide information on all those that have 'ever tried' a drug but this will include those that have used many times a day for decades as well as those for whom that first experience was the cause of them *not* continuing. Simply using prevalence data – as many governments do – as a straight-forward indicator of the nature of the drug problem is thus unhelpful. Prevalence data should be treated with due caution. That said, and with due caution noted, what follows now is an indicative outline of some drug use trends.

THE REALLY BIG PICTURE

In terms of prevalence and drug use patterns, the really big picture is that the last 50 to 100 years has seen an enormous growth in drug use around the world, both in terms of types of drugs being used and the populations that use them. The modern context is one in which there have never been so many drugs taken by so many people for so many different objectives. Within this shift, however, there have been some definite patterns that have emerged around specific types of drugs and drug using behaviour.

WORLDWIDE: PREVALENCE

According to the 2008 World Drug Report (UNODC, 2008a) the previous 10 years saw a relative stabilisation of drug use at around 5 per cent of the world's 15–64-year-old population. This means that around 208 million people around the world between the ages of 15 and 64 have used an illicit drug at least once in the previous 12 months and that that this has been more or less the case for the recent past. One drug that dominates nearly all the prevalence statistics is that of cannabis. With nearly 4 per cent of the global 15–64-year-old population (or 165.5 million people) using cannabis it literally dwarfs all other forms of drug use by comparison. The next closest – ATS, the amphetamine type stimulants – a group that combines the various amphetamines and various other 'dance drugs' such as ecstasy or ketamine accounts for less than 1 per cent (0.6 per cent) of the global 15–64-year-old population or 24.7 million. Cannabis use is thus nearly seven times more prevalent globally than the use of ATS, 14 times more prevalent than the use of heroin (0.3 per cent or 12 million) and 10 times more so than cocaine (0.4 per cent or 16 million). These figures compare to tobacco use of around 25 per cent of the global population (approximately 825 million) and relative mortality figures, where deaths from all illicit drugs is estimated at around 200,000 a year compared to 5 million a year from tobacco.

REGIONAL PREVALENCE AND TRENDS

ATS (amphetamine type substances)

A regional picture provides a little more detail. A recent United Nations report on ATS trends (UNODC, 2008b), for example, helpfully points out that ATS use, relatively stable and even in moderate decline in some 'mature' drug market nations in the 'West' and other developed nations, continues to be offset by growths in consumption in the developing world. Europe and North America for example, both regions that are close to the global average of ATS use, show little change in ATS and ecstasy use while ATS use in Africa and the Near and Middle East doubled between 2002 and 2006 (from a threshold lower than the global average). Nearly 55 per cent of the world's amphetamine users (around 14 million) are estimated to be in Asia and most of these to be methamphetamine users in East and South-East Asia. However, while ATS use overall has more or less stabilised, ecstasy use itself has grown in most parts of the world since 2002.

Ecstasy (MDMA) and ecstasy-group substances

Oceania (a region including Australia, Indonesia and New Zealand and numerous smaller nations), Europe and the Americas have consumption rates for ecstasy-group substances significantly above the global average and remain the primary consumption areas but the highest levels of growth were experienced in East and South-East Asia where they tripled between 2002 and 2006. Most growth of ecstasy use in the developed nations took place prior to 2001 and, at present at least appears to have plateaued, albeit at a comparatively high level. Prevalence of ecstasy-group substances nationally however, compared to cannabis is small. Regionally, ATS/ecstasy usage rates are below 1 per cent of the 15–64-year-old population and are often less than 0.5 per cent.

Cannabis

Cannabis use, as the global data shows, is much more prevalent and cannabis is the most used drug in most nations and regions. Table 1 shows this clearly.

Table 1 Global cannabis use

Geographical averages (Cannabis)	Cannabis users in 15–64-year-old population (5)
Global average	3.9
Oceania	14.5
North America	10.5
Africa	8
Europe	7

Overall, annual prevalence rates in Oceania declined slightly between 2002 and 2006. Western Europe and North America (despite Mexico showing an increase) have seen moderate declines in recent years while large *increases* in cannabis consumption have been reported for South America and for West and Central Africa.

Heroin and other opiates

The major opiate-based drugs are opium, morphine and other opiate-based pharmaceuticals, such as heroin. Heroin users constitute three-quarters of the 16 million opiate users globally or 0.4 per cent of the global 15–64-year-old population. Regionally we find that opiate use in Western and Central Europe along with North America has stabilised in recent years while parts of Eastern Europe, countries bordering Afghanistan (the world's leading opium producer) and East and Southern Africa have all seen a growth of use.

Cocaine

There is some argument for placing cocaine use within that of amphetamine type substances but cocaine has been part of the street drug scene for a longer period of time than most other ATS and is historically part of a distinct drug taking scene. As such cocaine data is often presented separately from other ATS data. Cocaine use on a worldwide scale has risen slightly in recent years with around 14.3 million users but has remained fairly steady at approximately 0.3 per cent of the global 15–64-year-old population (UNODC 2007). National and regional trends are more indicative however with 88 per cent of global cocaine use taking place in North America (44 per cent), in West and Central Europe (28 per cent) and South America (16 per cent – which includes Central America and the Caribbean).

Trends in cocaine use around the world are also meaningful. In North America (USA and Canada) the largest consuming region, some reduction has taken place in recent years but this has been offset in the global figures by increases in a number of South and Central American countries, such as Bolivia and Peru, and perhaps most significantly in Europe where the 2007 World Drug Report states 'Cocaine use … in contrast, continued to increase unabated' (UNODC, 2007: 84). In Europe the UK reports the highest levels of cocaine use with 6.8 per cent of the adult population reporting having 'ever used' cocaine with Italy and Spain reporting similarly high rates at 4.6 and 4.9 per cent, respectively. For recent use rates, most countries in Europe reported rates of less than 1 per cent whereas in the UK and Spain more than 2 per cent reported use in the previous 12 months (EMCDDA, 2005). For some of those countries in Europe where cocaine use continues to rise, regular use among younger urban groups looks set to consistently outstrip rates by young adults in the USA for the first time. Pockets elsewhere, such as in South Africa, are also seeing rapid rises in cocaine use whereas Australia and New Zealand have recently seen some moderate decline (UNODC, 2007). Whereas increased use of heroin mostly indicates a rise in addicted heroin use, the rise in cocaine use has been strongly associated with occasional and recreational use (for example, special occasions or use at weekends when at dance clubs or parties).

Other drugs

A range of other drugs, such as the psychedelics LSD and hallucinogenic 'magic' mushrooms, are also consumed (as are a range of 'legal highs' (see **18 novel psychoactive substances**) where users attempt to get a drug 'high' from legally available substances (such as nitrous oxide or 'laughing gas') intended for other uses. Prevalence of LSD and magic mushrooms is generally very low. Last year use rates for LSD in Europe in 2007 among the 15–24 age group was above 1 per cent in only three countries (Czech Republic, Estonia and Italy) and ever (lifetime) use for most European countries was less than 2 per cent. Prevalence rates for hallucinogenic mushrooms in Europe show lifetime use rates for the 15–24 age group that range from 0.3 to 8.3 per cent and last year rates that range from 0.2 to 2.8 per cent.

PREVALENCE INDICATORS AND WAYS OF USING DRUGS

All of the above only makes sense if we have a sense of *how* the various drugs are used. In the most simplistic of senses most drug use is moderate and will cause few harms. Prevalence simply relating to use therefore is not necessarily indicative of the amount of harm taking place. One example of this would be that of mephedrone – a synthetic compound that has some effects similar to ampheta-mine and MDMA – brought under control in the UK in 2010. Most illicit recreational drug use starts with moderate use and patterns of use develop. Although both cocaine and ecstasy were used more prevalently during 2009 and have many similar risk attributes, mephedrone, perhaps because of its legality, suddenly burst onto the drug scene and use among young people was rapid and (unusually) often excessive almost straight away. Simply looking at the prevalence figures would not reveal what was important about mephedrone use.

In a similar vein, a country may see a significant drop in drug use and hail its drugs policy as successful while at the same time have a worsening problem – as has been the case in the USA for much of the last 15 years. This is because recreational drug use of substances such as cannabis but also cocaine fell overall but problem drug use related to substances such as heroin and crack cocaine rose.

Prevalence indicators alone therefore are not a reliable indicator of the drug problem and the nature of it.

REFERENCES

European Monitoring Centre for Drugs and Drug Addiction (EMCDDA) (2005) *Annual Report: The State of the Drugs Problem in Europe.* Lisbon: EMCDDA.

UNODC (2007*) The World Drug Report.* Vienna: The United Nations Office on Drugs and Crime.

UNDOC (2008a) *The World Drug Report.* Vienna: The United Nations Office on Drugs and Crime.

UNODC (2008b) *Annual Report: Covering Activities in 2007.* Vienna: The United Nations Office on Drugs and Crime

Schivelbusch, W. (1993) *Tastes of Paradise: A Social History of Spices, Stimulants and Intoxicants.* New York: Vintage Books.

3

Why Do People Take Drugs?

Explanations for why people take drugs are typically based on individuals' biological and psychological traits, or are located within the historical, economic, social and cultural contexts in which an individual or social group is situated. There is no singular authoritative reason for drug taking.

In order to reduce drug use or harm from drug use, it is necessary to understand why people take drugs. Explanations can be divided into three broad types: biological, psychological and environmental, with the last including historical, economic, social and cultural factors. Explanations as to why people start taking drugs, known as initiation, may or may not be satisfactory in accounting for why people continue to take drugs or why people become dependent on drugs. It is most helpful to consider the ways in which biological, psychological and environmental factors overlap and less helpful to assume that there is a sole definitive reason as to why a person takes drugs.

Explanations for drug taking can be considered in terms of a continuum, from casual, experimental and recreational use through to heavy, dependent and problematic use. Some drug use is occasional and controlled, or regular but controlled, even with drugs widely deemed to be inherently 'problematic' such as heroin and cocaine. In addition, widespread, casual and relatively unproblematic use of legal drugs such as caffeine and painkillers is endemic to Western societies. Other forms of substance use include prescription drug use for minor and/or serious medical conditions alongside 'non-medical' use of prescription drugs, such as benzodiazepines.

BIOLOGICAL EXPLANATIONS

Research suggests that one of the reasons people take drugs is a biological or inherited, genetic predisposition to do so, as a result of a particular combination of genes rather than a specific gene (Muscat et al., 2009). However, genetic research is at its strongest when looking at why people continue to take drugs, rather than why people start to take them. Studies of twins have been used to identify genetic factors for drug and alcohol misuse, although there remain difficulties in separating genetic and environmental influences on drug use behaviours, even when adopted and non-adopted sibling pairs are compared. Genetic factors are 'risk' factors, which may have an influence on, but are not predictors of, drug and alcohol use. Drug use, particularly alcoholism and dependent opiate use, may be the result of a complex interaction between biological factors, familial transmission or hereditary factors, and social and economic circumstances.

PSYCHOLOGICAL EXPLANATIONS

Within psychological explanations as to why people take drugs, drug users are typically seen as distinct from 'normal' people (non-drug users) in terms of certain personality characteristics, such as being more or less neurotic, extrovert, impulsive or sensation-seeking (Muscat et al., 2009). In this model for explaining why people take drugs, certain 'abnormal' personality characteristics are thought to coalesce into an addictive personality that results in unhealthy behaviours. However, there remains little evidence of a unique 'addictive personality' that can be plainly recognised in individuals *prior* to drug and alcohol addiction (see also **4 addiction**). Perhaps more useful than the notion of an 'addictive personality' is the assertion that at certain points in their lives individuals may psychologically be in 'need' of drugs or alcohol (for example, at adolescence, during significant life events), but that only some then go on to develop patterns of use which prove to be problematic.

Severe mental illness is highly correlated with substance dependence or abuse. Many dependent drug users have a history of mental illness that leads to either self-medication with drugs or a tendency to find drugs helpful in some other way as a means of fulfilling psychological needs. It is often difficult to untangle from case history data whether a psychiatrically disturbed individual's drug use was caused by, or resulted in, mental illness. In such cases, comorbidity is used to denote an individual with a dual diagnosis of, for example, bipolar disorder and opiate misuse. Comorbidity of severe mental illness and alcohol and drug misuse is associated with increased risk of psychiatric admission, suicidal behaviour and poor treatment outcomes. One further suggestion is that those with psychological difficulties may take drugs not as an act of self-medication, but as a form of chronic self-harm and a means of self-destruction.

Other psychological explanations for why people take drugs rest on perceived differences between genders. Men are more likely to take psychoactive drugs than women and are more likely to be heavy and/or dependent users. This may signal an interaction between biological and psychological differences between males and females, as well as social and cultural factors such as gender expectations surrounding 'appropriate' behaviours. For example, it may be more socially acceptable for women to take prescribed tranquilisers as a coping mechanism, or for men to drink to excess in public places as a show of 'masculinity'. Gender differences in the use of various illicit and licit drugs are narrowing in certain contexts, suggesting that socio-cultural change has an important impact on use patterns.

Age is another factor related to patterns of drug use. Young people are more likely to use drugs, possibly to combat adolescent anxieties and to aid relaxation through intoxication. There may also be structural reasons as to why young people are more likely to take drugs related to the life-course, such as the likelihood that young people have more leisure time and fewer responsibilities than adults. Research with young people (and adults) highlights the ways in which they actively use alcohol and drugs to create 'time-out' from their daily routines. Young people may simply be curious about drugs and seek 'risky' new experiences through them, with 'risk-adversity' tending to develop later on in the life-course.

ENVIRONMENTAL EXPLANATIONS

A chaotic home life, family breakdown, child neglect or abuse, being a looked-after child in institutional care, educational underachievement and related problems such as truancy and exclusion from school, unemployment and underemployment, being of a lower socio-economic class and having parents and siblings who condone drug use or are dependent drug users themselves, have all been suggested as reasons why some people use drugs. 'Risk factors' should not be put forward as causal explanations for why people take drugs. Although, it may be useful to identify such risk factors in order to undertake targeted interventions or to prevent problematic drug use, locating the 'cause' of drug use solely in one or even several of these factors can result in stigmatising individuals and social groups. Alongside looking at why people take drugs, we can ask why people do not take drugs, or why they abstain. Abstention from drug use is conceptualised in terms of 'protective factors', namely what might 'protect' people from taking drugs; having a stable family life is one example. Protective factors tend to be the inverse of risk factors.

British young people who are socially excluded, specifically being 'not in education, employment or training' (NEET), are more likely to develop problematic adolescent drug use patterns. In the USA, severe social deprivation has been linked to crack cocaine use, while in Australia and New Zealand, dependence on methamphetamine is more likely to be experienced by materially deprived individuals, particularly members of indigenous cultures. Broadly speaking, research demonstrates that economic deprivation and social exclusion are correlated to drug taking, particularly problematic forms such as dependent use. However a direct causal relationship has been harder to prove, with the notion of risk factors moving in to fill this explanatory gap in recent times.

Other environmental explanations for why people take drugs rest on explorations of the kind of societies we live in. Sociological theorists have long argued that widespread drug taking apparent in the post-war era of Western capitalist societies is a result of an erosion of norms, morals and values defined as anomie, which includes forms of personal and societal alienation. In the face of pressures to achieve social status and be successful in mainstream society by obtaining a good education, a well-paid job and a stable family life, some people become alienated, 'drop out' from 'straight' society and instead take up 'alternative' drug-orientated lifestyles offering a different form of subcultural outsider status. Such individuals or subcultural groups are then labelled as deviant as a result of their drug taking, leading them to become further distanced from mainstream culture in a process of deviancy amplification, which may in turn further entrench drug taking. Another classic sociological explanation of drug use is reference group theory which states that most drug use originates in previously developed intimate personal groups (Dull, 1983). Simply put, if your friends use drugs then it is likely that you will too. It is within such groups of friends and associates that people learn to take drugs and to enjoy their effects.

What such sociological explanations highlight is that we cannot seek to explain why people use drugs without reference to the historical, social and cultural contexts in which they do so. It has been argued for example that there has been a **14 normalisation** of 'sensible' controlled 'recreational' illegal drug use among UK young adults (particularly in relation to cannabis), which goes some way to explain high rates of drug use prevalence in the country, rates which rapidly increased in the late 1980s, 1990s and early 2000s. While not explicitly concerned with why people take drugs, normalisation theory does illuminate the context in which individuals and their immediate personal groups may consume drugs. Normalisation may be differentiated. This means that within certain social groupings, use of specific drugs is accepted as 'normal' or socially acceptable, as with cannabis use among jazz musicians in the 1950s, ecstasy use among ravers in the 1990s, or alcohol use among some North American student fraternities or sororities. More generally, in terms of historical changes in Western societies in the post-war era, 'recreational' drug use is but one expression of consumer-based youth cultural lifestyles, often played out in profitable night-time economies, where a 'controlled loss of control' or calculated hedonism achieved through drug intoxication is widely accepted and even expected in some youth scenes.

PERCEPTIONS OF DIFFERENT DRUGS

An important consideration as to why people take drugs relates to perceptions of certain drugs. As Schivelbusch (1992) notes, in the past it was acceptable to consume 'beer for breakfast', while such behaviour in contemporary Western society is likely to be interpreted as the actions of an 'alcoholic'. Some people take 'soft' drugs, such as cannabis, but would not consume what are perceived to be 'hard' drugs, such as heroin. The legality or illegality of a drug may have an impact on how people perceive that drug and its users and in turn whether they would take it themselves. It is in this sense that people's perceptions of different drugs may be related to the fashions and social mores of the era in which they live. That people perceive particular drugs differently alerts us to the multiple reasons as to why people do or do not take specific substances, including historical changes in their social acceptability, of which tobacco smoking in Westernised countries is a prime example.

TAKING DRUGS FOR FUNCTION, FUN AND PLEASURE

A final explanation as to why people take drugs rests on the assertion that drug users experience pleasure from drugs and from being intoxicated, or that specific drugs fulfil particular functions in people's lives, as with tobacco users gaining confidence, feeling calmer or relieving boredom through cigarette smoking. Researchers have tended to frame pleasure as the outcome of a cost-benefit analysis of the user as a 'rational actor'. This rational user decides which drug or combination of drugs carries least likelihood of harm and is most likely to benefit them in terms of reaching a desired 'function' or effect such as enhancing wakefulness or confidence (Boys et al., 2001). In contrast, Duff (2006) argues that pleasure as a reason for taking drugs needs to be considered in the context (or setting) the user is in, and that functionalist 'rational actor' theories of drug taking ignore this context. This body of work's contribution to understanding why people take drugs rests on the somewhat controversial acknowledgment that it is possible to enjoy, have fun and gain pleasure from drug taking (Decorte and Fountain, 2009). This possibility has largely been ignored by drugs research and drug policy with its focus on risk and harm. By framing all (illicit) drug use as inherently problematic, drug research and policy have tended to obscure the possibility that one of the main reasons people take drugs is that they perceive various states of intoxication to be profoundly pleasurable.

REFERENCES

Boys, A., Marsden, J. and Strang, J. (2001) 'Understanding reasons for drug use amongst young people: a functional perspective', *Health Education Research*, 16 (4): 457–69.

Decorte, T. and Fountain, J. (eds) (2009) *Pleasure, Pain and Profit: European Perspectives on Drugs*. Lengerich: Pabst.

Duff, C. (2006) 'The pleasure in context', *International Journal of Drug Policy*, 19 (5): 384–92.

Dull, R. T. (1983) 'An empirical examination of competing sociological theories of drug use', *Criminal Justice Review*, 8 (1): 17–23.

Muscat, R., Korf, D.J., Neigreiros, J. and Vuillame, D. (2009) *Signals From Drug Research*. Strasbourg: Council of Europe.

Schivelbusch, W. (1992) *Tastes of Paradise: A Social History of Spices, Stimulants, and Intoxicants*. New York: Vintage/Random House.

Addiction

> *For an individual whose drug or alcohol use becomes a daily activity, for whom consumption proves difficult to limit, reduce or stop and where that consumption interferes with the health and/or well-being of the individual concerned that person is commonly said to be **addicted** or **dependent** on the substance(s) in question. Exactly what that means however is open to debate. A strongly pharmacological, chemically based, view would suggest that addiction is mainly caused by the ability of the substance to 'addict'; a bio-chemical view that both genetic predisposition and substance are of primary importance and a more 'social' and psychological view that addiction to drugs may be but one form of addictive behaviour where substances play a part but perhaps not the primary one in knowing what addiction is.*

Pinning down exactly what 'addiction' is has proven difficult. What may appear to be a straightforward and easily definable phenomenon for many, does in fact, when considered closely, have characteristics that confound most theories about what *it* is. In the USA the idea that addiction is a *disease* is the prevailing belief whereas in Europe and the rest of the Western world the disease model is considered far less convincing and problematised to a greater degree. Ultimately, addicted drug and alcohol use is the continued use of a substance that somehow becomes repetitive 'compelled' use, where desisting from that use is very difficult and for some, seemingly impossible. Knowing the roots or essence of that behaviour is more difficult.

HISTORICAL VIEWS

Understandings of what addiction or dependency is however are themselves subject to the context in which they arise. Prior to medical definitions such as those laid down by the World Health Organization (WHO) or the American Psychological Association, or pseudo-medical definitions such as those provided by organisations such as Alcoholics Anonymous (AA) and Narcotics Anonymous (NA), addiction was variously understood more simply as a habit or a weakness of will. Common to many ancient and contemporary religions and philosophies (for example, Protestantism, Islam, Catholicism, Buddhism, Taoism, Confucianism) is a condemnation of 'excess' (around almost any behaviour), a concern that excess leads to behaviour that is uncontrolled and as such transgresses 'good' appropriate – and thus moral – behaviour. Controlled and abstemious (sober, temperate) behaviour thus has a long tradition with being associated with good and moral conduct and excess as being synonymous with immorality. From the early 18th century, various temperance movements (temperance means 'restraint', to temper, to control) – mostly religious in origin and motivation – and focusing mainly on alcohol, sprung up in various locations around the world. Ideas around temperance became influential and impacted upon government thinking and policy in many countries. This influence reached its zenith in 1919 in the USA when Congress prohibited the manufacture, transportation, sale and importation of alcohol – a period known as *prohibition*. This early view that associated excessive and habitual drinking with immoral behaviour essentially saw evil in the alcohol being consumed and the consequent weaknesses of those consuming it.

Although many doctors were also involved in temperance lobbying and activities, these doctors were often religious and morally motivated first and scientists second (Harding, 1998). The late 19th and early 20th centuries were also periods when doctors and pharmacists were seeking to gain control over various areas of public life as which they perceived to fall properly under the remit of medicine. Seeing addiction as a disease was consistent with medical thinking of the time and beneficial to it as an emergent profession (Berridge, 1999). Addiction as a disease, and one which robbed the 'good' individual of self-control and free will, became the dominant way of talking about and thinking about it.

BIO-CHEMICAL POSITIONS AND CONTEMPORARY 'DISEASE' POSITIONS

The current dominant medical/'scientific' position (at least in the USA) on the nature of 'addiction' is that it is essentially a brain disease. Neuroscientific evidence that the brain undergoes physical changes when drugs are used – some of which are permanent – has been used to argue that the effect of drug use is to produce progressive disease states which have negative health effects on the body. A number of studies (mostly 'twin' studies) have also shown that there is a genetic aspect to addiction whereby some people are more likely, because of their genes, to succumb to addiction (although which people exactly will succumb cannot be predicted, even if those genes are found as not all these people will). This provides a dominant view of addiction as bio-chemical in nature – that both biology and substance 'produce' an addictive state or disease.

RESEARCH THAT CONFOUNDS SIMPLE UNDERSTANDINGS OF 'ADDICTION'

Problematically however there is a range of research that confounds many conventional and even recent theories of addiction and behaviours assumed to be requisite of the addicted state. No one really questions that the brain is involved when a person takes psychoactive drugs (if it was not involved the drugs would not be psychoactive), however the questions that remain are whether these changes and the substances used 'produce' addiction. There are circumstances, for example, when people who use drugs deemed addictive, such as heroin, do not become addicted; when chronically addicted persons are able to become un-addicted; when individuals display addictive or compulsive type behaviours but no drug is present. All are examples that confound simple disease or bio-chemical notions of addiction or addiction connected simply to substances. Similarly, although some people may be more biologically predisposed to succumbing to an addictive state, it is far from the case, to the point that reliable prediction is *not* possible, that all those genetically predisposed will become addicted and to understand why we have to look beyond biology and chemicals.

Older research (pre-1970s) appeared to confirm that addiction was almost definitely permanent. Treatment populations were thought of as being in a 'revolving door', 'chronically relapsing' scenario whereby they would be treated, they would relapse and they would return to treatment. Addicts that did not reappear or the relative absence of older addicts and/or the relative absence of older addicts led to the belief that they were thought to have died off. Relatively recent research on addicted individuals, research that does not simply focus on treatment populations (the most chronic of addicts), confounds notions that addiction is permanent, a disease, necessarily uncontrolled or substance/biologically determined. As we shall see, such research is more consistent with seeing addiction as a syndrome (or a set of symptoms) rather than a disease.

VIETNAM VETERANS

When Lee Robins and colleagues published their research on returning Vietnam soldiers in the early 1970s, the findings impacted enormously on thinking around addiction, effectively 'turning it on its head'. The research looked at a group of over 900 returning US soldiers in 1972. Roughly 700 of these had either tested positive for opiates prior to leaving Vietnam and/or admitted to having developed either physical or psychological dependence on them. A follow-up of these soldiers 8–12 months after their return (83 per cent now civilians) found that only 5 per cent showed signs of dependence, even though around 20 per cent had continued to use in some form over the previous year. The research indicated that opiate dependency was not necessarily a chronic relapsing condition and suggested that the context in which drug use takes place as well as people's attitudes to why they are using impacts strongly on the motivation or not to continue to use even drugs of addiction such as heroin (Robins et al., 1974). Vietnam was, for many soldiers, a horrific place combined with boredom and uncertainty. Drug use was prevalent. On their return soldiers' re-entered an old familiar context that appears to have enabled and facilitated a return to a non-dependent and diminished drug using–lifestyle.

'MEDICAL ADDICTS'

Other physically dependent groups have also been observed to be able to give up opiates (heroin and morphine) relatively easily. Therapeutic patients, for example, those recovering from operations or injury, prescribed opiates for pain relief and who develop a physical dependency have fewer problems stopping opiate use because they are not using it for pleasure but for medical purposes. As such their association with the drug and the way they 'connect' to it is not psychologically strong. Dealing with the physical discomfort – and thus the physical dependency – of withdrawal for these individuals is relatively easy to manage and 'addiction' is not fully achieved.

CLINICAL POPULATIONS

Clinical populations tend to be different from non-clinical populations. Robins' returning veterans did not seek help for their drug use and represent a group of dependent and regular users that were able to manage, control and mostly leave dependent use behind them. Clinical populations tend to be of the most severely affected individuals that struggle to do this more than others. Simply studying clinical populations thus distorts how we understand problems such as addiction as it provides examples of the condition at its very worst. In a similar way if we only studied lifelong pathological criminals it would only provide a partial picture of what criminality is as many people 'grow out' or 'mature out' of criminality.

MATURING OUT, DESISTING FROM SUBSTANCE USE AND ADDICTION

Just as many people – for various reasons - 'mature out' of criminality, many heroin or other drug users 'mature out' of drug use and even of dependent heroin use. This clearly indicates to us that life circumstances – as indicated by the Robins' studies – and individuals play a stronger part in the process of being addicted than a focus of the drug alone or on addictive personalities or brain disease would allow. Studies of people that leave their addictions behind show that people (sometimes after many attempts) become 'ready' to give up. This may involve new motivating factors such as a new relationship, the end of a relationship, a death, a new opportunity – the list can be long but what is meaningful is that an individual, when ready and given facilitative circumstances (despite genetic predisposition and/or level of use) can decide to leave their addiction behind.

ADDICTIVE PERSONALITY

There is no research evidence of the 'addictive personality' existing in terms of a specified set of behaviours related to particular personality traits or groups of people. Some people do believe they have an addictive personality and indeed some people act this way and follow through on their belief, providing little personal resistance to compulsive behaviours. In Coomber and Sutton (2006), for example, a small group of people moved to daily use straight away because they believed 'that's what you do' or 'that's how it is done' – they were neither physically nor psychologically addicted at that point – their daily use was driven by their expectation of how to use the drug, not chemicals or personality.

NON-ADDICTED, CONTROLLED AND RECREATIONAL HEROIN USE

One of the reasons that addiction is understood as relating primarily to substances is because the substances themselves have been imbued with powers they do not have. Heroin is not simply addicting and not immediately so. Addiction is a process. Addiction to heroin 'on the street' regularly takes more than a year and often more than six months (Coomber and Sutton, 2006). Zinberg (1986) and numerous other studies since have found heroin users and even crack cocaine users (some that have never been addicted and others that have recovered) that use in non-dependent ways, in a controlled manner, for recreational purposes. This fundamentally under-mines both our conventional understanding of both the drugs themselves and the nature of them to addiction.

OTHER COMPULSIVE BEHAVIOURS: NON-SUBSTANCE BASED 'ADDICTIONS'

It is now widely accepted in the addictions field (other than by those bent on stipu-lating addiction to be a disease – despite the broader research evidence) that there are a number of excessive compulsive behaviours that are non-substance based but mirror the symptoms of substance-based addictions, that is, the behaviours are rela-tively uncontrolled and compulsive, excessive, cause individual and family problems and relate to a particularised entity such as pathological: gambling; sexual activity; shopping; eating; online gaming; or exercise. Importantly, excessive compulsive behaviours such as these conform to the various clinical addiction indexes (which are symptom based) that are used to diagnose a substance addiction.

ADDICTION AS A BEHAVIOURAL PROCESS, NOT A DISEASE OR RESULT OF SUBSTANCE ALONE

This leads us to a point whereby we might recognise addiction to be a process that can be strongly influenced by the context and circumstance in which it emerges – and, just as importantly, in which it recedes. An individual may immerse them-selves in a stimulus (drug or activity) to a harmful degree and find themselves in a situation where they are involved in excessive compulsive and problem drug use, gambling and so on but choices and circumstance play an important part in how this develops. We know, for example, that some social structures, such as good social support and religion, are protective against addiction.

Exactly how we understand addiction, therefore, that is whether it is a 'syn-drome' (Shaffer et al., 2004) where a range of symptoms form something that has been classified as addiction, or as a mostly psychosocial phenomena (Peele, 1998) that suggests we are all capable of succumbing to varying levels of dependence (dependence on parents; on significant others) and that this underlying propen-sity sometime spirals and focuses on specific drugs or behaviours, is difficult to pin down exactly at this stage. What we do know is what it is not. The broader social scientific research evidence suggests that the position that argues it is sim-ply about bio-pharmacological relationships is overly simple and cannot account for the numerous research examples, such as those listed above, that confound it.

REFERENCES

Berridge, V. (1999) *Opium and the People: Opiate Use and Drug Control Policy in Nineteenth and Early Twentieth Century England*. London: Free Association Books.

Coomber, R. and Sutton, C. (2006) 'How quick to heroin dependence', *Drug & Alcohol Review*, 25 (5): 463–71.

Harding, G. (1998) 'Pathologising the soul: the construction of a 19th century analysis of opiate addiction', in Ross Coomber (ed.), *The Control of Drugs and Drug Users: Reason or Reaction?* Amsterdam: Harwood Academic Publishers. pp. 1–12.

Peele (1998) *Visions of Addiction: Major Contemporary Perspectives on Addiction and Alcoholism.* Lexington, MA: Lexington Books.

Robins, L.N., Davis, D.H. and Goodwin, D.W. (1974) 'Drug use by U.S. army enlisted men in Vietnam: a follow-up on their return home', *American Journal of Epidemiology*, 99 (4): 235–49.

Shaffer, H.J., LaPlante, D.A., LaBrie, R.A., Kidman, R.C., Donato, A.N. and Stanton, M.V. (2004) 'Toward a syndrome model of addiction: multiple expressions, common etiology', *Harvard Review of Psychiatry*, 12(6): 367–74.

Zinberg, N. (1986) *Drug, Set and Setting.* New Haven, CT: Yale University Press.

5
Legal Drugs: Alcohol and Tobacco

> *While social and legal structures discourage or ban the use of many drugs, some drugs are not outlawed. These legal drugs are subject to forms of regulation to reduce prevalence, control use and minimise harm. Control policies, such as restrictions on pricing, availability, advertising and retail practices, have varied effect, with taxation being the most effective way to control use at the population level and voluntary advertising codes of practice being the least effective.*

Drugs that are legal to sell, possess or use are subject to certain forms of regulation. Broadly, drugs that have been controlled through regulation rather than prohibition have tended to be those with a longer history of both use and misuse, as well as perceived medicinal or spiritual benefits rather than recreational (see also **8 typologies of drug use**). Novel psychoactive substances whose recent emergence means that they have not yet been assessed and regulated, are covered elsewhere (see **18 novel psychoactive substances**).

PREVALENCE

Alcohol

In countries where alcohol is legal, adult prevalence rates are very high with the majority of the population drinking on at least an occasional basis, although wide variations exist within populations influenced by ethnicity, religion and other factors (see also **13 gender, ethnicity and social class**). Patterns of consumption also vary markedly across the world. For example, in Europe a distinction is made between 'dry', northern European beer and spirit drinking countries and 'wet', southern European wine drinking countries. Traditionally in 'wet' countries, smaller amounts of wine are consumed on a daily basis with family-based meals. In 'dry' countries, consumption focuses on less frequent consumption of larger quantities of alcohol for the purpose of intoxication at non-family-based social gatherings. From the mid-1990s, initially in northern European countries, such as Ireland, Denmark and the UK, young people developed a pattern of increased sessional consumption (see 9 **binge drinking**), although recent general population and schools surveys suggest that this is now declining, with evidence of growing numbers of abstainers and light drinkers. There is also evidence that these northern/southern European distinctions are blurring: previously lower consumption countries, such as Ireland and Finland, are now exceeding previously higher consumption countries, such as France and Italy; young people in southern Europe increasingly drink spirits and beer; and wine consumption has increased in northern Europe. In the UK, the real price of alcohol has halved since the 1960s and adult consumption has risen in parallel with this increasing affordability, along with increased sales outlets and extended trading hours (as discussed later).

Tobacco

Tobacco was imported to Europe and North America from South America from the 16th century onwards. Smoking increased significantly in the late 19th and early 20th centuries with the advent of commercially manufactured cigarettes and peaked in developed countries around the time of the Second World War. For example, in the UK at its peak, nearly three-quarters of men and one-half of women smoked. However, with the discovery of a confirmed link between smoking and lung cancer in Richard Doll's ground breaking report of 1950, as well as the development of public health campaigns and a growing acceptance of the role of government in directing individual lifestyle choices, smoking fell in developed countries in the later decades of the 20th century. For example, currently 19 per cent of men and 15 per cent of women smoke in the USA; 25 per cent of men and 23 per cent of women smoke in the UK; and 35 per cent of men and 26 per cent of women smoke in the Netherlands.

Smoking continues to rise in developing countries, however, with cigarettes being both a symbol of adulthood for youth and an identification with Western consumer branding, associated with more aggressive advertising in less robust regulatory environments. As with developed countries, the increase in smoking occurs first among men, then women. For example, 47 per cent of men and 17 per cent of women smoke in India; 60 per cent of men and 16 per cent of women smoke in the Russian Federation; and 82 per cent of men and 17 per cent of women smoke in Afghanistan. It is estimated that 1.1 billion people (one-third of adults) currently smoke across the world and that this will rise to 1.6 billion people by 2025. Annual deaths are expected to rise to at least 10 million people every year by 2030.

POLICY: TYPES OF REGULATION

Regarding regulation, a key distinction is whether the target audience for interventions is the whole population (favoured by public health bodies), target subgroups of the population who are at greater risk of harm (favoured by the alcohol and leisure industries) or a combination of the two strategies. Further differences arise from distinctions between mandatory regulations and voluntary codes of practice within the alcohol, leisure and advertising industries.

Brand et al. (2007) conducted a comparative analysis of alcohol control policies in 30 countries across the world and developed an Alcohol Policy Index to gauge the strength of each individual country's alcohol regulation. Overall, they estimated that alcohol consumption causes 4 per cent of the global disease burden. Based on five areas of regulation: (1) physical availability; (2) drinking context; (3) price; (4) advertising; and (5) use of motor vehicles – Brand et al.'s index showed that alcohol controls vary widely between countries, ranging from Luxembourg at the bottom to Norway at the top, with the UK and USA in the middle. The study revealed a strong inverse relationship between alcohol consumption and strength of alcohol controls: a 10 per cent increase in the strength of controls was associated with a 1 litre decrease in alcohol consumption per person per year.

Physical availability

Alcohol and minimum purchase age

In most countries, in most circumstances young people under 16 cannot buy alcohol although many teenagers can acquire alcohol from friends or relatives; at first drinking at home with parents from their early teens and later with friends at unsupervised parties and outdoors. A substantial minority buy alcohol underage from off licences and shops, or from licensed premises, although this is increasingly difficult with proof of age and identity card schemes. For both alcohol and tobacco sales, rigorous enforcement and intensive staff training substantially increase the effectiveness of the law on minimum purchase age.

In most countries it is legal to buy alcohol from the age of 18. Two systematic reviews have concluded that raising the minimum purchase age reduces consumption and alcohol-related road traffic accidents involving young people. In the USA, the National Minimum Drinking Age Act 1984 operates across all 50 states and establishes the legal drinking age at 21 years old, one of the highest in the world. A 40-year review of the evidence in the USA by Wagenaar and Toomey (2002) concluded that raising the minimum legal drinking age and enforcing this action reduced alcohol-related harms to young people. Maintaining a minimum drinking age of 21 rather than 18 is estimated to save approximately 1000 lives each year in the USA, particularly young people in road traffic accidents.

Tobacco and minimum purchase age

In most countries tobacco is sold to customers aged 18 and over. As with alcohol, underage smokers can buy or acquire cigarettes from friends, relatives or peers but are increasingly likely to be refused service from shops as stricter identity checks have been introduced in many countries. In the USA, young people are less likely to smoke if living in areas with more stringent policies regarding tobacco sales to underage customers. However, research suggests that while enforcing the minimum purchase age for cigarettes can reduce illegal sales, the evidence that it reduces prevalence of smoking is weaker because underage smokers acquire cigarettes from other sources.

One of the most rapid recent changes in cultural attitudes towards smoking has been the ban on smoking in public places. In 2003, with mounting evidence of the negative impact of passive smoking, New York City became the first city in the world to introduce a smoking ban in public buildings, such as bars and restaurants, followed by 100 other US cities. In 2004 Ireland became the first country in the world to introduce a nationwide ban on smoking in the workplace. In the UK a ban on smoking in enclosed spaces was introduced in 2007 and the minimum purchase age for cigarettes was raised from 16 to 18 in 2008. Ideological criticisms have focused on health 'fascism' and 'nanny state' interventions in individual lifestyle choices, as well as practical concerns about a displacement of smoking from public to domestic spaces negatively impacting upon the health of smokers' families.

Other restrictions on availability

Aside from minimum purchase age, other restrictions on availability include: restrictions on types and strengths of products sold; number, location and density of retail outlets; trading hours of outlets; and server/retailer liability for costs resulting from consumption of intoxicants. There are also regulations restricting the blood alcohol concentration (BAC) for drivers which can influence consumption levels and associated harms. For example, in the USA fatalities dropped by 14 per cent in 1980–1997 across 50 states when the legal BAC was reduced from 0.1 per cent to 0.08 per cent. Conversely, in Portugal, fatalities increased by 10 per cent when the legal BAC was raised from 0.02 to 0.05 per cent.

In terms of changes in licensing hours, the effect on consumption is mixed and limited. Studies in Nordic countries with state alcohol monopolies have shown that a major relaxation in controls on alcohol strength or sales outlets results in increased alcohol consumption (and associated drunkenness and hospital admissions), and conversely that consumption falls after controls are reintroduced. An international review by Stockwell and Chikritzhs (2009) concluded that in countries where trading hours were extended (for example, Australia, New Zealand, Ireland and the UK) increased trading hours led to increased consumption and increased alcohol-related problems. In the UK, a liberalisation of licensing hours in 2005 resulted in people drinking later into the night with a consequent reduction in the closing-time peak of disorder, but an extension of problems into the early morning.

Pricing

Alcohol

There is a strong inverse relationship between price and consumption of legal drugs. Demand for alcohol is price sensitive, therefore the most effective way to reduce alcohol consumption at the population level is to increase the price through taxation. For example, an increase in price (from increased taxation or increased minimum pricing) can result in delayed onset of initiation, reduced frequency and quantity of use, and delayed onset of problem use. Alcohol price is also inversely associated with harmful outcomes, including drink driving and fatal road traffic accidents involving young people (particularly in the USA), as well as the prevalence of problem drinkers and mortality rates for liver cirrhosis in the general population. Some studies suggest that young people are more price sensitive than adults, but there is little evidence that price increases result in a significant reduction in binge drinking, and therefore opponents of population-based alcohol control measures advocate interventions targeted at problem drinking instead.

A review by Ogilvie et al. (2005) looked at the effectiveness of measures controlling the availability of alcohol, tobacco and other drugs on patterns of use and health outcomes for young people. Ogilvie and colleagues calculated that a 10 per cent increase in price would reduce demand for beer by about 5 per cent (drinking on licensed premises) or about 10 per cent (bought and consumed off trade), for wine by about 8 per cent, and for spirits by about 13 per cent.

Tobacco

Demand for tobacco is also price sensitive. Ogilvie et al. calculated that a 10 per cent increase in price results in a 4 per cent reduction in demand in higher income countries. In the UK, a rise in tobacco taxation in the 1970s and 1980s resulted in a reduction in smoking. Again young people are more price sensitive than older adults. A systematic review of studies in the USA found an association between price and both prevalence of smoking and numbers of cigarettes smoked by young people.

This inverse relationship is itself price sensitive, however. If taxation is too high, as has been argued is the case with tobacco in Europe, an illegal market can develop with the product smuggled into that country from a lower taxation country. It has been estimated that Western European countries lose £7 billion in lost tax revenue each year because of tobacco and cigarette smuggling from former Soviet bloc and developing countries. Some have argued that lower tobacco taxes would reduce the incentive for smuggling, but it could have other negative effects: when several Canadian provinces cut taxes, the downward trend in teenage smoking was reversed.

Advertising

Alcohol

Brand et al. (2007) noted that in countries where there was a voluntary code of practice on advertising there were generally lower levels of compliance and higher levels of alcohol-related problems than where a national mandatory code exists. A review by Hastings et al. (2005) also found an association between advertising and alcohol consumption levels.

In the UK, both mandatory and voluntary advertising codes exist. The voluntary Portman Group Code of Practice on advertising for alcohol retailers (introduced in 1996 and since updated) recommends that the naming, packaging and merchandising of alcoholic drinks should not 'suggest any association with, acceptance of, or allusion to illicit drugs'; should not 'encourage illegal, irresponsible or immoderate consumption such as binge drinking, drunkenness or drink-driving'; and should not be more likely to appeal to under 18s than adults through the use of 'imagery or allusion to under 18s culture' (The Portman Group, 2001). Periodically alcoholic beverages are withdrawn from distribution that do not comply with this code.

Tobacco

Tobacco advertising has been banned in some countries with a resultant fall in smoking levels that surpasses reductions in neighbouring countries. Thailand has some of the strictest tobacco control policies in the world including high levels of taxation on cigarettes, no advertising of cigarettes permitted anywhere in the media and strong and varied warning labels on cigarette packets. Smoking prevalence is falling faster in Thailand than in neighbouring countries.

SUMMARY

The regulation of legal drugs involves a delicate balance between government, public health and criminal justice bodies: the alcohol, tobacco and leisure industries, and the wishes of the tax paying, and (mostly) alcohol consuming, adult electorate. A key debate relates to whether control policies should be directed at the general public to reduce harms at the population level or whether they should be targeted at problem or at-risk groups. Price controls are particularly effective at reducing consumption at the population level whereas secondary prevention, harm reduction and brief interventions are more effective at reducing harm within targeted groups. Unenforced voluntary agreements, educational interventions and information through retail outlets are among the least effective means to reduce the consumption of legal drugs and/or associated harms.

REFERENCES

Brand, D., Saisana, M., Rynn, L. Pennoni, F. and Lowenfels, A. (2007) 'Comparative analysis of alcohol control policies in 30 countries', *PLoS Medicine*, 4 (4): 752–59.
Hastings, G., Anderson, S., Cooke, E. and Gordon, R. (2005) 'Alcohol marketing and young people's drinking: a review of the research', *Journal of Public Health Policy*, 26: 296–311.
Ogilvie, D., Gruer, L. and Haw, S. (2005) Young people's access to tobacco, alcohol, and other drugs', *British Medical Journal*, 331: 393–6.
Stockwell, T. and Chikritzhs, T. (2009) 'Do relaxed trading hours for bars and clubs mean more relaxed drinking? A review of international research on the impacts of changes to permitted hours of drinking', *Crime Prevention and Community Safety*, 11 (3): 153–70.
The Portman Group (2002) *Code of Practice on the Naming, Packaging and Promotion of Alcohol Drinks: Encouraging Responsible Marketing*, 3rd edn. London: The Portman Group.
Wagenaar, A. and Toomey, T. (2002) 'Effects of minimum drinking age laws: review and analyses of the literature from 1960 to 2000', *Journal of Studies in Alcohol*, 14 (Supplement): 206–25.

key concepts in
drugs and society

6
Polydrug Use/ Polysubstance Use

Definitions of polydrug use vary but generally refer to the purposeful consumption of two or more psychoactive substances in order to enhance, reduce or extend the effects of each other. Polydrug use may be distinguished from polysubstance use in that polydrug use includes at least one drug which is controlled, whereas polysubstance use includes at least one drug which is legal, usually alcohol.

Polydrug use is the practice whereby two or more psychoactive substances are purposefully consumed together. The definitions and features of polydrug use vary, depending on the minimum number of drugs included, the legal status of each drug, route of ingestion, the combinations involved, the time frame of consumption, the sequence of consumption, agency/intentionality in the selection of drugs, and potential addictive, synergistic and pharmacodynamic effects. For example, we can distinguish between shorter and longer time frames for consumption. A shorter time frame usually focuses on one acute drug-taking *episode* or session, which can be measured by the time period or by the drugs' effects (for example, two or more drugs overlap in their acute effect half-life). Within a shorter time frame drugs can be mixed together in a combination formula and consumed at the same time, known as *simultaneous polydrug use*; or they may be taken *consecutively* across the course of the drug-taking episode.

When drugs are taken together across a longer time frame it is known as *concurrent polydrug use*. Concurrent use focuses on multiple drug use in the drug users' career or *repertoire* (the range of drugs used) rather than multiple drug use within an individual drug episode. For example, the ESPAD school surveys define polydrug use as the use of two or more substances, legal or illegal, in the 30 days prior to the survey (Olszewski et al., 2010). In the UK, the annual British Crime Survey (BCS) (Hoare and Moon, 2010) has a broader concurrent measure than ESPAD, defining polydrug use as self-reported consumption of two or more illicit drugs within a time period of 12 months.

In terms of legal status, polydrug use usually refers to the consumption of a combination of drugs which includes at least one whose possession or use is controlled or illegal within that country's legislature. For example, in the British Crime Survey a distinction is made between polydrug use (two or more illicit drugs) and polysubstance use (two or more drugs, one of which is alcohol). In French surveys, tobacco is often included in polydrug definitions, whereas in the BCS and ECMDDA definitions, tobacco is excluded from the definition.

PREVALENCE

Given the wide variations in definitions it is unclear how widespread polydrug use is but it is suspected that polydrug use is a usual rather than unusual pattern of consumption, evident in the traditional combined use of tobacco and alcohol in bars, and tobacco and caffeine in coffee shops, which can be traced back several centuries. A lower number of drugs and wider time frame will produce a higher estimated prevalence of polydrug use. For example, the BCS, using a generous concurrent measure of polydrug use, found that 4 in 10 of those British adults who reported past year drug use reported past year polydrug use (3.3 per cent of all adults) (Hoare and Moon, 2010). Furthermore, past year polydrug use was associated with younger adults and adults who attended nightclubs within the last month; suggesting that polydrug use may be particularly a feature of the drug profiles of young adult clubbers.

KEY POLYDRUG COMBINATIONS

Given the challenges of standardising definitions, measurements and features of polydrug use, some studies of polydrug use focus instead on key polydrug combinations and their consequences. Three key combinations which have been identified in studies are as follows:

1 Adolescent polydrug repertoires, particularly the combined use of alcohol, tobacco and cannabis. ESPAD studies of European school pupils aged 15–16 show that alcohol, tobacco and cannabis are the three highest self-reported drugs used in the last month. The centrality of these three substances to adolescent polydrug repertoires is evident in further analysis by Olszewski et al. (2010). Secondary analysis of ESPAD 2003 data for over 70,000 15–16-year-olds from 22 countries by Olszewski et al. found that about 3 in 10 reported having had two or more of any substances, legal or illegal, in the previous month: the ESPAD definition of polydrug use. Although there were 91 different drug combinations reported, for just over 20 per cent of the sample (two-thirds of polydrug users) their last month polydrug combination was alcohol and tobacco, for 6 per cent it was cannabis and either alcohol or tobacco, whereas only 1 per cent of the sample reported polydrug use which included any other drugs (ecstasy, cocaine and so forth).
2 Polydrug combinations among problem drug users include heroin and crack (known as piggybacking and speedballing) and other opioid/depressant combinations such as combinations of heroin, alcohol and benzodiazepines.
3 Polystimulant repertoires, sometimes combined with consecutive depressant use before or afterwards to reduce the negative after-effects or the 'come down' from stimulants. More recently, polydrug repertoires among clubbers and customers across the night-time economy have increased in popularity, particularly combinations of stimulants (MDMA, amphetamines, cocaine) and depressants/deliriants (cannabis, ketamine, GHB/GBL) with evidence of increasingly diverse polydrug combinations within prolific weekend repertoires (Measham and Moore, 2009) (see also **11 dance drugs/club drugs**).

A study of persistent young offenders aged 12–18 by Hammersley et al. (2003) identified three categories of drug users similar to the three polydrug combinations discussed above. Hammersley et al. estimated that about 1 in 2 of drug users were users of the 'socially acceptable' or 'normalised' drugs (alcohol, tobacco and cannabis); about 1 in 10 drug users were 'stimulant and polydrug' users; and about 1 in 20 could be characterised as 'addictive' or problem drug users (see also **14 normalisation**).

MOTIVATIONS FOR POLYDRUG USE

Motivations for polydrug use vary depending on the individual drugs which are combined, the circumstances of usage and the effect desired by the user. Each drug may be taken to enhance or to ameliorate the effects of the other drug(s) consumed, whether taken simultaneously, consecutively or concurrently, or may be taken to extend the effects of another drug.

It should be noted, however, that far from a recent or rare pattern of use, polydrug use is widespread and can be considered a not unusual attempt by drug users to balance the effects of different drugs and to manage the fluctuations in availability, price and purity of their preferred psychoactive substance through substitute displacement, alongside changes in legislation, enforcement and fashion. Typical polydrug repertoires include stimulants consumed earlier in the evening and depressants later on, a formula used across the developed world for decades, covering both street drugs and prescription medicines. For example, traditional stimulant/depressant combinations include prescription 'uppers' and 'downers', which have been linked to celebrity lifestyles and high profile deaths such as Elvis Presley and Michael Jackson.

Primary and secondary drug use relates to the level of importance given to different drugs within a polydrug repertoire. For example, among dance drug users, ecstasy is often cited as their primary or 'favourite' club drug, but other drugs are taken to enhance the overall drug experience, prolong or increase the intensity of ecstasy or to reduce what may be perceived as negative side effects of ecstasy.

It has been suggested (EMCDDA, 2009) that polydrug use is increasing. This is because the availability and use of drugs such as alcohol, cannabis, ecstasy, cocaine and ketamine have increased in the last two decades across much of the world, resulting in a growing range of drugs available for consumption. Concerns about this growing tendency towards polydrug use comes from survey evidence that increasing numbers of drugs are being taken before, during and after a night out, particularly in relation to weekend nights out at clubs and bars. What is significant here is the specific ordering, as well as quantities consumed, of the different individual drugs within the polydrug experience. Recent patterns in this growing polydrug use link the trend to issues of price, availability and the extended structure of leisure events with a 'night out' including the possibility of pre-loading at home, bar-hopping, dancing in clubs, then afterwards visiting breakfast bars or 'chill out' after parties before returning home.

RISKS OF POLYDRUG USE

Polydrug use can result in any or all of the potential health and social harms across the whole span of drug use, including increased toxicity, risk of overdose, road traffic accidents, and other acute and chronic harms. For example, many deaths that are supposedly caused by heroin overdose are in fact the result of heroin being consumed alongside other depressant drugs, such as alcohol or benzodiazepines, and therefore the risk factor may be the combination of drugs.

A second concern relates to the inadvertent consumption of more than one psychoactive drug. Many drug users may consume more than one drug simultaneously due to the adulteration or addition of other active ingredients to street supplies. Laboratory analyses of cocaine seizures in the UK, for example, show that 2009 street seizures contained an average of 22 per cent cocaine with the remainder including both inactive bulking agents and also varying amounts of psychoactive adulterants such as benzocaine, lignocaine and caffeine.

Alongside the added problems that polydrug use can produce, in itself polydrug use is seen as a risk factor for other risk-taking behaviours. Much research on polydrug use has focused on the correlation between patterns of multiple drug use and other risk indicators of harm such as social exclusion, offending and sexual risk taking. For example, Patterson et al. (2005) studied 261 HIV-positive, methamphetamine-using men who had sex with men. In the previous two months, they found that only 5 per cent of the sample had used only methamphetamine. They divided the other 95 per cent of their sample into light polydrug users (31 per cent) who had taken methamphetamine along with cannabis and/or poppers, and heavy polydrug users (64 per cent) who had taken methamphetamine alongside other drugs including cocaine, heroin, hallucinogens or ketamine. Heavy polydrug use was associated with being younger, having used methamphetamine for fewer years, having more sexual partners, more high risk sexual behaviours, such as unprotected sex including with partners of unknown serostatus, and scoring higher on impulsivity and negative self perceptions. However, the quantity and frequency of both methamphetamine and alcohol consumed did not vary between light and heavy polydrug users.

Given the variations in definitions and measurements of polydrug use, it is not surprising that polydrug use has tended to be neglected in terms of drug policy and drug treatment. Particular challenges relate to presenting problems, issues of displacement between primary and secondary drugs, and escalation. This has led some (for example, Gossop, 2001) to suggest that polydrug users are *more difficult* to successfully treat for addiction than non-polydrug users because of the complicating issues in assessment and treatment. Others have argued that drugs education and prevention programmes which target multiple drug use may be *more effective* in reducing overall harm given the high levels of polydrug use among users.

SUMMARY

Polydrug use is widespread among drug users and can be considered a usual rather than unusual practice, evident in the traditional combined use of tobacco and alcohol in bars, and tobacco and caffeine in coffee shops. The motivations for, and consequences of, polydrug use are dependent upon the combinations of drugs consumed, quantity, method of ingestion, whether taken simultaneously, consecutively or concurrently and the time frame of the polydrug episode or repertoire, as well as displacement between drugs due to variable purity, price and availability. Our understanding of the combined and cumulative effects of polydrug use is currently limited but acute toxicity and overdose are identified risks and studies also indicate that polydrug use is associated with other high-risk behaviours including sexual risk taking.

REFERENCES

EMCDDA (2009) *Polydrug Use: Patterns and Responses*. Lisbon: EMCDDA.

Gossop, M. (2001) 'A web of dependence', *Addiction*, 96: 677–8.

Hammersley, R., Marsland, L. and Reid, M. (2003) *Substance Use by Young Offenders: The Impact of the Normalisation of Drug Use in the Early Years of the 21st Century*. Home Office Research Study 261. London: Home Office.

Hoare, J. and Moon, D. (2010) *Drug Misuse Declared: Findings from the 2009/10 British Crime Survey England and Wales, Home Office Statistical Bulletin 13/10*. London: Home Office. http://www.homeoffice.gov.uk/rds/pdfs10/hosb1310.pdf

Olszewski, D., Matias, J., Monshouwer, K. and Kokkevi, A. (2010) 'Polydrug use among 15-to-16-year olds: similarities and differences in Europe', *Drugs: Education, Prevention and Policy*, 17 (4): 287–302.

Measham, F. and Moore, K. (2009) 'Repertoires of distinction: exploring patterns of weekend polydrug use within local leisure scenes across the English night time economy', *Criminology and Criminal Justice*, 9 (4): 437–64.

Patterson, T., Semple, S., Zians, K. and Strathdee, S. (2005) 'Methamphetamine-using HIV-positive men who have sex with men: correlates of polydrug use', *Journal of Urban Health*, 82 (1): 120-6.

7

Common Illicit Drugs

'Common illicit drugs' refers to substances (such as cocaine) that are illegal under national and international laws to supply and, in most but not all cases, to possess. Common illicit drugs also refer to those substances (such as minor tranquilisers) which are lawful to possess with a medical prescription but are used illicitly for non-medicinal purposes.

The term 'illicit drugs' generally refers to illegal or unlawfully possessed substances. The term 'drug' tends to denote an illegal substance. However, if the term 'drug' is used more broadly to mean any form of intoxicant, then legal substances, such as alcohol and nicotine, may be included. The term 'drug' is also widely used to mean substances used for medicinal purposes. Within the medical community 'narcotic' is specifically used to describe natural opioid drugs derived from the Asian poppy (*Papaver somniferous*), alongside semi-synthetic or synthetic substitutes, which dull pain and cause drowsiness or sleep. However the term 'opioid' is preferred within medical professions given the broader use of the term 'narcotic', notably in the USA. In the US legal context, 'narcotic' refers to opium, cocaine and coca leaves. The term 'narcotic' has strong negative connotations and tends to be used in US and international political contexts, as with the United Nations International Narcotics Control Board (UNINCB) and the United Nations Commission for Narcotic Drugs (UNCND).

CANNABIS/MARIJUANA/'SKUNK'

Globally, one of the most commonly used illicit drugs is cannabis (see also **2 prevalence and trends in drug use**), a mild sedative and hallucinogen illegal to supply and possess in most but not all countries. In Mexico, for example, possession of a small amount of the drug for 'personal use' has been de-criminalised. The term marijuana (or more colloquially 'dope') is used in the USA and Central and South American countries. Extracts from the cannabis plant include non-psychoactive hemp fibre and psychoactive hashish resin ('black' or 'solid'). Herbal cannabis flowers and leaves are dried out in preparation for smoking. Herbal cannabis ('weed') can be smoked with or without tobacco. Cannabis can also be eaten, for example, baked into biscuits/cookies or cakes. More recently there has been concern over strains of cannabis – known in the UK as 'skunk' or as 'super pot' in the USA – which have higher levels of the psychoactive agent A-tetrahydrocannabinol (THQ) than herbal cannabis and cannabis resin.

Cannabis users report a 'euphoric high', alongside decreased anxiety and increased alertness and sociability. Other more negative effects on mood include anxiety, paranoia and in some cases psychosis, although cannabis' relationship with pre-existing mental health problems remains unclear. Cannabis effects users' perceptions, with colours and music seeming brighter and more vivid. In high doses users may experience hallucinations. Cannabis is illegal to possess and supply in most countries across the globe, although in some countries (for example, Belgium) or states within countries (for example, Colorado, USA), possession of a small amount of cannabis for personal use in private settings is decriminalised, unenforced, subject to police discretion, or subject to a fine and confiscation (for example, Germany). In other countries, such as Finland, medicinal use of cannabis is decriminalised. Cannabis has a long history of medicinal or therapeutic use. In terms of cannabis addiction (see also **4 addiction**), there remains debate as to whether it is possible to become physically dependent, although evidence suggests that users can become psychologically dependent. When users stop they may experience psychological craving for the drug, feel lethargic, lose their appetite and find it hard to sleep.

POWDER COCAINE

Produced from the coca leaf, powder cocaine was first synthesised in Germany in 1860, although coca leaf chewing among indigenous peoples in South America has a much longer history. Cocaine is a white powder usually ingested intra-nasally ('snorted') through a rolled-up note or straw. Powder cocaine has a short-acting stimulant effect on the user, raising the body's temperature and heart rate. Users report increased energy, confidence and sociability, although cocaine's stimulant properties can also result in anxiety and paranoia. In high doses, powder cocaine can result in convulsions, respiratory problems and heart failure. When powder cocaine is consumed alongside alcohol the human body produces a chemical called cocaethylene which is more toxic to the human cardiovascular system then either drug taken alone. Cocaine is currently illegal to produce, supply and possess in all nation states who are signatories to the various international treaties attempting to control drug production, distribution and consumption, such as the United Nations Convention Against Illicit Traffic in Narcotic Drugs and Psychotropic Substances (see also **30 international drug control history/prohibition**). Powder cocaine can be described as a psychological drug of addiction. Regular heavy powder cocaine users may become tolerant to the drug and reliant on its effects. Stopping cocaine consumption can prove difficult as users may develop symptoms including exhaustion, insomnia, diarrhoea, vomiting and excessive sweating.

CRACK COCAINE

Crack cocaine is produced or 'cooked' using sodium bicarbonate ('baking soda') and a small amount of water to convert powder cocaine (see above) to freebase cocaine. When this mixture is heated, small crack cocaine 'rocks' form in the mixture. Crack is produced via either this one-stage process (converting the drug from a salt to a base, commonly known as 'freebasing') or a two-stage process (converting the drug from salt to base but also refining it). Hence crack is only 'purer' than the cocaine from which it is produced if the cutting agents (see also **34 drug markets**) present in the cocaine are removed. Users tend to purchase crack cocaine in 'rock' form. Crack cocaine is either smoked, or dissolved and injected, allowing for quick absorption into the blood stream, whereas powder cocaine is typically taken intra-nasally ('snorted'). Crack cocaine acts to rapidly release dopamine, a chemical in the brain which produces an intense 'euphoric high' coupled with an increase in confidence, alertness and energy. Initial effects typically last between 5 to 10 minutes. The rapid and intense high and comedown from crack increases the likelihood of dependency among users and can lead to 'binge' patterns of use. Repeated use of crack cocaine at high dosage levels can produce cravings, depression, irritability, restlessness (including the development of severe muscle 'tics'), paranoia and psychosis. Crack cocaine users may develop 'delusional parasitosis' – the feeling of having insects crawl under the skin – leading some users to develop skin damage from intense bouts of scratching. Crack cocaine is currently illegal to produce, supply and possess in all nation states signed up to international treaties.

Crack cocaine is widely perceived as highly addictive, with many users becoming daily dependent users, although some only try the drug once and others are able to control their use.

HEROIN

Heroin (medical name diamorphine) is one of a 'family' of drugs called opiates that are derived from the Asian poppy (*P. somniferous*). Heroin usually appears as a white or brown powder. Heroin's street names include 'smack', 'H', 'skag' and 'junk'. Heroin can be smoked, snorted or injected. Street heroin in the UK, the USA and Australia is typically exported from Afghanistan, Iraq and Pakistan. Heroin and other opiates are sedative drugs that depress the nervous system, slowing down body functioning and reducing physical pain and psychological distress. Although initial use can produce feelings of nausea and result in vomiting, these unpleasant effects usually diminish with regular use. Heroin users typically report feelings of warmth, relaxation and a reduction in anxiety through feelings of detachment. Heroin has a short onset and effects can last several hours depending on dosage. Users may become drowsy and 'nod off' following heroin consumption. When used regularly, users can develop tolerance to heroin, meaning that more is needed in order to acquire the same initial effect. Since heroin is often injected, regular users can suffer health problems associated with (unsafe) injecting practices, including damaged veins, and exposure to infection from HIV and Hepatitis C Virus (HCV). Excessive dosages of heroin can result in coma and death through respiratory failure. Methadone, a heroin substitute prescribed in some countries as part of drug treatment programmes, is also used illicitly. Heroin is currently illegal to produce, supply and possess in all nation states who are signatories to international drug treaties. Heroin use can lead to both physical and psychological addiction, with users consuming the drug on a daily basis, often to avoid feeling ill. Withdrawal symptoms on cessation of dependent heroin use may include aches, tremors, chills and muscular spasms and intense emotional distress. However, heroin addiction is not an inevitable effect of taking the drug, with some users able to control their use.

'ECSTASY' AND MDMA

Created and patented by German scientists in 1916, 'Ecstasy' was rediscovered in the 1960s by Alexander Shulgin and used as a psychotherapeutic adjunct. Recreational use emerged in Ibiza and the UK within the 'acid house' and rave scenes of the late-1980s. Ecstasy, commonly known as 'pills' or 'E', is now closely associated with the global rave and dance music club scene, and has been described as 'the cultural signifier of a generation' (Shapiro, 1999). The chemical name of pure ecstasy is 3,4 methylenedioxymethamphetamine or MDMA. Ecstasy is usually sold in pill or capsule form, which users ingest, although it is also sold as MDMA powder or MDMA crystal which users snort or 'bomb' orally. Ecstasy is a stimulant drug with mild hallucinogenic properties. It works to release serotonin, norepinephrine and dopamine into the brain. Ecstasy users typically report euphoric effects with feelings of energy and well-being alongside feelings of empathy with others.

Immediate negative physical effects include raised body temperature, heart rate and blood pressure, urinary retention and sometimes excessive teeth grinding. Immediate negative mood effects include feeling anxious and panicky. Users may experience feeling very tired and 'low' for up to three or four days after use; this is known as a 'comedown'. There are enduring concerns about the long-term neurotoxicity of ecstasy, including possible links to depression and memory deficits in heavy regular users, although evidence remains contradictory. Ecstasy is a globally controlled substance, a Schedule I substance in the USA, and a Class A substance in the UK, Australia and New Zealand. Ecstasy has been implicated in cases of heatstroke resulting in respiratory collapse. The risk of heatstroke can be reduced by drinking fluids. However, ecstasy has been related to deaths as a result of the intake of too much fluid, possibly related to the mistaken belief that large quantities are needed to prevent or reverse overheating. Excessive fluid consumption is problematic when coupled with the restrictive effect ecstasy places on the user's ability to urinate, which can in turn contribute to abnormal water retention (dilutional hyponatraemia), kidney malfunction, and water swelling around the brain. Regular users may develop tolerance to ecstasy, and some become psychologically dependent on the drug experience (as a way of escaping reality, for example). However, few users exhibit physical symptoms of dependence on cessation, while daily dependent use is extremely rare.

KETAMINE

Ketamine is a dissociate anaesthetic originally developed in the 1960s and still used legitimately by medical and veterinary professions. It is also taken illicitly for non-medicinal purposes. Ketamine is sold illicitly in powder form which is taken intra-nasally ('snorted') or in liquid form which can be ingested or injected. It is thought that street supplies of ketamine in the UK, USA, Western Europe, Australia and New Zealand come from diverted legitimate supplies or more commonly via importation from Asian manufacturers. Ketamine is valued by users for its short-onset and short-acting hallucinogenic properties and the dissociative state it can produce – known as depersonalisation – where the users feels as if he or she is 'floating' outside of their own body. The effects of ketamine vary with dosage, with low doses producing mild hallucinations and feelings of euphoria, while higher dosages – the effects of which have been termed 'the k-hole' – may produce intense hallucinations and render users unable to move. Heavy regular use of ketamine has been linked to memory impairment, and severe urinary tract and bladder problems including ketamine-associated ulcerative cystitis. Ketamine is a Schedule III drug in the USA, a Schedule I drug in Canada, a Class C drug in the UK (following its criminalisation in 2005) and a Schedule I drug in Hong Kong, where the drug is popular among young party-goers (Joe-Laidler and Hunt, 2008). Ketamine users can rapidly develop tolerance to the drug and may become psychologically addicted.

AMPHETAMINES AND METHAMPHETAMINE

Users of amphetamines report feeling alert, energetic and confident, although taking high doses over a short period of time can lead to bouts of anxiety and paranoia. Long-term regular use can mean users become 'run-down' though lack of sleep and food. This is because amphetamines and methamphetamine are stimulant drugs which work on the body's central nervous system, causing the user's heart and breathing rate to increase while suppressing appetite. Indeed in the 1950s and 1960s such stimulants were widely available as slimming aids. However, in more recent times medical prescribing of amphetamines has all but ceased, although methylphenidate (Ritalin), an amphetamine-like drug, is commonly used to treat hyperactivity in children, particularly in the USA. In the UK amphetamines are controlled as Class B drugs under the Misuse of Drugs Act. When amphetamines are prepared for injection they become Class A drugs and increased penalties apply. When smoked, snorted or injected (as opposed to swallowed), onset of effects is more rapid and the 'high' users experience is more intense. In these forms amphetamines can be particularly addictive. Methamphetamine was reclassified in 2007 from a Class B to a Class A drug in the UK. In the USA, both amphetamine and methamphetamine are Schedule II drugs, and Schedule I drugs in Canada, attracting high penalties for non-medicinal use. There has been concern in the USA about the use of methamphetamine among the country's rural poor population, while in Australia and New Zealand 'Meth', 'Ice' or 'P' as it is known has been subject to repeated crackdowns by law enforcement agencies. Users of amphetamine or methamphetamine may become dependent, experiencing physical and psychological withdrawal symptoms on cessation of use.

LSD

Discovered by American research chemist Albert Hoffman in 1938, lysergic acid diethylamide, or 'LSD', is a hallucinogenic drug. It derived originally from ergot, a fungus found growing wild on rye and other grasses. As a street drug, LSD is found as a liquid which is dropped onto sugar cubes, or is absorbed into paper sheets which are then cut into squares or 'acid tabs', often with printed pictures on them. The strength of these tabs may vary considerably. Only a tiny amount of LSD is needed to feel its mild hallucinogenic effects, while higher doses can result in a 'trip' which may last 12 hours or more. While it is thought that overdose on LSD is impossible, some users have died from accidents while under the influence of the drug. As with ketamine (see above), LSD users may experience dissociation from the self known as depersonalisation. LSD is known to have a potentially profound effect on individuals' perceptions; colours become intensified, while time, space, sounds, shapes and sizes become distorted and inert objects may 'move'. The user's experience of LSD depends greatly on their state of mind before consuming the drug and on their immediate surroundings. Users may experience a 'good trip', even likening the self-exploratory aspects of LSD to religious or spiritual experiences. However, it is possible to have a 'bad trip' (even within an overall relatively 'good trip') which can render the person severely anxious, afraid and paranoid. Although some people do report dependent behaviour, LSD and other hallucinogenics are not generally considered to be addictive. Indeed repeated doses of LSD over a short period render the drug psychoactively inactive. LSD is prohibited under the United Nations Convention against Illicit Traffic in Narcotic Drugs and Psychotropic Substances, whose signatories include the USA, the UK, Australia, New Zealand and most of Europe.

'MAGIC MUSHROOMS'

'Magic mushrooms' (naturally occurring fungi) contain the active substances psilocin and psilocybin, which have hallucinogenic qualities similar to LSD or 'acid', though typically milder and more manageable. The onset of effects from 'magic mushrooms' is between 30 to 60 minutes, typically lasting between 5 to 7 hours. Mushrooms can be eaten raw, but are more often dried, made into drinks or eaten with food. About 180 kinds of mushrooms are known to contain psilocybin and/or psilocin. Psilocybin and psilocin belong to the tryptamine family and their effect resembles the natural neurotransmitter serotonin. Fly agaric mushrooms are also used for their hallucinogenic properties but they do not contain psilocin or psilocybin. Fly agaric use has been found to produce unpleasant effects, including nausea and vomiting, stiffness of joints and lack of co-ordination. However, fly agaric has not been brought under the UK Misuse of Drugs Act 1971. The UK Drugs Act 2005 made fungi containing psilocin or psilocybin Class A drugs, in both fresh and prepared forms. The Act also made the sale and importation of 'grow kits' illegal. A similar legal situation exists in the USA, Australia, New Zealand, and as of 2008, the Netherlands. It is possible to become psychologically addicted to 'magic mushrooms' whereby users remember the pleasant feeling of the 'high', making them long for the next dose, with a very small proportion of users developing daily use patterns.

GHB, GBL AND 4-BD

GHB stands for gamma-hydroxybutyrate or gamma-hydroxybutyric acid. GBL is made from gamma-1,4-butanediol (also referred to as 4-BD) is a prodrug or precursor chemical of GHB. When GBL or 4-BD is ingested, GHB is produced in the body. GHB, GBL and 4-BD are used as 'recreational' drugs, commonly referred to as 'G'. GBL is longer acting and has a shorter onset than GHB, otherwise its effects are similar. GHB, GBL and and 4-BD tend to be purchased in clear liquid form (although all come in powder form) which is then mixed with water. Taken undiluted or under-diluted, GHB, GBL and 4-BD burns the mouth and oesophagus. All have an unpleasant salty taste when mixed with water. The effects of GHB, GBL and 4-BD include increased energy, happiness, desire to socialise, feeling affectionate and playful, disinhibition, sensuality, enhanced sexual experience, muscle relaxation, loss of coordination, nausea, difficulty concentrating, and potential loss of the gag reflex. GHB was classified as Class C drug in the UK in 2003, GBL and

4-BD were classified as Class C drugs in 2009. GHB, GBL and 4-BD are drugs of **4 addiction**, with long-term users building up a high tolerance, while displaying symptoms of both physical and psychological dependence. Sudden withdrawal can be extremely dangerous.

TRANQUILISERS

Tranquilisers fall into two main classes, major and minor. Major and minor tranquilisers bear only a superficial resemblance to each other, although the terms persist in popular usage. It is more useful to distinguish between benzodiazepines, the most commonly prescribed minor tranquilisers in the USA, which include anxiolytics (anti-anxiety agents) and hypnotics (which promote sleep); and neuroleptics, also known as anti-psychotic agents, used to treat major states of mental disturbance in people suffering with schizophrenia. Benzodiazepines have a sedative effect on users, making them feel calm and relaxed, but also forgetful, confused and lethargic. Tolerance to minor tranquilisers builds up quickly and users can become dependent on them. Benzodiazepines are used illicitly, usually after being sold on by those with legitimate prescriptions or stolen from legitimate suppliers, such as pharmacies. In the UK, a minority of users of hallucinogens, such as LSD, and stimulants, such as ecstasy, were found to take minor tranquilisers such as temazepam illicitly to ease their 'comedown'.

Flunitrazepam (most common brand name, Rohypnol, known colloquially as 'roofies') is also a minor tranquiliser which has been implicated in acquaintance (date) rape in the USA. Used in the short-term treatment of sleep disorders, flunitrazepam produces sedative effects including possible amnesia. In the UK flunitrazepam is legal to possess under prescription, but is classified as a Class C substance (as with other minor tranquilisers such as temazepam) under the Misuse of Drugs Act 1971 when supplied illicitly and/or when an individual in possession cannot produce a legitimate prescription. Tranquilisers can be addictive, with users becoming both physically and psychologically dependent on them, experiencing distressing withdrawal symptoms on cessation, while sudden withdrawal can be extremely dangerous.

ANABOLIC STEROIDS

Not to be confused with corticosteroids which are used for medical purposes, anabolic steroids are used non-medically for their body-building and performance-enhancing properties. Anabolic steroids are found in tablet form, or in liquid form that is injected. They may make users feel more aggressive, competitive and confident (Wright et al., 2001). Anabolic steroids can also lead to acute acne, hypertension, blood-clotting, jaundice, tendon damage and reduced fertility. Research in the USA with anabolic steroid-using weightlifters and body builders found that key motivations for use were to 'get huge and get ripped' (to have large, clearly defined muscles), coupled with frustration at being unable to do so via 'legitimate' means (Petrocelli et al., 2008). In the USA anabolic steroids are classified as Schedule III drugs under the Controlled Substances Act. In the UK anabolic steroids are prescription only drugs under the Medicines Act. This means that they are illegal to sell without a prescription, although they are not currently illegal to possess for personal use, although a growing list of anabolic steroids are being classified as Class C substances (making them both illegal to sell and to possess). There remains controversy as to whether anabolic steroids cause dependence and addiction, with doubt cast over the psychoactive physical dependence-forming properties of anabolic steroids. Instead a 'secondary reinforcement' mechanism of dependence seems to be at work, where users come to rely on the social reinforcement and pleasure of experiencing improved performance in sport and/or having a muscular body.

REFERENCES

European Monitoring Centre for Drugs and Drug Addiction (EMCDDA) (2006) *Hallucinogenic Mushrooms*. Lisbon: EMCDDA.

European Monitoring Centre for Drugs and Drug Addiction (2008) *GHB and Its Precursor GBL: An Emerging Trend Case Study*. Lisbon: EMCDDA

Joe-Laidler, K. and Hunt, G. (2008) 'Sit down to float: the cultural meaning of ketamine in Hong Kong', *Addiction Research and Theory*, 16 (3): 259–71.

Petrocelli, M., Oberweis, T. and Petrocelli, J. (2008) 'Getting huge, getting ripped: a qualitative exploration of recreational steroid use', *Journal of Drug Issues*, 38 (4): 1087–206.

Shapiro, H. (1999) 'Dances with drugs: pop music, drugs and youth culture', in N. South (ed.), *Drugs: Cultures, Controls and Everyday Life*. London: Sage. pp. 17–35.

Wright, S., Grogan, S. and Hunter, G. (2001) 'Motivations for anabolic steroid use among body builders', *Journal of Health Psychology*, 5 (4): 566–71.

8

Typologies of Drug Use: Use–Misuse–Abuse and Problematic–Recreational Use

Two key typologies of drug use are the use–misuse-abuse typology and the problematic–recreational typology.

1 The *use–misuse–abuse* typology characterises the degrees of social acceptability of drug use and distinguishes between perceptions of legitimate drug *use*; legally, medically or socially unsanctioned *misuse*; and problematic use with

(Continued)

(Continued)

harmful consequences for the individual or society termed *abuse*. *Addiction* or dependency may be included as the final category.

2 The *problematic–recreational* typology characterises the motivation or pattern of drug use. *Recreational* drug use is (usually) non-problematic drug use during leisure periods and in social settings. *Problem* drug use is later 'career' drug use when daily use, dependency, injecting or other problematic patterns of use have developed.

These typologies are not objective categories, rather they are imbued with morality and politics.

Drug use can be defined or categorised according to the ways in which drugs are used; where they appear in the sequence or 'career' of a drug user; the motivations, patterns and consequences of use; and the degrees of official or social acceptability of consumption within specific historical and cultural contexts. Two key typologies described below are the use–misuse–abuse typology and the problematic–recreational typology.

USE–MISUSE–ABUSE TYPOLOGY

This typology of drug use focuses on the perceived social acceptability of use and specifically medical and legal attitudes towards consumption. Some characterise this as a spectrum or 'career' of identified stages from use at one end to addiction at the other.

This differentiation can be defined in legal terms. For example, *use* is the consumption of psychoactive drugs that is allowed by law and/or sanctioned by medical practitioners (see also **1 what is a drug/medicine?**). Which drugs are legally or socially acceptable will change over time, between jurisdictions and depending on the purpose for which they are consumed. Looking at cannabis as an example, 'medical marijuana' is currently legally sanctioned for medical prescribing in many individual states in the USA for medical conditions for which cannabis might offer some relief, but the same drug is not sanctioned for recreational use in many states. In the Netherlands, cannabis supply is illegal but possession is (partially) sanctioned when consumed for recreational purposes in a small number of designated cannabis cafés. In Portugal possession of cannabis and other drugs for any purposes, including self-medication and recreation, has been decriminalised for under 10 days' personal supply.

Misuse is the consumption of drugs that have a legitimate clinical role but are being used in ways for which they have not been approved – for example, taken more frequently, in greater quantities and/or for reasons for which the drugs were not intended or prescribed.

Abuse refers to the non-medical use (or misuse) of psychoactive drugs to such an extent that it results in problems for the user such as anxiety, psychosis or dependency. *Addiction* may also be included as the final category in this typology when daily, dependent or uncontrolled consumption patterns have developed.

Critique

For medical and legal practitioners the boundaries between use, misuse and abuse are agreed even if the criteria for these distinctions are disputed. For social researchers, by contrast, there is no one accepted definition of misuse or abuse as they are seen as multidimensional and historically and culturally context specific. Nevertheless, some researchers (for example, Newcomb and Bentler, 1989) have argued that there is some value in distinguishing between the use and abuse of licit and illicit drugs, embedded within their socio-cultural context, in order to address issues of prevention, harm and treatment and to justify societal limitations on access to some drugs rather than others. Newcomb and Bentler identified a range of physiological, environmental and socio-cultural factors which together can assess whether use has shifted towards abuse, or an identifiable potential for harm. However, these different perspectives illustrate the complexity of making judgements between sanctioned *use* and unsanctioned *abuse* of psychoactive drugs in societies where a wide range of licit and illicit substances are consumed by the population, from daily caffeine to over-the-counter analgesics and beyond.

PROBLEMATIC–RECREATIONAL DRUG USE TYPOLOGY

A second key typology – problematic–recreational drug use – developed in the 1990s out of Newcombe's 'group model' approach, which contrasted problem drug users with recreational drug users. In Newcombe's original model (1990) drug users were separated on the basis of (1) consumption patterns and consequences (risks and harms); (2) demographic and personal characteristics; and (3) the nature and extent of their contact with drugs services. Group A included opiate users and injectors, Group B were non-injecting stimulant and hallucinogen users, Group C were predominantly cannabis users, Group D were volatile substance users and Group E were image/performance enhancing users of drugs such as anabolic steroids, with some overlap between the groups.

The group model was subsequently simplified and developed into a problematic–recreational typology, broadly similar to the 'hard'/'soft' drug dichotomy (Newcombe, 2007). Problem drug users (PDUs) – Group A in Newcombe's model – were estimated to make up about 5 per cent of the total number of drug users in the UK and were characterised by their use of opiates such as heroin, crack cocaine, and sometimes benzodiazepines or amphetamines, in patterns of daily or dependent use, often by the route of intravenous injection. Recreational drug users, by contrast, accounted for the rest (about 95 per cent) of illegal drug users and included occasional and regular users of cannabis, and weekend users of psychostimulants such as amphetamines and MDMA. Implicit in this 'problematic–recreational' model of users is the recognition that higher visibility PDUs, despite only being a small minority of the total number of drug users, are a focus for criminal justice and medical interventions as well as media and public concerns.

Definitions of problem drug use

The term problem drug user (PDU) has risen to take prominence in research and policy over the last 25 years, over and above concepts such as addiction (Seddon, 2011). However a review of definitions in the international literature (Cave et al., 2009) suggests that there is little agreement on the types of drugs, patterns of drug use or consequences of use which might be considered 'problematic', with many studies focusing on harmful outcomes of use rather than specific types of drugs taken. Nevertheless, treatment has prioritised opiate and/or crack cocaine use and tackling the problems for communities associated with problem drug use, such as open drug markets, acquisitive crime, health needs, supporting children at risk and harm reduction services.

Some countries define problem drug use by the drugs consumed. In the UK, official documents refer to 'problem drug users' rather than 'problem drug use', and define these as people using opiates and/or crack cocaine, whose use is more likely to be daily or dependent, and who may have a range of associated problems linked with their drug use.

Numbers of problem drug users

A variety of methods and indicators can be used to estimate the numbers of PDUs. For example, in the UK there has been a series of Home Office feasibility studies, a study of the market for illegal drugs, and a study on the social and economic costs of Class A drug use. Singleton et al. (2006) provided an overview of the various models used to estimate prevalence of PDUs and concluded that there were approximately 327,000 PDUs in the UK, drawn from a wider cohort of over four million self-reported past year drug users according to the annual national BCS, that is, about 8 per cent of drug users. However, it has been argued that estimates of PDUs rely on flawed data while indicators such as prevalence of opiate use, drug-related hospital episodes and deaths suggest that problem drug use has been on a downward trajectory since the millennium.

Policy implications of problem drug use

Interventions with PDUs have been partly prompted by concerns surrounding the drugs–crime relationship (see also **21 drugs and crime**) and partly linked to public health initiatives. With the advent of the HIV/AIDS pandemic, the pendulum of drugs policy for PDUs swung from criminal justice interventions to public health interventions including the advent of harm reduction (see also **26 harm reduction**). In particular, the policy focus on problem drug use was consolidated in the late 1980s with the identification of the link between injecting drug use, shared needles and blood-borne viruses. In the UK for a short period the government prioritised innovative harm reduction programmes such as syringe distribution and methadone treatment over the criminal justice issues relating to Class A drug use and associated acquisitive and trafficking crimes.

In policy terms, the problematic–recreational dichotomy has served to highlight both the prioritisation of the drugs–crime relationship and the predominance of the classic medical model of addiction as a way of understanding the underlying causes of problem drug use (see also **4 addiction**). It also poses questions regarding what are the appropriate policy responses and resource allocations proportionate to different types of drug users, the problems they create and how society should respond.

Recreational drug use

The much larger group of 'recreational' drug users is in part characterised in opposition to problem drug users. Recreational drug use can refer to the types of drugs consumed, patterns of drug use, the social circumstances and consequences. For instance, recreational usage may involve the purposeful consumption, occasionally or more regularly, of drugs other than heroin and crack cocaine, most usually at social gatherings in leisure venues. While intoxication may be an aim and a desirable effect, drug use is not the sole or primary function of the social gatherings and usage can be characterised as controlled rather than compulsive or chaotic. Cannabis is the most widely used of psychoactive drugs consumed across the world, taken for relaxation and recreational purposes in social contexts, although use has fallen in Europe in recent years. Other illegal drugs that are used on an occasional or regular basis in recreational settings include cocaine, MDMA, amphetamines and more recently novel psychoactive substances or 'legal highs' (see also **5 legal drugs**).

Policy implications of recreational drug use

The policy implications of the large numbers of recreational users of controlled drugs who have appeared in the last two decades relate primarily to the potential criminalisation of otherwise law-abiding young people whose controlled drug use in leisure settings may not have significant negative consequences on their health or social circumstances, nor for their communities or wider society beyond the law-breaking itself.

A critique of the problematic–recreational typology

The problematic–recreational typology has been challenged since its inception. First, to categorise people as problem drug users on the basis of whether or not they consume specific illegal drugs is flawed because not all opiate and crack cocaine use is necessarily problematic and not all drug problems are related to opiate and crack cocaine. For example, in relation to the former point, McSweeney and Turnbull (2007) challenge some of the myths surrounding patterns of heroin use including the inevitability of daily and dependent heroin use. They interviewed occasional and non-problematic heroin users, many of whom were not in touch with criminal justice or health services and for whom, for at least part of their drug taking careers, heroin use could be considered controlled and unproblematic aside from the illegality of their actions.

Second, it has been noted that in areas of poverty and social exclusion, the distinction between recreational and problematic drug use may break down, resulting in patterns of use not typically associated with recreational drugs. Simpson (2003) challenged the notion that recreational drug use is unproblematic in his ethnographic study in the north east of England. He proposed a third category – 'persistent' drug use –alongside recreational and dependent use, and suggested that drug use careers could slip between these three characterisations. However, in defence of the group model, it should be noted that the problematic–recreational typology was not envisaged in terms of mutually exclusive groups and recognised overlaps between the groups.

Nevertheless, despite the drawbacks identified above, the problematic–recreational distinction has retained some salience to our understanding of patterns of drug use. This can be illustrated in research on drug use in dance clubs (see also **11 dance drugs/club drugs**). First, in terms of sheer numbers, surveys of clubbers have noted very high levels of regular use of a wide range of illegal drugs including ecstasy, cocaine, amphetamines and cannabis at weekends, but very low levels of use of heroin, crack cocaine and benzodiazepines suggesting that in general terms, there is some empirical grounding to making a distinction between these two general clusters of drug use, even among regular and prolific users. Second, dance club surveys locate drug use away from the sphere of poverty and social exclusion and instead contextualised within the social setting of leisure time consumption, for example, as part of the night-time economy of clubs and pubs, with different challenges in terms of public health, public order and service provision.

Additionally, if focusing on motivations for drug use, this typology can also include experimental, spiritual and image/performance enhancing drug use. *Experimental* drug use can be characterised as initiation and early career drug use by inexperienced users or as exploratory in terms of motivations. *Spiritual* drug use is motivated by wanting to experience religious, expansive or euphoric feelings or by the broader symbolic or proscribed role of psychoactive drugs within a religious belief system, such as cannabis within Rastafarianism and Hinduism. *Cognitive enhancers* are stimulant drugs such as caffeine and amphetamines taken to improve stamina, memory or performance in work-related tasks. Other drugs taken to enhance image and/or performance include anabolic steroids and melanotan.

SUMMARY

Two key typologies of drug users are the *use–misuse–abuse* typology and the *problematic–recreational* typology. The *use–misuse–abuse* typology indicates the social acceptability of drug use and distinguishes between perceived legitimate consumption which is legally, medically or socially sanctioned and unsanctioned use which is problematic for the individual or society. The *problematic–recreational* typology characterises the motivations or patterns of drug use. The majority of drug users are *recreational* users who take psychoactive drugs during leisure periods, in leisure venues and social settings. A minority of users develop *problem* drug use when daily use (particularly of opiates and crack cocaine) results in dependency, injecting or other problematic patterns of use.

The wide variety of patterns of drug use, motivations to take drugs and consequences of use mean that there is no simple understanding of what a 'drug user' is and the problems faced by or caused by drug use. It is necessary to understand drug-using careers in their historical and socio-cultural context before considering the ways in which drug use may impact upon or cause possible harms to users, communities and wider society. Furthermore, the political reasons for the differentiations within these typologies are salient in terms of criminal justice, health service provision and resource allocation.

REFERENCES

Cave, J., Hunt, P., Ismail, S., Levitt, R., Pacula, R., Rabinovich, L., Rubin, J. and Weed, K. (2009) *Tackling Problem Drug Use*. RAND Europe Report. London: National Audit Office.

McSweeney, T. and Turnbull, P. (2007) *Exploring User Perceptions of Occasional and Controlled Heroin Use: A Follow up Study*. York: Joseph Rowntree Foundation.

Newcomb, M. and Bentler, P. (1989) 'Substance use and abuse among children and teenagers', *American Psychologist*, 44 (2): 242–8.

Newcomb, R. (1990) 'Drug use and drug policy in Merseyside, report for Mersey regional health authority', in W. Schneider (ed.), *First Conference of European Cities at the Centre of the Illegal Drug Trade*. Frankfurt: Conference City Reader.

Newcombe, R. (2007) 'Trends in the prevalence of illicit drug use in Britain', in M. Simpson, T. Shildrick and R. MacDonald (eds), *Drugs in Britain: Supply, Consumption and Control*. Basingstoke: Palgrave Macmillan, pp. 13–38.

Seddon, T. (2011) 'What is a problem drug user?', *Addiction Research and Theory*, 19 (4): 334–43.

Simpson, M. (2003) 'The relationship between drug use and crime: a puzzle inside an enigma', *International Journal of Drug Policy*, 14 (4): 307–19.

Singleton, N., Murray, R. and Tinsley, L. (eds) (2006) *Measuring Different Aspects of Problem Drug Use: Methodological Problems*, 2nd edn. Home Office Online Report 16/06. London: Home Office.

9
Binge Drinking

Binge drinking refers to the excessive consumption of alcohol within one drinking episode. The term was originally used in clinical practice to refer to an extended drinking session from which everyday life was suspended. From the 1990s, the term was more narrowly defined as a (much lower) quantity of alcohol consumed over and above recommended health limits within one drinking session.

The original clinical definition of a binge referred to both the excessive consumption of alcohol across an extended time period and also the consequence of such consumption for the user. Clinical definitions of the length and outcome of a binge vary and can include characteristics such as continuous dependent drinking over a period of a day or more to the point where the drinker becomes unconscious, to two days or more, resulting in the suspension of normal activities. Moreover, the drinker indulging in a 'binge' – or 'bender' in popular culture – is a clinical concern because a 'binge' is usually not just a one-off occasion of excessive consumption but a more frequent occurrence, often associated with alcohol dependency or problem drinking.

More recently the term has moved away from the 'bender' definition of prolonged consumption lasting over a day, possibly to the point of unconsciousness, towards a clearly measurable definition of excessive drinking. Since the 1990s binge drinking has been defined as consumption above the recommended daily limits set by public health professionals and measured by a specified number of drinks within an unspecified time period. The shift to numbered drinks was linked to growing concerns in the USA about excessive sessional drinking particularly among students on college campuses away from the potentially moderating influences of their families and communities. Thus in the US context, binge drinking came to be understood as men drinking more than five standard alcoholic drinks and women drinking more than four standard drinks on a drinking occasion, the so-called 'five/four measure' in the research by Wechsler et al. (1994).

The development of measurable, unit-based definitions of binge drinking in line with sensible drinking messages became a key aspect of public health promotion and alcohol education campaigns in many countries from the 1990s, although the definition of a binge varies considerably between countries. For example, in the UK the Department of Health in 1995 defined a 'binge' as either drinking one-half the recommended weekly sensible drinking maximum or, more usually, drinking more than double the recommended daily sensible drinking maximum, in a single drinking session, the latter being termed the 8/6 unit measure. Thus, a man consuming 64 grams of alcohol and a woman consuming 48 grams of alcohol would be classified as binge drinking in the UK whereas a man would need to drink 70 grams of alcohol and a woman 56 grams to be classified as binge drinking in the USA.

LIMITATIONS OF THE TERM

Binge drinking has been described as a 'confused concept' (Herring et al., 2008) with considerable drawbacks. First, as noted above, while the quantitative definition clearly specifies the number of drinks or units of alcohol to be imbibed in a drinking session, it does not make allowance for the length of the session, the individual drinker's characteristics or other factors. Therefore a specified number of drinks consumed over a prolonged drinking session alongside food could result in a low blood alcohol content with no subjective feelings of drunkenness whereas the same quantity consumed rapidly on an empty stomach could result in intoxication. Second, the benchmark used, the public health sensible drinking guidelines, is a simple measure and does not incorporate individual differences such as body mass index, physical exertion or other factors that may influence the experience of rapid alcohol consumption and associated harms. Such individual differences will influence levels of harm associated with alcohol consumption.

Given the limitations of the quantitative measure, a second and more subjective measure of binge drinking developed in parallel which used the drinker's experience of drunkenness instead. Some studies combine both these objective and subjective measures of drunkenness; for example, the ESPAD project schools surveys which are conducted every four years in 35 European countries uses both a numeric measurement of heavy episodic drinking (five drinks or more in one episode) and also asks about the frequency of experiencing drunkenness.

Given that binge drinking is a 'confused concept', some American clinicians have attempted to reinstate the original definition of consumption over 24 hours or more, resulting in everyday life being suspended (Schuckit, 1998). Alternative terms have also been used to capture the phenomenon of binge drinking including 'determined drunkenness' (Measham, 2004), 'intense intoxication', 'calculated hedonism' and 'extreme drinking' (Martinic and Measham, 2008). A range of studies have suggested that drunkenness is not only considered a motivation for consumption but a *positive* outcome in some societies (Martinic and Measham, 2008). Also it is not necessarily an activity preserved only for the young or manual workers, with consumption increasing among women, professional groups and the over 30s. Thus binge drinking can take the form of teenagers drinking illicit alcohol in the local park; young adults 'out on the town' in city centre bars and professionals drinking wine at home. There are huge cultural differences in attitudes to excessive drinking around the world, however. In some southern European countries such as Italy, for example, drunkenness still appears to be less socially acceptable than some northern European countries (Martinic and Measham 2008), although this is changing, for example, with the appearance of public gatherings whose primary purpose is to get drunk by consuming cheap off-trade alcohol, such as the *botellón* in Spain.

EXPLANATIONS FOR THE RECENT EMERGENCE OF THE CULTURAL PHENOMENON OF BINGE DRINKING

In northern European countries, such as the UK, Ireland and Denmark, from the mid 1990s there was an increase in the quantity of alcohol consumed by young people during a drinking session. In the UK and Ireland, these changing patterns of youthful and young adult consumption were linked to rapid changes in the alcohol industry, the expansion of the night-time economy and associated concerns about public drunkenness. Several changes coalesced including: first, the emergence and growing popularity of high-strength alcoholic beverages, such as 'alcopops' (ready-to-drink flavoured alcoholic beverages), shots and bottled beers. Second, drinking venues shifted from traditional pubs with intergenerational drinking, to continental-style café bars and fun pubs marketed at young people, some of which specialised in 'vertical drinking', and associated promotional activities encouraging excessive consumption (Measham and Brain, 2005). Third, urban regeneration in many cities has been based on the expansion of alcohol-focused leisure with the emergence of what came to be known as the night-time economy (Hobbs et al., 2003) whereby northern European weekend binge drinking patterns have been incorporated into a southern European café bar context associated with more leisurely consumption. This has led some (for example, Measham and Brain,

2005) to suggest that we saw a 'new culture of intoxication' emerge, linked to the use of legal and illegal substances with public drunkenness no longer as socially unacceptable as it once was.

POLICY RESPONSES

Trading hours

Initial attempts to reduce the binge drinking frenzy of 'last orders' in countries with restricted trading hours led Australia, New Zealand and Ireland, followed by the UK, to experiment with extended trading hours with the aim of reducing binge drinking, staggering venue closing times, reducing tensions at disorder 'hot-spots' and thus promoting a more leisurely Mediterranean model of consumption. The liberalisation of licensing had a mixed response, but in general drinkers extended their night out later into the night with an associated increase in alcohol consumption and alcohol-related crime.

Marketing and promotional restrictions

The increased quantity of alcohol consumed by young people on a night out, followed by associated increases in alcohol-related disorder and health problems, was evident, for example, not just in the growth in liver cirrhosis mortality, particularly in the UK, but also the lower age of onset of the disease. Media coverage of binge drinking by young people led to calls for greater restrictions on the marketing and sale of alcohol, both through state regulation and stricter industry self-regulation. There are concerns that restrictions on drinks promotions in licensed premises to promote more responsible drinking, in contrast to cheaper off-licence alcohol prices and supermarket 'deep discounting', has produced a growing discrepancy in prices between the on-trade and off-trade and the emergence of a phenomenon known as pre-loading or drinking at home before going to leisure venues. Early indications are that pre-loading on alcohol before going out can be associated with higher levels of drunkenness, disorder and vulnerability to assault in the night-time economy once drinkers go out.

Pricing

A strong association has been identified between alcohol pricing and consumption levels across the world. In order to reduce alcohol-related consumption levels and associated harms, increased taxation and/or minimum pricing of alcohol can be an effective tool at the population level, although very high levels of tax for legal drugs like alcohol and tobacco (see also **5 legal drugs**) can result in the increased likelihood of smuggling duty-free goods into a country. Increased retail prices in licensed premises have led to a growing discrepancy between on-trade and off-trade prices and have been linked to increased pre-loading as discussed above. Minimum pricing per unit of alcohol, as introduced in Scotland, increases the price of the cheapest drinks and therefore is seen as a more targeted policy measure than blanket taxation of all alcoholic products. Minimum pricing is most likely to affect street drinkers and younger drinkers with less disposable income who are more likely to drink cheaper alcoholic beverages and for whom drinking may be problematic or risky. It has little effect on on-trade sales (whose prices are rarely as low as the off trade) or on those on higher incomes and/or those who purchase alcoholic beverages priced above the threshold of the minimum price per unit. Minimum pricing can be seen as a regressive form of taxation because it disproportionately affects lower income drinkers and/or those who favour cheaper alcoholic beverages. Furthermore, increasing the cost and reducing the consumption of alcohol for those on low incomes does not necessarily address possible underlying problems of poverty and social exclusion and may have unintended consequences such as displacement to other cheap and easily available psychoactive substances such as solvents or other forms of ethanol.

DECLINE IN BINGE DRINKING

After an increase in heavy episodic drinking in the 1990s, there is evidence from international surveys (for example, ESPAD) and national surveys (for example, UK General Lifestyle Survey) that binge drinking, or excessive sessional consumption, has remained stable or declined slightly in some countries since the early 2000s. The fall in consumption is linked to a decline in beer drinking among young people, while alcopops, spirit and wine consumption has increased, as has older adult women's consumption, particularly of wine at home. This may be because high levels of drinking have reached a plateau with market saturation but other possible changes include a fall among a new generation of young people who find binge drinking less culturally appealing and/or economically feasible in the wake of worldwide recession, a downturn in youth employment, an increase in the real price of alcohol and general economic insecurity.

ALTERNATIVES TO 'BINGE DRINKING' IN PUBLIC HEALTH

Recently, in recognition of the limitations of public health policy focused on unit-based definitions of binge drinking, there has been a shift in emphasis to the harm or potential harm from drinking. While some alcohol researchers have called for the term binge to be reclaimed for its original clinical application, alcohol policy in many countries is shifting towards a focus on the consequences of problem drinking rather than just the amount of alcohol consumed, such as the WHO definitions of hazardous, harmful and dependent drinking.

REFERENCES

Herring, R., Berridge, V. and Thom, B. (2008) 'Binge drinking: an exploration of a confused concept', *Journal of Epidemiology and Community Health*, 62: 476–9.
Hobbs, D., Hadfield, P., Lister, S. and Winlow, S. (2003) *Bouncers: Violence and Governance in the Night-time Economy*. Oxford: Oxford University Press.

Martinic, M. and Measham, F. (eds) (2008) *Swimming With Crocodiles: The Culture of Extreme Drinking*. New York: Routledge.

Measham, F. (2004) 'The decline of ecstasy, the rise of 'binge' drinking and the persistence of pleasure', *Probation Journal*, 51 (4): 309–26.

Measham, F. and Brain, K. (2005) '"Binge" drinking, British alcohol policy and the new culture of intoxication', *Crime, Media, Culture: An International Journal*, 1: 263–84.

Schuckit, M. (1998) 'Binge drinking: the five/four measure', *Journal of Studies on Alcohol*, 59: 123–24.

Wechsler, H., Davenport, A., Dowdall, G., Moeykens, B., and Castillo, S. (1994) 'Health and behavioral consequences of binge drinking in college: a national survey of students at 140 campuses', *Journal of the American Medical Association*, 272: 1672–7.

NOTES

In the UK a unit of alcohol is defined as 10 ml of pure ethanol. This is equivalent to a standard measure of spirits (25 ml at 40 per cent alcohol by volume) or half a pint of standard strength beer (284 ml at 3.6 per cent alcohol by volume). Thus a man drinking more than four pints of average strength beer (or 8 standard spirit measures or shots) and a woman drinking more than three pints of average strength beer (or 6 standard spirit measures or shots) would be classified as binge drinking.

10
Raves and Circuit Parties

Raves were venues associated with particular music styles, dance and youth culture. The term is used less frequently in contemporary culture, compared to its usage during the 1980s and 1990s. Circuit parties are commercialised dance music events that are attended largely by gay males.

A unique music and dance scene emerged on the Mediterranean island of Ibiza in the mid-1980s. According to folklore, a small group of DJs from England who were visiting the island in 1987 consumed ecstasy during a night out in a local club. The effects of ecstasy and the DJ's unique music encouraged the group to recreate the scene in London. Referred to as acid house, the music was a collective sound of various other music genres that had roots in Chicago and Detroit. Although its origins are debated, most reports suggest that the rave scene emerged from the acid house phenomena and techno music parties in Goa. Organised as all-night unlicensed events and sometimes extending over several days, raves were held in abandoned warehouses, factories, fields and other secluded locations. The 'rave scene' blossomed into a 'movement' that was shaped by solidarity among friends, acquaintances and strangers, and collective identity. Various informal norms regulated the scene that was characterised by symbolic logos (for example, smiley face) and unique fashion. The diffusion of the rave scene spread to various countries in what some have described as an international phenomenon, firmly embraced by various youth subcultures. Over time, 'rave music' became increasingly diversified, to include techno, house, hardcore, garage, trance and other music genres.

Beginning in the early 1990s, raves began to be subsumed into mainstream club culture. This transition occurred in the UK in part due to increasing pressure from law enforcement via new legislation, and occurred in selected Canadian cities when promoters sought legal venues to accommodate large crowds of people. Mainstream clubs featured 'rave music,' drew disc jockeys that specialised in this music, and altered lighting and other aspects of the physical environment that enhanced the dance experience, particularly under the influence of ecstasy.

In the move from unlicensed to legal commercialised venues, some club owners were increasingly motivated by profit and less concerned about patrons' health. For example, although some clubs were known for their 'user friendly' atmosphere, observations in other clubs noted the lack of 'chill out' space, limited availability of free water, astronomical prices for bottled water, and cold water taps/faucets being shut off in public bathrooms.[1] Raves organised in unlicensed as well as club venues are still held in various European countries, where information on upcoming events can be located via the Internet and social networking via mobile/ cell phones. The Internet sites feature sponsored advertisements from well-known commercial airlines and hotels, which suggests that the rave scene has been economically viable for tour operators and travel agents (Sellers, 1998). In some countries, the term 'rave' is no longer used; rather, the scene has been described as electronic dance music, or EDM, which incorporates both rave and club cultures (Anderson and Kavanagh, 2007). Music genres associated with the scene are highly debated among listeners.

RAVES, EDM SCENES AND DRUG TAKING

Several historical and contemporary examples have linked drug use to particular venues, for example, opium dens, shooting galleries, crack houses. In the UK, raves became associated with drug taking (namely ecstasy use) beginning in the late 1980s and early 1990s. It was an association that was in some ways misguided in that ecstasy was used in various social settings outside rave venues, and some rave participants never consumed ecstasy. The association with ecstasy, coupled with large crowds and music that was misunderstood by mainstream culture contributed to moral panic. Reports of alleged ecstasy-related fatalities surfaced in several countries and these deaths further fuelled the panic. Rave organisers, participants and the scene itself were perceived as threats to the dominant social order.

---

[1]Ecstasy can dehydrate. This effect combined with long periods of dancing can pose dangers to users' health. Drinking water while under the influence of ecstasy helps to prevent dehydration.

Although a causal link between drug use and rave/club settings has not been demonstrated, substantial use of ecstasy, other drugs, or polydrug combinations among rave or club patrons has been reported in several counties, including Australia, Canada, Northern Ireland, Scotland, and the USA. In Manchester (England), club patrons reported substantially higher rates of drug use than bar patrons, and this difference extended to drugs that were used prior to entering the venues (Measham and Moore, 2009). A study of club-goers in New York City found that 91.7 per cent of respondents had engaged in polydrug use, and the authors of that study documented over 1600 polydrug combinations (Grov et al., 2009). In most countries, the disappearance of unlicensed raves did not deter drug use when scenes shifted to EDM.

THE SOCIAL CONTROL OF RAVES

Viewed as deviant and threatening, raves became the focus of increasing social control through various state mechanisms. In the USA, the Illicit Drug Anti-Proliferation Act was passed in 2003, which targets managers, and business and property owners who organise events for the purpose of distributing or using illicit drugs. Although the law does not specify any association between drug use and dance music, it has been referred to as the RAVE Act. A new classification of substances was devised, originating in the USA: 'club drugs' represented the latest menace that required intervention from drug policymakers.

Elsewhere, state controls followed the pattern in the USA, and in some countries these controls were quite rigid. A participant-observation study of club culture in China found that initially, the government was slow to respond to the developing rave culture in the late 1990s (Chew, 2009). For example, people openly consumed ecstasy tablets within rave venues as late as 1998. Government suppression of raves followed, and the movement was driven underground. In 'up-ground' clubs, clubbers often altered their style of dance to avoid the association with ecstasy. Chew (2009) concluded that state suppression in China contributed to a segregated club scene that tended to polarise participants based on their social class.

CIRCUIT PARTIES

In the early stages of the HIV/AIDS epidemic, unprotected anal intercourse between gay males was identified as a risk factor for disease transmission (see also **24 HIV/AIDS and other blood-borne viruses**). In response to limited government expenditures allocated for prevention of HIV, grassroots and voluntary agencies developed proactive initiatives that attempted to address the alarming rates of HIV among gay males. Fundraisers were organised in the early stages of the epidemic in an effort to raise money for not-for-profit agencies that catered to gay males. In 1982, a dance party was held in New York City and attended by several hundred gay males. Entrance fees for the party were donated to the Gay Men's Health Crisis to support HIV/AIDS initiatives. A few years later, the White Party was organised in Miami, so named for the clothing worn by participants who dressed in white. Currently, at least 100 themed circuit parties are held every year in the USA and Canada, including the Winter Party (Miami), Fireball (Chicago), Black Party (New York), and the Black and Blue Ball (Montreal). White parties are now held in various locations throughout the USA, and more generally, circuit parties have spread to other regions of the world, for example, Australia and Brazil. Although once organised as one-night events, some circuit parties now extend over several days. Information about the now highly commercialised events is circulated through magazines that cater to potential participants (Kurtz and Inciardi, 2003) as well as Internet websites.

Circuit parties feature music, dance, flamboyant entertainment, after-hours parties and a host of other events. Each event can draw thousands of party-goers, and the entrance fees alone have raised millions of dollars for voluntary agencies each year. Participants tend to be males who work in professional occupations and who have the salaries to travel. Indeed, some participants attend several circuit parties annually. The communities in which the parties are held benefit greatly from the tourist economy. One circuit party alone can bring in millions of dollars for local hotels, restaurants and the service industry in general.

Although originally organised as a means to fundraise for HIV/AIDS initiatives, circuit parties help to reinforce gay identity and pride, and provide gay males with feelings of liberation and space in which to openly share pleasure and affection. For some participants, circuit parties provide a venue for a stigma-free celebration of gay lifestyle.

Drug use and the circuit

Similar to rave scenes, circuit parties have been described as places characterised by high prevalence of drug use among participants who attend the events. Participants have reported extensive drug use during the past year and while attending the events. Use of ecstasy is relatively common as circuit parties incorporated elements of the rave scene. Furthermore, crystal methamphetamine has been increasingly linked with circuit parties, and more so than ecstasy, the effects of crystal can contribute to sexual behaviours that pose risk for HIV transmission. A survey of gay males attending a circuit party in Miami in 2003 found that 60 per cent of attendees had tried crystal methamphetamine and the most common polydrug combination included crystal, ecstasy and GHB (Kurtz and Inciardi, 2003). The authors found that although the use of crystal was unrelated to (self-reported) HIV infection, attendees who had used the drug were approximately twice as likely as non-users to report having a sexually transmitted disease within the last six months.

The relatively common patterns of drug use among circuit party participants have created concern among some critics, including individuals from the gay community. Drug and sexual risk taking at the parties appears to be at odds with the HIV prevention messages that have been promoted among gay males. In response to these concerns, several parties have organised on-site condom distribution, health promotion, ambulances, drug outreach, counsellors and physicians.

The costs of these services is said to be well below the profit that is earned from the events.

SUMMARY

Although not all participants engage in drug use, raves and circuit parties are venues where drugs are consumed, and polydrug use combinations are extensive. The scenes that have emerged from these settings have encouraged collective identity and have expanded social networks. In some ways, these venues are contemporary examples of opium dens, roadhouses, and shebeens – settings from another era that permitted drug or alcohol use in environments that were relatively safe from the gaze of mainstream culture.

REFERENCES

Anderson, T.L. and Kavanagh, P.R. (2007) 'A "rave" review: conceptual interests and analytical shifts in research on rave culture', *Sociology Compass*, 1 (2): 499–519.

Chew, M.M. (2009) 'Decline of the rave inspired club culture in China: state suppression, clubber adaptations and socio-cultural transformations', *Dancecult: Journal of Electronic Dance Music Culture*, 1 (1): 22–34. Available at: http://dj.dancecult.net/index.php/journal/article/view-File/20/4 (accessed 16 October 2012).

Grov, C., Kelly, B.C. and Parsons, J.T. (2009) 'Polydrug use among club-going young adults recruited through time-space sampling', *Substance Use and Misuse*, 44 (6): 848–64.

Kurtz, S.P. and Inciardi, J.A. (2003) 'Crystal meth, gay men and circuit parties', *Law Enforcement Executive Forum*, 3 (4): 97–114.

Measham, F. and Moore, K. (2009) 'Repertoires of distinction: exploring patterns of weekend polydrug use within local leisure scenes across the English night time economy', *Criminology and Criminal Justice*, 9 (4): 437–64.

Sellers, A. (1998) 'The influence of dance music on the UK youth tourism market', *Tourism Management*, 19 (6): 611–15.

Dance Drugs/Club Drugs

Dance drugs or club drugs are associated with attendance at dance clubs or events playing electronic dance music. Surveys suggest that ecstasy is a favourite dance drug although reduced purity and availability, regional differences and changing fashions have led to other illegal drugs such as cocaine and ketamine becoming more popular club drugs in recent years.

There is no simple answer to the question of which drugs are dance drugs or club drugs. A wide range of drugs have been taken by people throughout history to enhance music and dancing, with music and dancing also being used to enhance the effects of psychoactive drugs. The consumption of drugs alongside dancing has been associated with specific subcultural groups and music scenes, and associated public anxieties (Kohn, 1997), from amphetamine use by 1960s British mods and Northern Soul aficionados in the UK through to cocaine use in the 1970s American gay/disco scene such as at the infamous Studio 54 night-club in Manhattan. The term dance drugs developed in the UK in the early 1990s when the 'acid house' and 'rave' scene developed along with the emer-gence in consumption of ecstasy pills (containing MDMA) and other stimulant drugs at raves and unlicensed warehouse parties (see also **10 raves and circuit parties**). As raves evolved into commercial dance events in licensed nightclubs, and as drug use was seen to extend across a weekend and beyond the primary function of facilitating prolonged dancing, the term club drugs superseded the term dance drugs in the early 21st century.

Potentially almost any drug could be included in the category club drug – as have various stimulants, hallucinogens, depressants and deliriants – with the pri-mary criterion for inclusion being a drug that is taken during a night out which involves dancing and/or attendance at a dance event. Stimulants and psychostimu-lants, however, are the most prevalent and most popular of club drugs.

PREVALENCE

Studies suggest that 'clubbers' are more drug experienced than the general popu-lation, have higher levels of current drug use and broader repertoires of use. For example, in the UK the general population survey undertaken in private house-holds on an annual basis – the BCS – records self-reported prevalence of use of any drug among 16–24-year-olds as 40 per cent in their lifetime and 11 per cent in the past month. Regarding self-reported ecstasy use among this age group, lifetime prevalence is 10 per cent and past month ecstasy use is just over 1 per cent (Smith and Flatley, 2011). However, this survey also found that those respondents who visited nightclubs and pubs were more likely to take illegal drugs and that more frequent attendance was positively associated with higher levels of drug use.

Surveys of dance club customers were undertaken from the 1990s as dance club culture became increasingly popular and dance drug use became a cause for public concern and press attention (see also **32 drug scares and moral panics**). In the UK, a Home Office-funded survey reported a lifetime prevalence rate of 79 per cent for clubbers' use of any drug. In Australia, lifetime prevalence of use of any illegal drug was also reported by almost all ravers, for example over 96 per cent of a sample of Perth ravers in the 1990s reported having taken an illegal drug at least once.

In the USA, a study compared customers attending clubs playing electronic dance music with those attending clubs playing hip hop music. For those attending dance clubs, rates of drug use tended to be higher and/or more recent, but they had less interest in getting drunk or in meeting sexual partners at venues compared with those attending hip hop clubs.

The use of club drugs is not confined just to clubs, however. Surveys of Manchester bar customers in the 2000s found that although bar customers were significantly less likely to take drugs than club customers on a night out, nevertheless one-fifth either had consumed or planned to consume cocaine or ecstasy during their night out. Relatedly, the association between an appreciation of dance music and the consumption of dance drugs is evident in non-club customers as well, including those who are too young to attend clubs. For example, self-reported lifetime prevalence of ecstasy use is higher for adolescent fans of rave music than non-rave music fans.

Even among those who take club drugs and go clubbing, it appears that increased drug use is associated with increased attendance at clubs. For example, British holidaymakers in Spain attend dance clubs, consume more club drugs, drink alcohol and have more sexual partners on holiday than they usually do when at home. Those attending dance clubs and taking club drugs in Ibiza, however, have lower levels of drunkenness and alcohol-related violence and risk taking than British holidaymakers elsewhere in Spain. As with the American and Spanish studies, a study of Glasgow nightclubs also suggested that those attending dance clubs and consuming club drugs may be more likely to prioritise music and dancing as a motive for their club attendance, and less likely to be involved in alcohol-related incidents of violence and disorder. Zero incidents of violence were observed at the Glasgow 'old-skool' hardcore rave fieldwork venue, for example. Similarly a study comparing drug use at standard nightclubs and dance events in Lancashire in the UK found drug use was twice as high at a dance event as at a standard nightclub, but alcohol consumption was lower.

THEORETICAL DEBATE

Given the higher incidence of drug use among clubbers, a debate developed regarding the theoretical significance of the emergence of dance drug use and wider dance club culture and specifically whether it could be characterised as a subculture, neo-tribe or scene. As dance drugs and dance clubs became increasingly popular from the early 1990s in Europe and Australasia, it was suggested that rave could not be characterised as a subcultural phenomenon due to its commercial success. Researchers challenged the relevance of subcultural theory in postmodern society and specifically the notion of an authentic underground subculture, suggesting instead that rave could be understood in terms of subcultural capital, which featured an underground 'cool' aesthetic rather than genuine underground movement (Thornton, 1995). Others argued that rave and other youth cultural forms could be characterised as a series of musical and stylistic neo-tribes in 1990s UK. Such post-subcultural theorists were themselves then challenged by youth studies researchers who reasserted the relevance of the concept of subculture to dance club culture. However, rather than being a working class rebellion through style, rave was characterised as a spectacular and higher income subculture associated with the middle class (Shildrick and MacDonald, 2006). Most recently, dance club cultures have been noted for their distinct yet pluralistic musical and stylistic sub-genres, characterised neither as subcultures nor neo-tribes, but rather as 'scenes' which each have distinctive patterns of club drug use (Anderson, 2009; Measham and Moore, 2009).

KEY CLUB DRUGS

Primary and secondary club drugs refer to the level of importance given to different drugs most usually consumed within a polydrug repertoire (see also **6 polydrug use/ polysubstance use**). Primary dance drugs are usually stimulant drugs such as ecstasy or amphetamines, with survey respondents often citing ecstasy as their primary or 'favourite' club drug, whose popularity emerged with the development of acid house, rave and electronic dance music scenes across the world (for example, Measham et al., 2001). Secondary dance drugs are taken to enhance the perceived positive effects of primary club drugs or to reduce the perceived negative effects, and can include hallucinogenic drugs, such as LSD, and depressant drugs, such as alcohol, GHB/GBL and cannabis. They are seen by the user as complementary to, rather than central to, the club drugs experience and are not exclusively or primarily used as drugs in the club drug repertoire: for example, cannabis, tobacco, poppers, alcohol, energy drinks containing caffeine and herbal stimulants, such as guarana.

A reduction in the purity and/or availability of primary club drugs such as ecstasy, along with national and regional differences and changing fashions have led to other illegal drugs such as cocaine, ketamine and mephedrone becoming more popular club drugs in recent years. In Hong Kong, ketamine has been the most popular club drug (Hunt et al., 2010) while in Japan hallucinogenic mushrooms have been popular. In the UK, use of amphetamines and LSD fell from the 1990s to 2000s, while cocaine increased in popularity both among clubbers and in the general young adult population from the late 1990s. Amphetamines have been popular in the European techno and hard house scenes whereas hallucinogens, such as LSD, magic mushrooms and ketamine, have been more popular in free party and festival scenes.

MOTIVATIONS

The motivations for club drug use are primarily stimulant, to provide extra energy for prolonged dancing, possibly with euphoric properties to increase sociability and empathy with fellow clubbers, alongside other drugs which may be taken to ameliorate, enhance or prolong the effects of the drug(s) consumed and the context to use, whether taken consecutively, concurrently or combined (see also **6 polydrug use/polysubstance use**). Hallucinogenic drugs have been favoured to enhance the audio-visual stimulus of the club environment and depressant drugs have been taken after clubbing either at 'chill out' parties or at home in order to counteract the stimulant drugs consumed earlier in the night out. While cannabis is the most widely used of 'chill-out' drugs, other drugs consumed after clubbing include alcohol, ketamine and sedatives.

CONSEQUENCES

Early studies of ecstasy hospital admissions and ecstasy-related deaths highlighted concerns about increased body temperature and associated complications, as well as kidney dysfunction and hyponatraemia, leading to a small number of high profile deaths of young people. It appeared that it was the context to club drug use – that is, specifically the consumption of stimulant drugs in hot dance clubs during prolonged dancing – which was of particular significance. While an average of 25 deaths per annum involving ecstasy were reported in the UK in the 1990s, it is notable that no ecstasy-related deaths were recorded among psychotherapy and counselling clients who took MDMA in therapeutic settings in 1970s America.

Studies exploring media coverage of these ecstasy-related deaths have questioned the extent to which such deaths were disproportionately covered in the press compared with other drug-related deaths and the extent to which the response of the media and the authorities to club drugs could be understood in terms of 'moral panic' (see also **32 drug scares and moral panics**). Critics have argued that due to the growth in alternative media forms such as the Internet it is no longer possible to have a moral consensus and therefore, a moral panic, around a drug (Murji, 1998). Others have pointed to the ongoing disproportionate press coverage of young, white and photogenic 'victims' of club drugs compared with problem drug users.

Combined polydrug use in hot dance club settings continues to be linked to hospital emergency admissions, however. Toxicologists have highlighted the numbers of acute emergency department admissions predominantly due either to GHB/GBL overdose or to excessive stimulant drug use (such as ecstasy, cocaine and more recently mephedrone), resulting in palpitations and unconsciousness. Other medical assessments of club drug users have suggested by contrast that regular clubbers may be fitter and have a lower body mass index than the general population, due to vigorous and prolonged dancing for many hours, aided by stimulant drug consumption (for example, Measham et al., 2001).

POLICY ISSUES

Criminal justice initiatives

The association between the consumption of illegal drugs and attendance at electronic dance music events led the authorities in many countries to regulate and restrict the occurrence of raves and electronic dance music events. For example, in the UK, the Criminal Justice and Public Order Act 1994 for the first time defined and criminalised a specific musical genre and its followers, if they attended an unlicensed music event playing rave music which was defined as 'sounds wholly or predominantly characterised by the emission of a succession of repetitive beats'.

In the USA, the Illicit Drug Anti Proliferation Act 2003 or so-called RAVE Act, was a federal law which held venue owners responsible for illicit drug use on their premises. The RAVE Act resulted in venue owners enforcing a zero tolerance approach to club drug use which led to delays in users receiving medical attention due to concerns about the club's liability. This federal law, along with local and state level drug-related rave laws, led to club closures or a switch to more commercially successful music events.

More recently, concerns have been expressed about the disproportionate policing and surveillance of club-goers through the use of searches upon entry into dance clubs, police sniffer dogs and drug testing. In Australia this has led to protests against perceived human rights violations.

Health initiatives

At a local level, harm reduction initiatives emerged alongside the development of the early rave and dance club scene (see also **26 harm reduction**). One early researcher into this phenomenon, Russell Newcombe, applied the harm reduction principles developed for problem drug users in Merseyside to dance events and formulated the 'Safer Dancing' policy together with Manchester City Council and Lifeline drugs agency, which established the first local authority harm reduction policy on dance drug use at dance events in the world. These ideas were subsequently picked up at a national level in Home Office guidelines for the management of nightclub venues. In the Netherlands the Drug Information and Monitoring System (DIMS) developed in the 1990s provides information and testing for individual drug users as well as acting as a public health early warning system regarding harmful contents such as variable purity or adulterants.

REFERENCES

Anderson, T. (2009) *Rave Culture: The Alteration and Decline of a Philadelphia Music Scene.* Philadelphia, PA: Temple University Press.

Hunt, G., Moloney, M. and Evans, K. (2010) *Youth, Drugs and Nightlife.* Abingdon: Routledge.

Kohn, M. (1997) 'The chemical generation and its ancestors: dance crazes and drug panics across eight decades', *International Journal of Drug Policy*, 8 (3): 137–42.

Measham, F. and Moore, K. (2009) 'Repertoires of distinction: exploring patterns of weekend polydrug use within local leisure scenes across the English night time economy', *Criminology and Criminal Justice*, 9 (4): 437–64.

Measham, F., Aldridge, J. and Parker, H. (2001) *Dancing on Drugs: Risk, Health and Hedonism in the British Club Scene.* London: Free Association Books.

Murji, K. (1998) 'The agony and the ecstasy: drugs, media and morality', in R. Coomber (ed.), *The Control of Drugs and Drug Users: Reason or Reaction?*, 1st edn. Amsterdam: Harwood Academic Publishers.

Shildrick, T. and MacDonald, R. (2006) 'In defence of subculture: young people, leisure and social divisions', *Journal of Youth Studies*, 9 (2): 125–40.

Smith, K. and Flatley, J. (eds) (2011) *Drug Misuse Declared: Findings from the 2010/11 British Crime Survey, England and Wales.* Home Office Statistical Bulletin 12/11. London: Home Office. http://www.homeoffice.gov.uk/scienceresearch (accessed 1 August 2012).

Thornton, S. (1995) *Club Cultures: Music, Media and Subcultural Capital.* Cambridge: Polity.

12
Cross-cultural and Traditional Drug Use

Drug use takes place in all sorts of contexts and locations. Sometimes by studying behaviours or actions such as drug use in different contexts, we find that things we assume from our experience to be either 'natural' or universal outcomes of that behaviour may not occur in the same way or even at all when looked at elsewhere. Traditional drug use refers to forms of drug use long embedded in a society's day-to-day life and/or traditions. In this section we will look at examples from tribal and other non-Western societies. Cross-cultural drug use refers to examples of drug use within different types of culture. This can be subcultures within a society such as the USA or between nations.

WESTERN VIEWS OF DRUGS AND DRUG USE

Broadly speaking, a modern view of those drugs that are controlled or illegal in Western countries such as the UK, much of Europe, the USA, Canada or Australia is that they have little or no benefit when used for non-medical reasons. In addition such use is seen as essentially destructive to individuals, families, communities and whole societies. Such a view is perhaps exemplified by a United Nations declaration in 1998 that stated:

Drugs destroy lives and communities, undermine sustainable human development and generate crime. Drugs affect all sectors of society in all countries; in particular, drug abuse affects the freedom and development of young people, the world's most valuable asset. Drugs are a grave threat to the health and well-being of all mankind, the independence of States, democracy, the stability of nations, the structure of all societies, and the dignity and hope of millions of people and their families. (United Nations General Assembly Political Declaration, 1998: 3)

The impression given by the United Nations, one repeated in similar form by governments around the world, is that it is inherent to drug use and to the drugs themselves that it/they will produce harms of this kind, that they are likely to fracture the social glue that helps keep individuals stable and societies functional. It is such a westernised view of the risks related to drug use that are embedded within the various international conventions and treaties that provide the framework for anti-drugs legislation around much of the world (Coomber, 2011). Such a position, however, ignores the different forms of traditional drug use that have existed both historically and contemporaneously in the non-Western world.

TRADITIONAL DRUG USE

Arguably this westernised view of the essentially destructive nature of commonly illicit drugs is one that is overly pharmacological in its assessment, that is, it suggests that the psychoactive properties of substances tend to lead, almost without fail, to negative or poor outcomes for individuals and society. As such it is inclined to ignore the context in which drug use takes place: the cultural and societal influences that provide a framework for such use and which help shape both the actual drug use experience and the eventual outcomes from it.

Different naturally occurring substances (for example, plants; fungi, and so on) have been used by different groups of people for thousands of years. There are hundreds of possible examples we could provide of this but for the purpose of illustration we shall focus here on just four – each different from the other but all providing evidence of drug use outcomes that, rather than acting as a mechanism of destruction, help provide structure and meaning to the groups described and thus acting as a relative cement to individual and social cohesion.

Ritual and meaning as key?

A great many examples of traditional drug use are heavily combined with meaningful ritual. Rituals take many forms. Some, like marriage, are considered special and (for the individuals involved) intended to be performed rarely. As such the meaning of marriage and the ritual of getting married takes on great significance. Other rituals such families eating at the table together for the evening meal or even just on Sundays are 'everyday' but are clearly also meaningful in terms of bonding. Drug use that is integrated and accepted into the fabric of a culture, community or society therefore has meaning that goes beyond simple individual pleasure. Indeed in many examples of traditional drug use there may be little pleasure derived from the activity and it can be restricted or controlled in all sorts of ways that take away the 'freedom' of using the drug and make sure the outcomes are constrained. In the West much drug use is hedonistic in nature, it is indulged in for the purposes of individual pleasure, it is not overtly constrained by any obvious set of rules and regulations and it is (i.e. excessive intoxication) in fact in most cases contrary to laws and what is considered (by the majority of the population) as acceptable behaviour. It is this absence of embeddedness, ritual and control that arguably provides a framework of drug use in the West that is has less meaning and thus is associated with less meaningful (and unwanted, problem) behaviour and ways of consuming.

Analysis of other modern forms of cross-cultural drug use allows us to see that the effects or outcomes of drug use can differ even within similar societies and groups.

Cross-cultural and intra-cultural drug use

Ayahuasca

Ayahuasca is a hallucinogenic brew that is made from the vines of an Amazonian tree and the leaves of local plants. It has been used variously over hundreds of years, including as an effective medicine for certain local ills, by groups all across South America. Use has involved ritual, shamanism and trance and been studied extensively. As with all psychoactive drugs the effects are partially dependent on dose, set and setting (see also **15 drug effects**).

Ayahuasca use in Brazil perhaps exemplifies all aspects of issues attaching to traditional and cross-cultural drug use: it is highly ritualised and controlled and is directly connected to religion but also to 'connective' social meaning and practices stretching back many centuries. It is also feared by mainstream society in Brazil and has been subject to sanction despite not presenting obvious health problems or problem behaviour either within or outside of the group that uses it.

The particular case of the church of the Santo Daime however enables us to see how tradition, culture and drug use can combine to be a positive contributor to both group and individual, rather than being something problematic. The founding of the church of the Santo Daime was a fairly recent (1930) event but the church, like Brazilian society in general, is a syncretic organisation, an organisation that is built upon the combining/mixing of European, Indian and African elements. As such Catholicism is combined with more traditional religious and other spiritual faiths. The founder of Santo Daime had been exposed to traditional shamanic (traditionally a tribal, indigenous Indian healer or priest that uses magic and/or potions to communicate with higher beings) practice and ayahuasca prior to founding the church. Indeed, it was while experiencing ayahuasca that he believed that he had seen 'Our Lady of the Immaculate Conception' who related to him the rules and principles of a new religious doctrine – one that is a heady mix of traditional South American practices with a strongly Catholic essence. In practice, this means that ayahuasca plays a central role in the church's ritual activities and intoxication – under highly controlled conditions (including the given dose) – is used to help followers achieve a higher spiritual state where meaningful visions are experienced (the ritual helps 'direct' the hallucinogenic experience so what is 'seen' confirms that the church and its teachings are true). All aspects of the worship/ritual are hierarchically managed and circumscribed with acts, clothing, posture and traditional gendered roles that reinforce the rules of the religious teachings and of the society around them. The consumption of the ayahuasca brew is both part and parcel of this and central to achieving it. For a more extensive overview into the various groups that use ayahuasca in this way and how it acts as social cement see MacRae (2004).

Opium

Opium is the raw product from which the drugs morphine and heroin are made. Opium is produced by cutting and extracting the (latex) sap from a particular variety of poppy (*P. somniferum*) and it has been grown and used medicinally and 'culturally' for thousands of years. Prior to the introduction of modern medicines in the 19th century, opium was in fact almost the only available substance to treat most ailments and was used widely by all sections of society (in nations East and West, North and South, industrialising and traditional) for all manner of purposes.

key concepts in drugs and society

Opiate use, however, has become highly problematised over the years and is now associated with being likely to spread (if not rigorously curtailed), through its addictive and degrading properties, speedily across nations to ravage all who come into contact with it. Perhaps the epitome of this image is 19th-century China through which it has been said opium ripped, leaving society ruined. This image, however, is reliant upon an exaggerated understanding of the power of opiates (including heroin) as almost instantly addicting (see also **4 addiction**) and as inherently destructive because that is how they have been commonly portrayed and how current anti-drug policy has been justified (see also **30 international drug control history/prohibition**). Traditional forms of opium use, however, indicate that it can be used in a multiplicity of contexts, be melded to a multiplicity of activities and meanings and, importantly produce a range of use outcomes, many of which do not result in addiction or destruction to society, group or individual but indeed add value to culture, activity and health.

While there are many examples of non-problematic opium use[2]: poppy-head tea was drunk in Norfolk in the 18th century; it was used as a substitute for wine in 16th-century Turkey; used in Chinese, Egyptian and other countries ritually and socially long before it emerged as a problem; there also remain forms of traditional use in rural India even today that demonstrate how opium can be integrated into everyday life both as ritual attached to the life-course (birth, coming-of-age) ceremonial rituals as well as into day-to-day work and cultural practices that confirm tradition and the existing structure of life. Just a few examples of the many found in the rural villages of the Rajasthan region of India are: the ritual welcoming of a new-born baby with a taste of opium to its tongue to 'socially prime' the newborn into the opium-using culture and where the family and friends present will sup of opium water; use as an ethno-medicine for a range of ailments but also to be used to aid sexual satisfaction and the rite of passage into sexual maturity; post-marital ritual use as part of the marriage ritual and day-to-day consumption relating to adult community meetings where opium is used in groups and by adolescents seeking to show how grown up they are (by emulating their elders in a fashion similar to the way that the use of alcohol and tobacco is clandestinely adopted by youth in the West). As Ganguly has stated:

> The cultural practices surrounding opium use make it an object central to the life of the people of Rajasthan. The users are mostly considered to be decent people, well accepted within their society [and opium] … has an evident symbolic and functional importance deriving from earlier times and now integrated into the contemporary setting. (2004: 97–8)

---

[2]Non-problematic can mean a number of things. For the purpose of this chapter we concur with Ganguly (2004) that addiction itself does not necessarily represent problematic use if the continued use of opium is not producing individual or social problems and is integrated into daily life such that it is complementary to that existence.

OTHER INDICATIVE TYPES OF TRADITIONAL AND CROSS-CULTURAL USE

Another form of 'drug' use that confounds a notion of predictable negative outcomes relates to alcohol. Heavy drunkenness is commonly understood in the West as likely to produce disinhibited and/or often aggressive or violent behaviour whereas reference to cross-cultural studies of groups not exposed to such a belief has found that these behaviours are not the necessary outcome (Heath, 2004; MacAndrew and Edgerton, 1969). Similarly the use of 'angel dust' or PCP (phencyclidine) while having a popularised reputation for producing a kind of egomania and increased likelihood of violent outcomes has been shown – even within the same society but among different subcultural groups – to not produce these outcomes for all groups (see also **20 drug-related violence**). There is a much longer list of such examples – both ones where substances traditionally thought to produce destructive outcomes for individual and society do not do so in traditional settings but also where contemporary settings also produce different outcomes depending on which individuals and groups are using them and how.

SUMMARY

The main conclusion to be drawn from an examination of drug use outcomes in some traditional and cross-cultural settings is that an overly simple pharmacological (that is, the 'power' and destructiveness is inherent to the substance and its interaction with the human host) understanding of what drug use will 'do' to individuals and society is unhelpful. Instead we find that rather than essentially destructive almost any kind of substance can, when used in a ritualised or meaningful (to the group/society) fashion, often constrained by group/ societal norms and expectations, be used not just relatively non-problematically but as a way of adding to the social cement of the group or society of which it is integrated. Understanding drugs as inherently destructive is not supported by the available evidence.

REFERENCES

Coomber, R. (2011) 'Social fear, drug related beliefs and drug policy', in G. Hunt, M. Milhet and H. Bergeron (eds), *Drugs and Culture: Knowledge, Consumption and Policy*. Aldershot: Ashgate.

Ganguly, K. (2004) 'Opium use in Rajasthan India: a socio cultural perspective', in R. Coomber and N. South (eds), *Drug Use and Cultural Contexts 'Beyond the West': Tradition, Change and Post-Colonialism*. London: Free Association Books. pp. 83–100.

Heath, D.B. (2004) 'Camba (Bolivia) drinking patterns in alcohol use, anthropology and research perspectives', in R. Coomber and N. South (eds), *Drug Use and Cultural Contexts 'Beyond the West': Tradition, Change and Post-Colonialism*. London: Free Association Books. pp. 119–136.

MacAndrew, D. and Edgerton, R.E. (1969) *Drunken Comportment: A Social Explanation*. Chicago, IL: Aldine.

MacRae, E. (2004) 'The ritual use of Ayahuasca by three Brazilian religions', in R. Coomber and N. South (eds), *Drug Use and Cultural Contexts 'Beyond the West': Tradition, Change and Post-Colonialism*. London: Free Association Books. pp. 27–45.

United Nations General Assembly Special Session (1998) 'Political Declaration: Guiding Principles of Drug Demand Reduction and Measures to Enhance International Cooperation to Counter the World Drug Problem', from Resolutions adopted at United Nations General Assembly Special Session on the World Drug Problem New York, 8–10 June 1998. Available at. http://www.unodc.org/pdf/report 1999–01–01_1.pdf (accessed 2 December 2012).

13
Gender, Ethnicity and Social Class

People's social position influences their involvement in drug use and supply, as well as the broader regulation and policing of drugs. While traditionally women have been less likely than men to both use and supply drugs, this gender gap is narrowing. Regarding ethnicity, different ethnic groups often take their indigenous drug consumption patterns with them when they migrate and those drugs or patterns of use become associated with minority ethnic immigrants and the social problems associated with discrimination, disadvantage and inequality. For minority ethnic nationals within developed countries, they may face disproportionate policing of their involvement in drug use and supply, with resulting social disaffection and political tension. Different patterns of drug use and supply occur across socio-economic groups with distinct patterns of problem drug use associated with lower income groups and social exclusion. Drug service provision often does not reflect this diversity of drug use, user groups and their circumstances.

In order to fully understand why people make, take and trade in psychoactive drugs, it is necessary to understand individual influences (such as biology, psychology, genetics and individual autonomy) and structural issues (such as age, gender, ethnicity, culture and social class). The structural, social and economic position of individual drug users often has a bearing on the type and extent of drug use and supply, as well as the ways that drug markets and drug-related cultures are policed and controlled. For researchers and policymakers, the challenge is to understand the ways in which these individual and structural influences combine in order to recommend appropriate, effective and non-discriminatory interventions in terms of education, regulation and treatment.

GENDER

As with wider social research on gender, up to the 1980s there was a paucity of research on women and drugs and a tendency to extrapolate to women the findings of research on men. Since then, a key focus regarding female drug users has been their perceived invisibility as users and service users alongside their added vulnerability to risk when intoxicated, for themselves and dependents: the 'mad, bad or sad' explanations for female criminality that dominated the field of criminology before the 1980s. For women, the regulation of their drug use has become an extension of the way that their bodies can be controlled in society – socially, legally or medically – as child bearers, child rearers, sex workers and romantic partners (Ettorre, 2007). A key policy debate has centred on the extent to which drug policy should be gender-neutral or gender-sensitive in relation to education, regulation and treatment. For men, differently gendered constructions of identity play out, with intoxication and involvement in drug markets associated with aggression and the performance of masculinity (Messerschmidt, 1997).

Gender and prevalence

Drug use and supply traditionally have been considered to be predominantly male activities with women's involvement dependent on male partners in terms of initiation and access: women's initiation into drug use tends to be related to a male partner who may provide the opportunity for use, if not the pressure. General population surveys suggest that the gender gap in drug use has narrowed in recent years, with a ratio of about 2:1 in men's to women's drug use in developed countries, alongside a growing recognition of women's autonomy and pleasure in drug use independent of male partners.

Gender and smoking

Advertising is seen as influential to the construction of adolescent identities and related patterns of consumption (see also **5 legal drugs**). In relation to tobacco, cigarette advertising since the early 20th century has targeted young women with unconventional images associated with freedom, defiance against social conventions and elders, upward mobility and the role of tobacco as an appetite suppressant and therefore slimming aid. For men by contrast, cigarette advertising has played on traditional gender identities: the rugged masculinity of the American cowboy was a key advertising image.

These gender differences in reasons for smoking are reflected in mortality rates for women from smoking-related diseases and cancers. The UK, Denmark and other northern European countries saw increased female mortality rates in the 1950s-1970s, while southern European countries such as Spain, Italy and Portugal saw a rapid increase in female deaths from the 1980s. In recent years, while smoking has fallen overall in developed countries, it has fallen less rapidly among young women than young men.

ETHNICITY

Migration and drugs

Historically, before the synthesis and manufacture of synthetic drugs, the types of psychoactive drugs that were used were dependent on the natural resources of individual countries. Specific plants, herbs and fungi have been utilised in most indigenous societies for spiritual, medicinal or experimental reasons across the world (Coomber and South, 2004; Klein, 2008) and consequently when people have migrated they have taken their drug-using traditions with them. This is well illustrated by the movement of cannabis-smoking migrant workers to new lands, such as Indian workers taking *bhang* (later to be known as *ganga*) to the West Indies. Similarly Mexican migrant workers took *marijuana* to North America from the late 19th century onwards. In the UK, an influx of Chinese migrant workers was associated with the supply of opium to East London opium dens and cocaine to the revellers at West End jazz clubs in the early 20th century, as was a wave of post-Second World War Jamaican migration to the UK and the use of cannabis.

Ethnicity and enforcement

This association of 'foreign' drug use with migrant workers fuelled a perceived threat of the unknown 'other', bringing their unfamiliar customs and 'dangerous' drugs with them, whether Mexican *marijuana* or Jamaican *ganga*. Alongside the social exclusion, poverty and discrimination faced by immigrant communities and subsequent genera-tions, the drugs themselves came to symbolise this threat of invasion, a changing way of life and associated tensions. Migrant workers were subject to disproportionate regulation and policing of their drug use by contrast with the sanctioned or semi-sanctioned drug use of the indigenous majority (for example, daily wine consumption with meals in Mediterranean countries), as an indirect form of social control of immi-grants per se. This was evident among second generation offspring of West Indian migrants to the UK, with the rise of Rastafarianism, reggae and cannabis use in the 1970s. The combination of unemployment and heavy-handed policing of young men on inner city streets led to disaffection, social unrest and media representations of Jamaican 'muggers' committing acquisitive crime in the late 1970s, and more recently as 'Yardie' gangsters embroiled in drug-related violence (Murji, 1999).

Enforcement of drug laws became a vehicle in some countries for disproportion-ate policing of minority ethnic communities and continues to be a source of ten-sion. In the UK a comparison of self-reported cannabis use in general population surveys with those netted in the criminal justice system indicates that drugs offenders are not a random sample of cannabis users: male and minority ethnic cannabis users are over-represented in the official statistics on cannabis offenders compared to self-reported cannabis use in the BCS (Smith and Flatley, 2011), in part the result of the UK having one of the widest 'race gaps' in police 'stop and search' techniques in the developed world, which disproportionately targets the black population (Ministry of Justice, 2010).

While such disparities are often the result of differences in enforcement of drug laws, they can also be enshrined in supposedly neutral legislation. In 1986, for example, the US Congress agreed to a sentencing disparity of 100:1 between powder cocaine and crack cocaine to reflect the perceived seriousness of crack cocaine use. Thus for the purposes of sentencing guidelines, the possession of 500g of cocaine was seen as the equivalent of 5g of crack with both receiving a recommended five-year prison term. Given that more black Americans used crack than white Americans, significantly more black Americans received lengthy prison sentences than white Americans for using the same drug (cocaine) because of this disparity between cocaine and crack possession in sentencing guidelines. Further-more, although black Americans make up only 13 per cent of regular drug users in the USA they make up 35 per cent of drug arrests, 55 per cent of drug convic-tions and 74 per cent drug possession offenders, with black Americans 13 times more likely to go to state prisons for drug offences. In 2010 the Obama adminis-tration supported the passing of the Fair Sentencing Act which reduced the sentencing disparity between cocaine and crack from 100:1 down to 18:1, resulting in a significant drop in black imprisonment. Therefore a supposedly neutral law resulted in gross disparities in justice because of ethnic differences in patterns of drug use.

Furthermore, once convicted, drugs offenders face a wide range of barriers to reintegration into society including discrimination in the employment market, and in some countries withdrawal of welfare benefits and loss of student educational loans. These all disproportionately impact on minority ethnic and lower-income drug users, despite prevalence being below the national average among minority ethnic groups. The longstanding and ongoing racial discrimination in the American employment market has been suggested as a partial reason for black American men's greater involvement in drug supply and the resulting need to resort to illegitimate means – to 'hustle' – to achieve normal aspirations such as providing economic support for their family or gaining status and respect with their peers in their local community (Whitehead et al., 1994). Thus the cycle of minority ethnic over-representation in criminal justice systems continues.

Prevalence

While the prevalence of drug use may not necessarily be higher for minority ethnic communities, and indeed in many countries is lower, they face a negative spiral of stereotyping, marginalisation and criminalisation. In the UK, self-reported drug use in the annual national household survey, the BCS, is highest among white and mixed ethnic origin respondents and lowest among Asian respondents (Smith and Flatley, 2011).

Longitudinal studies allow careful consideration of the relationship between drug use and structural factors such as ethnicity, gender, age and life-stage transitions by tracking individuals through adolescence and into adulthood. A longitudinal study by Aldridge et al. (2011) which tracked young people between the ages of 14 and 28 in the north west of England found that the protective factor of being minority ethnic in the early teens weakened by the late teens as young people left their families and communities, attended university and started their careers.

Ethnicity and alcohol

There are a growing number of abstainers and light drinkers in European countries, particularly among younger drinkers (see also 9 **binge drinking**). One reason suggested is that there are a growing number of minority ethnic young people and specifically Muslims who do not drink alcohol or at least do not drink at the frequency and in the quantities of white Europeans. While this might provide a partial explanation for increased numbers of abstainers, the expansion in abstainers and light drinkers is greater than the expansion in the Muslim population and therefore suggests that ethnicity and religious factors alone cannot explain these changes and that other factors are at work.

SOCIAL CLASS

Historically some forms of drug use have been associated with spiritual, creative and therapeutic motives for centuries, with widespread use of easily available opiate-based products in 19th-century Europe across all social groups from wealthy bohemians and patients whose medicinal usage had escalated, through to factory workers, rural labourers and their children, until growing control of medicines and the start of global regulation led to decreased availability just before and after the First World War. In the 20th century, as access was restricted due to global conventions and growing awareness of issues of dependency, problem drug use increasingly became associated with poverty, inequality and also acquisitive crime to fund drug dependency (see also **21 drugs and crime**).

Social class and prevalence

Given that the majority of drug users are neither daily nor dependent users, drug use can be found across the social spectrum and general population surveys show that some patterns of drug use (for example, weekend recreational use by clubbers) are associated neither with income nor social class (see also **11 dance drugs/club drugs**). Indeed a cornerstone of the normalisation thesis (see **14 normalisation**) is that social class, as well as gender and ethnicity, are neither predictors nor protectors from recreational drug use by young people. This draws on early drugs research by Young (1971) and others that linked drug use and deviancy to subterranean play by middle-class youth, as part of a 'work hard, play hard' ethos, whereby leisure time consumption stimulates production and production facilitates leisure consumption.

Nevertheless certain drugs are more likely to be used by certain socio-economic groups and poverty continues to be associated with problem drug use (as opposed to recreational drug use). For example, while there is no difference in prevalence of cocaine use between income groups in the UK, heroin use is more likely to occur among lower income groups and particularly among the unemployed and those receiving welfare benefits.

Class and drug treatment

While the majority of drug users in treatment are in treatment for problem and dependent use of opiates and crack cocaine, there is a mismatch between resources, service demands and service provision. For example, there are growing numbers of younger entrants into treatment with a background of family problems, economic deprivation, physical and mental health concerns, and low educational and employment aspirations and achievements (Aldridge et al., 2011). Younger drug users may feel discouraged from contacting services with drug problems because of treatment environments that have been traditionally tailored to the needs of older opiate users. Furthermore, these problem users of supposedly 'recreational' drugs, such as cannabis, psychostimulants and word psychoactive substances, are less likely to be employed, more often caught up in the criminal justice system and are presenting to services in growing numbers at a time of decreased opiate and crack cocaine presentations. This suggests that it is not simply the types of drugs used but the patterns of use and the broader social context that can result in drug-related problems.

SUMMARY

Gender, ethnicity and social class all intertwine to influence individual drug use and supply, with the illegal drug economy mirroring many of the structural determinants of the legal economy. While there is evidence that for certain patterns of recreational drug use social influences are no longer as significant in the developed world, social exclusion and poverty continue to be associated with problem drug use and dependency, and specifically the use of opiates and crack cocaine. Furthermore, drug laws and their enforcement can result in disproportionate or discriminatory policing of marginalised groups, adding to the social disaffection and political tensions between specific ethnic and social groups and the authorities.

REFERENCES

Aldridge, J., Measham, F. and Williams, L. (2011) *Illegal Leisure Revisited: Changing Patterns of Alcohol and Drug Use in Adolescents and Young Adults.* London: Routledge.

Coomber, R. and South, N. (eds) (2004) *Drug Use and Cultural Contexts 'Beyond the West': Tradition, Change and Post-Colonialism.* London: Free Association Books.

Ettorre, E. (2007) *Revisioning Women and Drug Use: Gender, Power and the Body.* Basingstoke: Palgrave Macmillan.

Klein, A. (2008) *Drugs and the World.* London: Reaktion.

Maher, L. (1997) *Sexed Work: Gender, Race, and Resistance in a Brooklyn Drug Market.* Oxford: Clarendon.

Messerschmidt, J. (1997) *Crime as Structured Action: Gender, Race, Class, and Crime in the Making.* Thousand Oaks, CA: Sage Publications.

Ministry of Justice (2010) *Statistics on Race and the Criminal Justice System – 2008/09.* London: Ministry of Justice.

Murji, K. (1999) 'White lines: culture, "race" and drugs', in N. South (ed.), *Drugs: Cultures, Controls and Everyday Life.* London: Sage.

Smith, K. and Flatley, J. (eds) (2011) 'Drug misuse declared: findings from the 2010/11 British Crime Survey, England and Wales', Home Office Statistical Bulletin 12/11, London: Home Office. Available at: http://www.homeoffice.gov.uk/scienceresearch (accessed 1 August 2012).

Whitehead, T., Peterson, J. and Kaljee, L. (1994) 'The "hustle": socioeconomic deprivation, urban drug trafficking, and low-income', *African-American Male Gender Identity, Pediatrics,* 93 (6): 1050–4.

Young, J. (1971) *The Drugtakers: The Social Meaning of Drug Use.* London: MacGibbon and Kee.

14
Normalisation

Normalisation is a concept which, when applied to drug use, describes a process of behavioural and cultural change whereby drug use is accepted or tolerated to a degree, by both users and non-users in wider society. The debate emerged in the UK in the early 1990s regarding the extent to which normalisation might better explain significant changes in drug use and users – particularly young people's 'recreational' use of cannabis and psychostimulants – than traditional structural, psychological and subcultural explanations. The ensuing normalisation debate has been applied, refined and contested across Europe, North America and Australasia for two decades.

The concept of normalisation developed in disability studies in the 1970s and was used to describe the reintegration of those with disabilities into wider society. The concept was applied to the drugs field to explain changing patterns of drug use by young people in the UK in the early 1990s. Normalisation was first applied to a study of school pupils in the north west of England who were surveyed each year from the age of 14 in 1991, when unexpectedly high prevalence rates identified the beginning of what was to become a significant increase in the use of certain drugs across the UK in the 1990s. The concept was fully discussed in a monograph on the first five years of the North West England Longitudinal Study (hereafter NWELS) when the pupils were aged 14–18 (Parker et al., 1998) and then in an updated monograph covering the same sample of young people up to the age of 28 (Aldridge et al., 2011).

Since the 1990s normalisation has developed into one of the key debates conceptualising changing patterns of drug use in the late 20th and early 21st centuries, adopted and adapted across the world.

DEVELOPMENT OF THE CONCEPT

Grounded in data obtained from a representative sample of school pupils from the age of 14 onwards, the NWELS reported high levels of exposure to and use of illegal drugs in annual surveys. Moreover, their drug use was not significantly related to their gender, ethnicity or socio-economic class (see also **13 gender, ethnicity and social class**), as previously had been the case with many studies of young people's drug use in the UK. This led the researchers to question the reasons why young people took drugs in early 1990s Britain, and the extent to which traditional explanations such as social exclusion, subcultural identities or individual pathology could no longer account for drug use (see also **3 why do people take drugs?**). Furthermore, it led the authors to consider the policy implications: if up to one-half of young people experiment with illegal drugs then this results in the potential criminalisation of large numbers of young people who might be otherwise law-abiding. Instead of peer pressure, psychological problems or poverty, young people in the study discussed their drug taking decision making in terms of rational, cost-benefit analyses of whether or not to take drugs, and the longitudinal design (which followed the same sample as they grew up) was able to explore how these drug decisions were made and remade by the young people throughout their teens and 20s. The very high prevalence figures, but not the conceptual debate surrounding the social and cultural context to normalisation, led to widespread media coverage and an ensuing and ongoing academic debate.

DEFINITION OF NORMALISATION

Normalisation refers to a process of growing accommodation, acceptance or tolerance of drug use by both drug users and wider society, in terms of drug-related attitudes and behaviours. It includes both increased levels of drug use – the behavioural component – and also increased understanding or social acceptance of drug use by wider society – the cultural component.

MEASUREMENTS

Six key features of normalisation were identified by Parker et al. (1998). The first measure is drug *availability* or the extent to which individuals are in situations where drugs are offered or available to them; second, drug *trying* which is most usually measured in terms of self-reported lifetime prevalence. Third, a measure of current drug *use* is included, although how this is defined may vary between studies (for example, past month drug use, a 'recency' measure, is sometimes used as a proxy measure for current or regular drug use for practicality in surveys). Fourth, respondents may be asked about future *intentions* in order to ascertain whether there is a sense of being open to the possibility of future experimentation, for adolescent non users as well as users. Fifth, the extent to which individuals were *drugwise*, familiar with or culturally knowledgeable about drugs was assessed: for example, do young people know about different drugs and their effects, regardless of whether or not they have tried them themselves? Sixth, the concept included the notion of *cultural accommodation* of illicit drug use at the societal level, an important (subjective) indicator of normalisation.

CRITIQUES OF NORMALISATION

The concept of normalisation was promptly and robustly challenged in a critique by Shiner and Newburn (1997) who felt that too much focus was given to lifetime prevalence and recency figures on young people's experimentation (the second and third measures) at the expense of much lower figures on regular usage. Applying Sykes and Matza's (1957) theory of techniques of neutralisation, Shiner and Newburn noted that among the 14-year-olds they had interviewed (a small, unrepresentative and openly anti-drugs sample), hostility to drugs and to drug users was evident which they argued illustrated that illegal drug use was not condoned or accepted either among adolescents or wider society. They further contended that the sharp increase in adolescent drug use in the UK in the 1990s was not such a significant break with the past, but part of the broader ebbs and flows in usage which could be tracked across the 20th century.

Various other researchers also refined or contested the concept of normalisation of recreational drug use. For example, Blackman (2004, 2010) has raised concerns about both its theoretical underpinnings in post modernism and the unintended consequences of widespread media coverage of increased adolescent recreational drug use and the subsequent policy ramifications.

The normalisation concept was restated by the Manchester University team with the publication of later years of the longitudinal survey and endorsed to varying degrees by other drugs researchers including Manning (2007). Subsequent modifications related to the degree of agency, or individual free will, given to adolescent drug users. If the original 1990s NWELS had been an attempt to recognise the agency and rationality within young people's drug use, the 2000s saw a move towards the re-emphasis of structural factors such as gender, ethnicity and socio-economic class. For example, Shildrick (2002) noted the continued importance of social exclusion in the lives of some young drug users in the north east of England. Measham (2004) also called for two shifts in emphasis in the debate. First, she reasserted the importance of cultural accommodation as a key indicator of normalisation, rather than behavioural components such as lifetime prevalence, which had dominated both the media and academic debate about increased drug use in the late 1990s. Second, she suggested modifying the earlier theoretical underpinnings to the cost-benefit analysis regarding rational actor theory. The original normalisation thesis had (over)emphasised rationality (rational thinking) and individual agency (free will) at the expense of structural factors including gender and social class: Measham called for a greater balance between agency and structure, and between rationality and emotionality (the experiences, passions and pleasures surrounding drug use).

A synergy came between two of the protagonists (Measham and Shiner, 2009) with an agreement on the need to reassert the role of structural influences, on the importance of the wider cultural context to drug use and a more historically sensitive approach to understanding the significance of contemporary drug use. They agreed to disagree, however, on both the extent to which the 1990s changes had been a significant break with the past or part of the historically omniscient ebbs and flows of drug-related attitudes and behaviours; and also on the extent of cultural accommodation of illicit drug use in wider society.

POLICY IMPLICATIONS

The original thesis concluded with policy recommendations which questioned the effectiveness of regulatory regimes which attempt to prohibit and thus criminalise such a large minority of young people who choose to take drugs because they see the benefits outweighing the costs. The implications of this policy debate led to a discussion regarding the decriminalisation of cannabis. Yet the impact of drug policy on the increasing numbers of recreational drug users in the UK in the 1990s and 2000s was increasing numbers of drug-related offenders being processed through the criminal justice system within a wider move towards a criminal rather than public health focus in government drug policy: with recreational drug users being treated first and foremost as criminals in need of punishment rather than in need of drugs education, treatment or harm reduction advice. Therefore the normalisation debate was diverted from the original thrust of the policy recommendations by alarmist media coverage and even used as fuel for strengthening the prohibitionist agenda (Blackman, 2010), in direct contrast to the original aims of its authors.

The concept has been refined from the original macro level exploration of changing attitudes and behaviours across society, to an exploration of its relevance at the micro level of individual drug users' lives (Pennay and Moore, 2010), for example in terms of which drugs are socially acceptable in certain social contexts but not others. However, rather than the continued refining of the concept, adding caveats, conditions or emergent drugs to the original thesis outlined in 1998, the original protagonists have suggested that the utility of the concept might lie in its broader conceptualisation of social change around illicit drug use and adaptability to different contexts (Aldridge et al., 2011).

SUMMARY

Normalisation is a concept which was developed and applied by Parker et al. (1998) to explain a significant increase in adolescent recreational drug use in the north west of England in the 1990s and associated changes in drug-related attitudes and behaviours by users and non-users. Given that drug use increased across the social spectrum in the UK in the 1990s traditional explanations such as structural, subcultural and psychological reasons did not seem adequate. Since then normalisation has been adopted and adapted to explain young people's increased recreational drug use in many other countries.

REFERENCES

Aldridge, J., Measham, F. and Williams, L. (2011) *Illegal Leisure Revisited*. London: Routledge.

Blackman, S. (2004) *Chilling Out: The Cultural Politics of Substance Consumption, Youth and Drug Policy*. Maidenhead: Open University Press.

Blackman, S. (2010) 'Youth subcultures, normalisation and drug prohibition: the politics of contemporary crisis and change?', *British Politics*, 5 (3): 337–66.

Manning, P. (2007) *Drugs and Popular Culture: Drugs, Media and Identity in Contemporary Society*. Cullompton: Willan.

Measham, F. (2004) 'Drug and alcohol research: the case for cultural criminology', in J. Ferrell, K. Hayward, W. Morrison and M. Presdee (eds), *Cultural Criminology Unleashed*. London: GlassHouse, pp. 207–18.

Measham, F. and Shiner, M. (2009) 'The legacy of normalisation: the role of classical and contemporary criminological theory in understanding young people's drug use', *International Journal of Drug Policy*, 20 (6): 502–8.

Parker, H., Aldridge, J. and Measham, F. (1998) *Illegal Leisure: The Normalisation of Adolescent Recreational Drug Use*. London: Routledge.

Pennay, A. and Moore, D. (2010) 'Exploring the micro-politics of normalisation: Narratives of pleasure, self-control and desire in a sample of young Australian "party drug" users', *Addiction Research and Theory*, 18(5): 557-71.

Shildrick, T. (2002) 'Young people, illicit drug use and the question of normalization', *Journal of Youth Studies*, 5 (1): 35–48.

Shiner, M. and Newburn, T. (1997) 'Definitely, maybe not: the normalisation of recreational drug use amongst young people', *Sociology*, 31 (3): 511–29.

Sykes, G. and Matza, D. (1957) 'Techniques of neutralization: a theory of delinquency', *American Sociological Review*, 22 (6): 664–70.

key concepts in
drugs and society

Section II
Drug Effects

15
Drug Effects: Drug, Set and Setting

> *A drug effect is what happens to the mind and/or body of an individual that uses it. The actual effect of a taking a drug however is not as simple as (1) the drug causes (2) the behaviour/psychedelic effect/the harm. A fuller understanding of drug effects goes beyond simply looking at the drug in question, the dose used and the host body – a bio-pharmacological perspective – and also needs to consider expectation/beliefs, the mood of the user, the environment use is taking place in and the ways that drug effects can differ significantly when each of these aspects vary.*

PSYCHOACTIVE DRUG EFFECTS

Psychoactive, or psychotropic, effects are those effects that are in some way 'mind or mood-altering'. Such effects can be relatively subtle/barely noticeable as in the case of tobacco, chocolate or caffeine (as found in tea and coffee), moderate, as with drugs such as ecstasy or cannabis, or extremely distorting of reality, as with drugs such as LSD or ketamine, which can produce hallucinations and/or out-of-body (dissociative) experiences.

For a drug to have psychoactive effects it has to enter the blood stream and then the active substances of the drug have to be small enough to pass the blood-brain barrier to enter the brain. Once this has been achieved the drug can act on the brain.

PHARMACOLOGICAL EFFECTS

Drugs have specific pharmacological effects on those that use them. Some of these effects are more predictable than others, however, and are dose related. If we consider alcohol we can see that consuming excessive amounts will have an effect on the central nervous system such that it becomes difficult to control speech, walking and other motor functions. At lower levels of consumption these effects are less and often not even present. Other behaviours, however, are still associated with moderate alcohol use such as enabling lowered inhibition (sometimes contradictory behaviours), for example: elevated mood, depressed mood, aggression, feelings of friendliness, well-being and many others. These non-extreme physiological reactions (that is, as opposed to overdose, incapacitation and so on) – as can be seen with alcohol – vary between individual and even for any one individual during the course of a single event or over different events. Such variation is observed with almost every licit and illicit drug that has psychoactive effects. This variation is mostly caused by the *set* and *setting* in which the drug is used and some effects assumed to be inherent to a particular drug, that is, directly caused by its pharmacological make-up, may not be true.

DRUG, SET AND SETTING

The notion of how variable drug effects related to social and psychological contexts was championed by American psychiatrist, Dr Norman Zinberg in his 1984 seminal text *Drug, Set, and Setting: The Basis for Controlled Intoxicant Use*. It is now widely accepted that depending on how a person is feeling (their *set*) before using a drug (scared, angry, confused, happy, sad and so on), what beliefs they have about that drug (what people or 'society' have/has told them to expect) and the kind of environment (the *setting*) in which they are taking it (relaxed, pressured, legal, illegal, around friends, in a familiar 'safe' place or in a strange 'unsafe' space and so on) will impact upon both short-term and long-term effects.

Short-term or immediate effects impacted on by set and setting may mean that different individuals using the same drug(s) in the same environment or setting (which may be experienced as 'safe' for some but 'unsafe' for others) have different experiences to the drug.

Long-term differences relate to drugs of addiction, such as heroin, and to the experience of addiction itself. Zinberg found that different users, depending on their personal circumstances, their motivations, the context in which heroin was being used and the choices they had open to them meant that addiction was experienced differently. Some were able to use heroin recreationally (non-addictively) and in a controlled manner for many years while others were able to make decisions to curtail or even stop their addiction. Large numbers of addicted Vietnam veterans returning from war were able, once in a new, less stressful environment to discontinue their use of heroin. Addiction, despite popular assumption, is itself much more than simply a dependence on a drug and is partly understood by reference to set and setting as well as particular drugs (see also **4 addiction**).

PLACEBO AND SUGGESTION

One way that we can see how beliefs, assumptions, set and setting can impact on drug effects is by referring to experiments on drug effects that use placebos – that is, pills or other 'medicines' that have no active substances in them – and deceptive substances – that is, where the suggested effect (by those carrying out the experiment) is different to the effect the substance *should* have. Gossop (2006) refers to a number of experiments where different groups of volunteers were split into groups: some were given (for example) a sedative and told that it would make then drowsy, others were given either a placebo or a drug with other non-sedative effects but also told they were receiving sedatives. The outcome was that many of those receiving placebos and/or non-sedative drugs felt equally drowsy as those given the 'control' drug. In other experiments, not telling the volunteers the effects of the drug they had been given but exposing them to actors pretending to be affected by a drug in a particular way also led to the volunteers mimicking that behaviour even when they had not been given an active substance or one that would produce that behaviour.

'MANAGED' FFFFCTS – RITUAL AND EXPECTATION

Now that we have seen how expectation can impact on perceived effects, we can further consider the role of ritual and how it can help shape and manage effects that some would think to be the result of bio-chemistry alone. Rituals are structured ways of behaving that reinforce group or cultural norms. Shaking hands when meeting people, offering them tea or coffee, having birthday cakes with candles, marriage and death (funerals) ceremonies are all activities or rituals which reinforce the way that these things are done in particular societies. Rituals act as cement, a behavioural bonding, that helps a group or culture 'know' itself and help reproduce itself. Other rituals such as those involved in some religious ceremonies are also designed to help the believer engage or get closer (bond) with their respective god(s), spirits or ancestors. To this end a number of groups (mostly those in traditional societies), such as some Indian tribes in the Amazonian rainforest, use naturally derived hallucinogenic substances during rituals. Despite extreme levels of intoxication from the use of a powerful drug understood in the West as producing 'loss of control' – these events produce fairly predictable drug effect outcomes. Guided by the structure of the ritual and the skill of the shaman or priests, the resulting hallucinations and visions often take the form of those things (ancestors/god(s)/sacred beings or animals) most sacred or meaningful to the specific group and the 'engagement' with them (for example, talking with the visions, receiving guidance and so on) succeeds, by extension, in guiding and reinforcing behaviour for both the individual and the group. This is what the aim of the ritual was to begin with. Very strong intoxicants and their psychoactive effects are thus partly managed by the ritual, expectation and belief as they combine with the drug effect to facilitate a desired, as opposed to random or wholly unpredictable outcome, (Dobkin de Rios, 1984; MacRae, 2004).

LEARNED DRUG USE AND EFFECTS

By acknowledging that there are outside influences and structures that impact, in part at least (e.g. ritual; social context; expectations fuelled by other people's experiences as well as one's own; initiation into drug use by others) on how users experience psychoactive drugs we are also in part acknowledging that some aspects of the drug using experience are *learned*. Howard Becker (1953) in his research into cannabis (marijuana/marihuana) use suggested that many people do not initially experience the pleasurable effects of cannabis, that people have to learn to recognise these effects and then learn how to manage and appreciate them. Learning takes the form of exposure to other experienced users who show new users how to smoke cannabis but also inform them and guide them to recognise the effects they can expect. Although Becker's early work is subject to some criticism, it is also acknowledged that many new users do struggle to get a 'high' from first and early use and that (unlike when Becker was doing his research) knowledge about drug effects are now so widespread that the 'learning' aspect of new drug use is partially overtaken by widely known drug effect expectation.

IMPORTANCE OF A NON-PHARMACOLOGICAL UNDERSTANDING OF DRUG EFFECTS

When understanding the psychoactive or mind-altering effects of drugs (both legal and illegal) we therefore need to move beyond simple bio-chemical/pharmaco-logical explanations. LSD, for example, does not simply cause the user to have effect (a) or (b). The outcome effect will depend on the pre-existing mood of the user, the expectations they have about the experience, the environment in which they take the drug, the extent to which either they or those around them are experienced in LSD use and how all these combine.

REFERENCES

Becker, H.S. (1953) 'Becoming a marihuana user', *The American Journal of Sociology*, 59 (3): 235–42.

Dobkin de Rios, M. (1984) *Hallucinogens: Cross-Cultural Perspectives*. Albuquerque, NM: University of New Mexico Press.

Gossop, M. (2006) *Living with Drugs*, 6th edn. Aldershot: Ashgate.

MacRae, E. (2004) 'The ritual use of ayahuasca in three Brazilian religions', in R. Coomber and N. South (eds), *Drug Use and Cultural Contexts 'Beyond the West'*. London: Free Association Books. pp. 27–45.

Zinberg, N. (1984) *Drug, Set, and Setting: The Basis for Controlled Intoxicant Use*. New Haven, CT: Yale University Press.

16

Medical Marijuana and Other Therapeutic Uses of Illicit Drugs

Therapeutic use of illicit drugs refers to the use of these substances to treat a physical or mental illness or condition. Marijuana that is used to treat illness or the symptoms associated with illness is known as medical marijuana. Medical marijuana is at times referred to as medicinal cannabis, or medicinal marijuana.

Cannabinoids are those substances that are found in the resin of the flowers and leaves of the female cannabis plant (*Cannabis sativa*). THC (delta-9-tetrahydrocannabinol) is the main active cannabinoid and the one that produces the primary psychoactive effects.[3] The leaves and flower tops (or buds) are known as marijuana; hashish[4] refers to cannabis resin and derives from a subspecies of the plant (C. *indica*). The term 'cannabis' is also used generically to refer to both hashish and marijuana.

Mechoulam (1986) describes the long history of medicinal cannabis, dating back at least 5000 years when it was used to treat symptoms of constipation, rheumatism and a host of other ailments. Cannabis preparations were used for analgesia, a practice that continued until the early 20th century. In the UK in the 19th century, various conditions, including migraine headaches (Russo, 1998), were treated with medicinal cannabis and patients included both adults and children. Beginning in the mid-1850s, the use of medicinal cannabis had spread to the USA where subsequently, a number of over-the-counter products containing cannabis or its derivatives became available. Cannabis preparations were used to treat tetanus, asthma, pain associated with childbirth and various other ailments (Grinspoon, 1971), although these practices declined when the drug was prohibited in the USA during the 1930s. In the UK, cannabis was available through prescription until 1973.

MEDICINAL MARIJUANA IN CONTEMPORARY SOCIETY

The interest in medicinal marijuana re-surfaced during the 1970s in the USA, when some cancer patients found that marijuana eased the nausea associated with chemotherapy (Grinspoon, 1971). The drug also was used to address symptoms of glaucoma and later, HIV and AIDS. In contemporary Western society, medicinal marijuana has been used to address dozens of ailments or the symptoms associated with ailments, although very often the use of the drug for these purposes is in violation of criminal law.

Synthetic cannabinoids are most often available in tablet form. The difference between marijuana and synthetic versions was observed quickly by cancer patients, who suggested that the latter are less effective than smoking marijuana. Claims surfaced that synthetic tablets produced only short-term relief, and took longer to take effect compared to smoked or inhaled marijuana. Initially, several governments failed to respond to consumers' preferences and various synthetic cannabinoids or cannabis extracts (for example, dronabinol/Marinol, Sativex) were approved for medical use in the UK and the USA. In 2005, the Spanish government approved the use of medical marijuana in the region of Catalonia. Physicians can prescribe the drug for four conditions: multiple sclerosis, chronic pain, as an appetite inducer for people living with AIDS, and nausea associated with chemotherapy.

To date, only two countries (the Netherlands and Canada) allow marijuana to be grown for and accessed by patients who have demonstrated that the drug is needed for therapeutic reasons. The Canadian Marihuana Medical Access Regulations provide legal access to marijuana for patients experiencing severe symptoms

---

[3]Interestingly, certain other cannabinoids can reduce the psychoactive effects of THC.

[4]Hashish is more available in Europe than in the USA.

related to cancer, HIV infection, spinal cord injury/disease, multiple sclerosis, arthritis and epilepsy. Under certain conditions, the Canadian government allows the use of medical marijuana for other illnesses. Physician authorisation is required. Canadian policy differs from other countries in that patients can apply to grow their own marijuana or appoint another person to grow it for them. Patients who wish to obtain medical marijuana from the government's appointed supplier, must pay for the drug, albeit at a considerably lower cost than through the illicit market.

The majority of US states have enacted statutes that acknowledge the benefits of medical marijuana. However, by late 2009, the drug could be legally accessed only in 14 states. Five states allow the drug to be accessed through 'dispensaries' and state legislation varies with regard to the kinds of ailments for which marijuana can be used for medical purposes. In California, registered patients are permitted to grow and cultivate marijuana for therapeutic use. Inadequate licensing regulations contributed in part to the large number of dispensaries in Los Angeles – upwards of 1000.

THE MEDICAL MARIJUANA MOVEMENT

The medical marijuana movement in both the USA and Canada originated through the work of several grassroots activists. In the USA, many recall the influential work of Robert Randall (now deceased). In the mid-1970s, Randall argued before a federal court that he needed marijuana to reduce the symptoms of glaucoma. He also presented his argument to the US Food and Drug Administration. In 1976, Randall was the first person in the USA to obtain authorised use of the drug since its prohibition 40 years earlier.

A few years later, a state legislative body (New Mexico) passed a law that acknowledged the role of marijuana in medicine. The legislation was influenced by accounts from physicians and their patients, many of whom had been diagnosed with cancer. Over the next two decades, other US states passed similar legislation fuelled largely by proactive grassroots organisations. In 1996, activists in California organised a major campaign that led to a state-wide vote in support of medical marijuana (Proposition 215, or the Compassionate Use Act 1996). US federal drug policy initiated several attempts to block state legislation, and intervention from federal law enforcement often hindered the provision of marijuana for medical purposes. The divisiveness between state and federal policy in the USA has continued well into the 21st century, although the Obama administration has indicated that the federal government will no longer target consumers and suppliers who comply with state laws, a major departure from previous presidential administrations. This change will no doubt be monitored closely by proponents of medical marijuana. State laws are increasingly being enforced. In California, local and state authorities shut down several dispensaries in 2009, and arrested proprietors for illegally distributing marijuana to customers who were not registered with the state.

EFFECTIVENESS OF MARIJUANA FOR MEDICAL PURPOSES

Case reports and clinical trials have demonstrated the therapeutic role of marijuana for treating the symptoms of various illnesses, for example, poor appetite associated with HIV and cancer, nausea produced by chemotherapy and chronic pain. The list of ailments for which marijuana might be beneficial appears to be expanding. For instance, THC may slow the progression of Alzheimer's disease and reduce the effects of muscle spasticity among people with multiple sclerosis. Clinical trials are currently underway in Plymouth (UK) to determine whether THC can slow the progression of multiple sclerosis.

Weak research designs characterise some studies that have investigated the role of medicinal marijuana, and similar to other politicised research topics, readers' opinions can determine the interpretation of findings (Robson, 2001). Two separate reviews of the therapeutic use of marijuana have found that more attention is paid to information that highlights negative effects, whereas positive outcomes tend to be overlooked (Hall et al., 1994; Robson, 2001).

Opponents of medical marijuana tend to minimise or ignore the potential benefits of the drug, and highlight or exaggerate the dangers. This position often fails to acknowledge that several conventional medicines can produce toxic or life-threatening outcomes. However, these effects are often rare in comparison to the benefits derived from the medicines.

THERAPEUTIC USES OF OTHER ILLICIT DRUGS

Various studies conducted in the 20th century focused on the therapeutic value of other illicit drugs in the treatment of medical conditions. These studies tended to receive little attention from mainstream scientific and medical audiences. However, there appears to be a growing interest in the therapeutic use of other drugs that are illegal in many countries.

MDMA

The biochemist, Dr Alexander Shulgin, self-experimented with MDMA in the 1970s and described the effects as euphoric. His observations had some influence on psychotherapy in the USA; by the early 1980s, several hundred professionals in the USA were advocating patient use of MDMA during therapeutic sessions. The drug was perceived to invoke feelings of empathy and introspection that enhanced the nature of therapy, but it was added to the list of illegal drugs in the USA in 1985.

The Multidisciplinary Association for Psychedelic Studies (MAPS) had provided funding and sought donations for several clinical trials that examine the impact of therapeutic doses of MDMA to treat post-traumatic stress disorder (PTSD). For example, research in Israel is investigating the role of MDMA and psychotherapy for addressing war-related PTSD. Results of the clinical trial are expected in 2010. Similar projects will take place in Vancouver (Canada).

Ketamine and hallucinogenic drugs

An emerging body of literature based on clinical trials suggests that ketamine, developed as an anaesthetic in the 1960s, might help people who experience clinical depression. The drug appears to produce a rapid antidepressant effect and has been tested with people who have not experienced successful outcomes using traditional treatment interventions. The relatively quick onset of ketamine is beneficial in that antidepressant drugs generally take several weeks to take effect. Few studies have investigated ketamine treatment over the long term. However, the potential for negative effects associated with currently available antidepressant drugs has been documented, and clearly are listed in the form of manufacturers' warnings. Moreover, although the clinical studies tend to rely on small sample sizes, investigators have observed few adverse effects when ketamine is administered intravenously in controlled settings. The role of ketamine for treating heroin dependence is also being investigated. Generally, ketamine is combined with psychotherapy and clinical trials have compared individuals who have been administered ketamine with those who have not.

Considerably fewer contemporary studies have focused on the therapeutic use of other drugs, for example, hallucinogens. However, Sessa (2005) provided a brief review of studies conducted in the 1960s and 1970s. Citing research evidence, he noted that hallucinogenic drugs were used to treat depression, anxiety, alcoholism and a host of other conditions. Further, few negative effects were reported in this body of research. More recent research has addressed the effects of psilocybin on obsessive compulsive disorder.

Heroin

In some countries, pharmaceutical heroin (diamorphine) is used as a form of treatment for heroin dependence. Known as 'heroin-assisted' treatment, the effectiveness of this intervention has been explored in several randomised clinical trials in Germany, Switzerland, Spain, Canada and elsewhere. Although this intervention has been debated widely, the programmes are generally restricted to supervised injecting facilities in which patients are monitored closely. In the UK, pharmaceutical heroin has been prescribed for palliative care and was used for decades to treat heroin dependence. Currently, the treatment is not widely available for opioid dependence in the UK, and is generally recommended only for patients who have demonstrated very poor outcomes with methadone maintenance (see also **27 substitute prescribing**). In contrast, US policy does not recognise any therapeutic benefit of diamorphine. Although widespread implementation of heroin-assisted treatment is probably unlikely for the foreseeable future, the accumulating evidence suggests positive outcomes for some individuals.

SUMMARY

Drug policy in several countries has been slow to recognise the therapeutic use of marijuana and other illicit drugs. Policy is often at odds with the views of physicians' organisations, patients' reports, and the preferences of the majority. The perceived contradiction between the therapeutic use of illicit drugs and the illegal status of these drugs is an important factor that appears to contribute to the opposition of marijuana and other illicit drugs for therapeutic use. An emerging body of research suggests that marijuana can ease the symptoms and help manage pain associated with various illnesses. In some countries, however, the debates around medical marijuana are highly politicised and this factor tends to influence policy. Other illegal psychoactive drugs also have been shown to have some therapeutic potential (ketamine, MDMA, heroin). From a historical perspective, we know that the legal status of drugs as well as the recognised therapeutic potential of some substances can change relatively quickly.

REFERENCES

Grinspoon, L. (1971) *Marijuana Reconsidered*. Cambridge, MA: Harvard University Press.
Hall, W., Solowij, N. and Lemon, J. (1994) *The Health and Psychological Consequences of Cannabis Use*. National Drug Strategy Monograph Series No. 25. Canberra: Australian Government Publishing Service.
Mechoulam, R. (1986) 'The pharmacohistory of *Cannabis sativa*', in R. Mechoulam (ed.), *Cannabinoids as Therapeutic Agents*. Boca Raton, FL: CRC Press. pp. 1–19.
Robson, P. (2001) 'Therapeutic aspects of cannabis and cannabinoids', *British Journal of Psychiatry*, 178: 107–15.
Russo, E. (1998) 'Cannabis for migraine treatment: the once and future prescription? An historical and scientific review', *Pain*, 76 (1): 3–8.
Sessa, B. (2005) 'Can psychedelics have a role in psychiatry once again?', *British Journal of Psychiatry*, 186: 457–8.

17
Prescribed and Over-the-Counter (OTC) Drugs

Psychoactive substances or medicines that are prescribed by a physician or other health professional are referred to as prescribed or prescription drugs. Prescribing and dispensing regulations vary considerably across countries. Over-the-counter drugs are medicines that can be purchased without a prescription.

Our interest in prescription drugs focuses on those medicines that produce psychoactive effects; prescribed drugs that alter our level of consciousness or our way of thinking. These drugs include: stimulants (for example, Ritalin, intended for use with Attention Deficit Hyperactivity Disorder), sedatives or anti-anxiety medication (for example, Xanax, Valium, Ativan), sleeping aids, and opioid-based pain medications (for example, hydromorphine, oxycodone). The substances are legal when prescribed by a physician and are used by a patient for whom the drug was prescribed. The legality of prescription drugs suggests societal acceptability which may encourage some people to perceive them as safe. However, some prescription drugs produce addiction, dependence, tolerance and withdrawal and can be implicated in overdoses. In some countries, prescribed drugs are more likely to contribute to fatal overdose than are heroin, cocaine and a host of other illegal drugs combined.

Prescription drugs are consumed at higher rates in the USA than any other country, a pattern that might be linked to several factors, including the privatisation of health care and pharmaceutical companies' aggressive marketing strategies. High rates of prescribing also occur outside the USA. For example, the number of opioid prescriptions nearly doubled in the UK from 1998 (5.5. million) to 2004 (9.5 million) (Coupe and Stannard, 2007), and an estimated 1.5 million people in the UK are dependent on benzodiazepines, for example, diazepam. Intended for use in the short term, repeat benzodiazepine prescriptions over long periods of time have been a cause of concern in several countries, for example, Ireland. Benzodiazepine withdrawal can produce serious and sometimes fatal consequences.

MISUSE OF PRESCRIPTION MEDICINE

The *availability* of prescribed drugs is one factor that contributes to the misuse of these drugs (McCabe et al., 2006). Non-medical or unregulated use refers to the consumption of a prescribed drug that was intended for another person, or the consumption of a prescribed drug in a manner that deviates from a physician's guidance (for example, increases in the dosage or frequency of consumption). Most research into misuse of prescribed medicine has occurred in Canada and the USA. The misuse of prescribed opioids, for example, codeine, hydromorphine, Fentanyl, oxycodone, are of particular concern and some authors have suggested that in Australia, Europe and North America, the street demand for these drugs now exceeds the demand for heroin (Fischer and Rehm, 2007). It is well documented that people dependent on heroin also misuse prescription drugs, for example, benzodiazepines. Emerging trends, however, show that vast numbers of people who misuse prescribed opioid medications have never used heroin.

Globally, the unregulated use of benzodiazepine, opioids and stimulants are available through illicit markets in both developing and developed nations. Several factors contribute to the demand for unregulated prescribed drugs. Some individuals become addicted or dependent on drugs that were originally prescribed for pain or another condition. Dependency presents additional problems for the consumer when physicians reduce the dosage or terminate the prescription. In turn, some individuals then obtain the substance through illicit drug markets. In other instances, structural barriers (for example, cost, availability) prevent access to health care professionals and consequently medicine is obtained through other means. Other people avoid presenting to physicians because of concern about confidentiality with regards to their medical conditions. Obtaining prescribed medicine through illicit markets helps maintain confidentiality and privacy. Others become involved in the misuse of prescription drugs in their pursuit of leisure.

Social context appears to contribute to some misuse of prescribed drugs. For example, US research showed that the misuse of Ritalin was higher among college students compared to individuals of similar ages who were not attending college (Johnston et al., 2005). That same study found that male students were somewhat more likely than females to report the misuse of prescription medicine. In other studies, women are more likely than men to report misuse of prescription drugs. Additionally, reports from several countries have documented fairly extensive benzodiazepine misuse among people who are dependent on heroin. High rates of prescription drug misuse have also been found among club-goers who use poly-drug combinations (Kelly and Parsons, 2007). Some reports from the USA have suggested that prescription drug misuse is rising among the elderly, although misuse may be unintentional within this group.

DIVERSION OF PRESCRIPTION MEDICINE

Prescription drugs are *diverted* when they pass from a medical or legitimate source to an individual for whom the prescribed drug was not intended. In many instances, the diverted drugs end up on the illegal market, and are then sold at a price several times higher than the cost of the prescription. In the USA, costs associated with the diversion of prescribed drugs have been estimated to be US$25 billion annually (United States General Accounting Office, 2003). These costs are associated with several factors, including health provision, loss of work and costs associated with criminal justice processing.

Prescribed drugs are diverted through different means. 'Doctor shopping' occurs when individuals present to more than one physician, and in turn receive multiple prescriptions for the same drug. Patients forge physicians' prescriptions (for example, change the dosage), or illegally obtain the forms on which prescriptions are written. Pharmacists, pharmacy counter staff, physicians and other health-care professionals have also been implicated in legal cases involving forged prescriptions. Diversion can occur through illegal Internet sales. Various psychotropic drugs and pain medicine are available through web-based companies, however, the vast majority of these sources are not designated as legitimate pharmacies. Internet supplies of prescribed medication occur frequently in some developing nations, where counterfeit medicine appears to be more common. A US study found that 'pill brokers' are actively involved in the supply of prescription medicine for non-medical use (Inciardi et al., 2009). 'Pill brokers' are individuals who obtain prescriptions from people who have been legally prescribed medicine, often for pain. The brokers pay a small fee to people for whom the medicine was originally prescribed and then sell the medicine on the illegal market.

MISUSE OF OVER-THE-COUNTER MEDICATION

Over-the-counter (OTC) products can contain ingredients that can produce psychoactive effects, and in some cases dependence or addiction. For example, codeine is an opioid that is found in some OTC medications (syrups or tablets) to treat coughs. Although less potent than morphine, codeine can produce dependence and withdrawal with chronic use. Between 1996 and 2002, prescribed and OTC opioid-based cough medicines were implicated in over 2000 deaths in England and Wales (Schifano et al., 2006). Although polydrug combinations were observed in some deaths, the finding suggests the potential danger of certain OTC medication.

Over 100 cold medications contain dextromethorphan (DXM), which can result in stimulant or disassociative effects with higher than recommended doses. These disassociative effects are similar to that produced by low doses of ketamine. Misuse of DXM has been reported in several countries, for example, the USA, Australia and Korea, and some medical case studies have described psychosis after ingesting high doses of DXM. The drug has been implicated in the deaths of young users, prompting the USA to pass legislation in 2007 to regulate the supply of the substance only to those manufacturers that are registered with the US Food and Drug Administration. However, the impact of the legislation is not yet known; a powder form of DXM can be purchased through Internet suppliers.

Ingredients used in OTC medicines are also used to prepare other drugs for sale on the illicit drug market. For example, pseudoephedrine has been extracted from OTC cold remedies and used to manufacture methamphetamine. In some countries, police have seized large amounts of pseudoephedrine in clandestine labs where methamphetamine is made. Customer purchasing restrictions of OTCs containing pseudoephedrine have been introduced in the USA, Canada, New Zealand and Australia. The issue is being debated in the UK.

SUMMARY

In summary, the misuse of prescription drugs is a global problem and has major implications for public health. McCabe et al. (2006) observed that people who misuse prescribed medicine are often unfamiliar with manufacturers' safety advice and warnings. They also lack knowledge about the effects of polydrug combinations. Diversion of prescribed medicine occurs through various means and diversion via street markets is well established in several countries. OTC medications represent another source of drug misuse and are difficult to regulate. Although the benefits generally outweigh their drawbacks, fairly extensive misuse of OTC medicine has been reported in several developed and developing nations.

REFERENCES

Coupe, M.H. and Stannard, C. (2007) 'Opioids in persistent non-cancer pain', *Continuing Education in Anaesthesia, Critical Care and Pain*, 7 (3): 100–3.

Fischer, B. and Rehm, J. (2007) 'Illicit opioid use in the 21st century: witnessing a paradigm shift?', *Addiction*, 102 (4): 499–501.

Inciardi, J.A., Surratt, H.L., Cicero, T.J. and Beard, R.A. (2009) 'Prescription opioid abuse and diversion in an urban community: the results of an ultrarapid assessment', *Pain Medicine*, 10 (3): 537–48.

Johnston, L.D., O'Malley, P.M., Bachman, J.G. and Schulenberg, J.E. (2005) *Monitoring the Future National Survey Results on Drug Use, 1975 2004 Volume II: College Students and Adults Ages 19–45*. Bethesda, MD: National Institute on Drug Abuse.

Kelly, B.C. and Parsons, J.T. (2007) 'Prescription drug misuse among club-drug using young adults', *American Journal of Drug and Alcohol Abuse*, 33 (6): 875–84.

McCabe, S.E., Boyd, C.J. and Teter, C.J. (2006) 'Medical use, illicit use, and diversion of abusable prescription drugs', *Journal of American College Health*, 54 (5): 269–78.

Schifano, F., Zamparutti, G., Zambello, F., Oyefeso, A, Deluca, P., Balestrieri, M., Little, D. and Ghodse, A.H. (2006) 'Review of deaths related to analgesic- and cough-suppressant opioids; England and Wales 1996–2002', *Pharmacopsychiatry*, 39 (5): 185–91.

United States General Accounting Office (2003) *Oxycontin Abuse and Diversion and Efforts to Address the Problem*. Report to Congressional Requesters, #GAO-04–110. Washington, DC: US Government Printing Office.

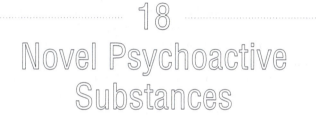

18
Novel Psychoactive Substances

Synthetic, semi-synthetic and natural substances that produce psychoactive effects and are legal to use, possess and supply.

To date, the physical and psychoactive effects of novel psychoactive substances (NPS) are broadly defined in terms of three categories: stimulants, depressants or hallucinogens. They are available in different forms (for example, tablets, mixtures, oils, powders, crystals) and have contained (1) plants, stems, leaves and herbs found in nature (for example, kava, kratom, salvia divinorum), (2) research chemicals produced in laboratories (for example, 2-aminoindan, butylone, mephedrone, methylone, synthetic cannabinoids, such as JWH-018 and JWH-073) or (3) semi-synthetic substances that are derived from natural oils (for example, DMAA). NPS are marketed in hundreds of different products and packaging often features 'hippy style', 'new age' or other symbols. Some product labels aim to remind consumers of illegal street drugs or their effects, for example, 'Snow Blow', 'White Ice Resin', 'Trip E', 'Charlie', 'Mary Jane' and 'X Pillz'. Drug scenes within a growing number of countries have expanded to include legal as well as illegal psychoactive substances.

Some nature-based legal highs have been used for hundreds of years by indigenous groups as part of social mores, ritual or ceremony (for example, khat). The use of NPS in this context sometimes creates problems for ethnic minorities who immigrate and settle in other cultures (see, for example, Armstrong, 2008). In contrast to the practices of indigenous people, the use of NPS as part of 'recreational' drug taking is primarily motivated by pleasure. In comparison, dosages are often higher than that taken by indigenous groups, routes of administration are different (Griffin et al., 2008) and polysubstance use is relatively common.

The market for synthetic NPS is quite different, in that the wide array of products makes it difficult to accurately describe the chemical make-up (including adulterants), potential side effects and drug interactions. Moreover, synthetic NPS are often sold under the guise of other purposes. For example, mephedrone products (recently banned in several European countries) were marketed as plant food and bath salts with the warning 'not fit for human consumption' presumably to avoid legislative controls.

Limited evidence suggests the availability of synthetic cathinones in Israel in 2004 (Power, 2009) and in selected European regions beginning in 2007–2008. Discussions focusing on mephedrone appeared on Internet forums beginning in 2007 (Psychonaut Web Mapping Research Group, 2009). In New Zealand, several European countries and Hong Kong, the legal market in synthetic stimulants has included piperazine derivatives, phenethylamines, tryptamines and cathinone derivatives. The development of this legal market has coincided with the rise of 'amphetamine-type stimulants' (ATS), major drugs of choice with an estimated 30–40 million users worldwide (United Nations Office on Drugs and Crime, 2010). In the UK and Ireland, mephedrone spread rapidly during 2009 and 2010 becoming embedded within several drug scenes within a span of 12 months. Post-criminalisation, concerns have been raised about the availability of mephedrone on the UK illegal street market and in other countries, and by late 2010, emerging reports described the availability of synthetic cathinones in Canada and the USA.

Research into NPS is limited, although the evidence is accumulating. Surveys conducted in schools or universities have described prevalence of NPS consumption. In a Florida study, conducted prior to legislative controls, approximately 4 per cent of females and 11 per cent of males reported ever using Salvia, with fewer than 1 per cent using in the past month (Khey et al., 2008). The authors noted that prevalence was higher among white students compared to African American or Hispanic students. Dargan et al. (2010) conducted a survey of 1006 individuals enrolled in schools, colleges and universities in one area of Scotland. The survey data were collected in February 2010, prior to the UK ban on mephedrone. Lifetime prevalence was 20.3 per cent, and of this group, 23.4 per cent used on one occasion only and 4.4 per cent reported using daily. A third study drew from a self-selecting sample of readers of a leading UK dance music magazine (Winstock et al., 2010). A total of 41.3 per cent of respondents had tried mephedrone (pre-ban) and approximately one-third had used the drug during the past month. Additionally, 15.1 per cent of respondents reported using mephedrone at least once a week.

The authors noted that respondents had prior experience with one or more illegal drugs, which might explain the higher prevalence rates among this purposive sample.

WHY USE NOVEL PSYCHOACTIVE SUBSTANCES

The rapid growth in popularity of NPS is an indication of the continued and wide-spread demand for psychoactive substances and altered states of consciousness. There is a range of motivating factors for the use of NPS, not least the pursuit of the pleasure of intoxication. More prosaically, the development of NPS needs to be put in the context of the illegal drug market (Measham et al., 2010). The sup-ply of legal NPS and the rapid growth in their popularity relates to experienced drug users' growing disillusionment with popular illegal street drugs. In the UK for example, rapid falls in the purity levels of powder cocaine and the MDMA content of ecstasy pills has meant that users were at least initially attracted to mephedrone, a substituted cathinone, owing to the relatively high purity levels. However, dis-placement from illegal street drugs to legal NPS highs may be temporary. Hammersley (2010) argues for example that in relation to smoking mixtures con-taining synthetic cannabinoids (for example, 'Spice'), once such mixtures are made illegal their appeal wanes and users return to their former use patterns of illegal drugs (for example, cannabis). The appeal of legal NPS may relate less to users' fear of arrest and prosecution than the surety and ease with which legal highs can be obtained compared to the unreliability and difficulties involved in purchasing illegal drugs. Some users may perceive legal NPS to be relatively 'safe' in com-parison to illegal drugs. Sheridan and Butler (2010) note that the formerly legal status of BZP 'party-pills' in New Zealand meant that some young people disregarded harm reduction advice relating to such party pills. Notably some users perceived BZPs to have inferior effects (that is, to be 'weaker') than other psychostimulants, such as ecstasy, precisely because they were legal, hence consuming greater quantities of BZPs than recommended, or more freely mixing BZPs with illicit drugs or alcohol. BZP users also reported that the drug's legal status reduced the social stigma attached to purchase and consumption, meaning they would more readily seek help and advice from parents, friends or 'official' sources than they might otherwise do in relation to illegal drugs.

ROUTES OF SUPPLY OF LEGAL HIGHS

NPS have been available through street-based and online headshops, specialty cloth-ing and music shops, adult shops (sex shops) and a host of other retail outlets. Availability through friends and dealers also has been noted. Media reports from the USA and selected European countries have voiced concern over Internet access to NPS. Although availability through online headshops is extensive, this source of supply may be over-stated by media. Routes of supply of NPS may be subject to change following their prohibition; there is evidence in the UK, for example, of the development of a street market in mephedrone following a banning of substituted cathinones in April 2010. However, routes of supply may not change following prohibition; GBL, banned in the UK in December 2009, remains widely available for purchase on the Internet.

POLICY RESPONSE

The emergence of NPS has led to considerable concern and anxiety, most notably among parents and guardians, teachers, politicians and drug workers. Popular media has been criticised for its sensationalist coverage of the issue of NPS. Both media and official reactions to NPS have tended to involve demands for the immediate banning of such substances (see also **32 drug scares and moral panics**). In this context those involved in the NPS trade, including users, have attracted negative attention. In Northern Ireland and the Republic of Ireland, for example, street-based headshops were blamed for the alleged widespread use of NPS, particularly among youth. In 2009–2010, community resistance towards street-based headshops and their owners included shop-front protests, 'Facebook' petitions, arson attacks, bomb threats, shootings and proposals to ban them altogether. This public reaction, along with adverse media attention and reports of young people experiencing problems with NPS, were three factors that contributed to legislative controls over synthetic cathinones and a host of other NPS by the Republic of Ireland in May 2010.

Policy responses have tended towards using existing prohibition frameworks to make both possession and supply of novel psychoactive substances illegal under individual list systems, whereby substances are added to banned 'lists' of substances, typically following risk assessments by expert bodies. By 2008 for example, 13 European Union (EU) member states had banned BZP. By September 2010, 13 European countries had introduced legislative controls over mephedrone (European Monitoring Centre for Drugs and Drug Addiction, 2010). In two other countries (Finland and the Netherlands) mephedrone is subjected to medicines control. In the UK all substituted cathinones, including mephedrone, were made illegal. Manufacturers responded by producing NPS that were not in the substituted cathinone family, notably naphyrone (NRG-1), which was subsequently banned in the UK. Calls have been made for more rapid official responses to emergent psychoactive substances in the forms of temporary banning orders to be put in place while evidence of harm is gathered. Elsewhere generic or analogue legislation works to ban all substances which may be used 'recreationally', In the USA, for example, the US Controlled Substance Analogue Enforcement Act 1986 outlaws the supply of all substances which are 'substantially similar' in chemical structure and/or effect to stimulant, depressant or hallucinogenic drugs that are already controlled, regardless of their individual harm. In criminal proceedings, however, government bears the responsibility of demonstrating that the analogue substance was specifically intended for human consumption.

REFERENCES

Armstrong, E.G. (2008) 'Research note: crime, chemicals and Khat', *Journal of Drug Issues*, 38 (2): 631–48.

key concepts in drugs and society

Dargan, P.I., Albert, S. and Wood, D.M. (2010) 'Mephedrone use and associated adverse effects in school and college/university students before the UK legislation change', *QJM*, 103: 875–9.

European Monitoring Centre for Drugs and Drug Addiction (2010) *Risk Assessment Report of a New Psychoactive Substance: 4-Methylmethcathinone (Mephedrone)*. Lisbon: European Monitoring Centre for Drugs and Drug Addiction.

Griffin, O.H., Miller, B.L. and Khey, D.N. (2008) 'Legally high? Legal considerations of *Salvia divinorum*', *Journal of Psychoactive Drugs*, 40 (2): 183–91.

Hammersley, R. (2010) 'The dangers of banning Spice and the synthetic cannabinoids agonists', *Addiction*, 105 (2): 373.

Khey, D.N., Miller, B.L. and Griffin, O.H. (2008) '*Salvia divinorum* use among a college student sample', *Journal of Drug Education*, 38 (3): 297–306.

Measham, F., Moore, K., Newcombe, R. and Welch, Z. (2010) 'Tweaking, bombing, dabbing and stockpiling: the emergence of mephedrone and the perversity of prohibition', *Drugs and Alcohol Today*, 10 (1): 14–21.

Power, M. (2009) 'Mephedrone: the future of drug dealing', *DrugLink*, March/April (6–7): 9.

Psychonaut Web Mapping Research Group (2009) 'Mephedrone report'. Available at: http://194.83.136.209/documents/reports/Mephedrone.pdf (accessed 16 October 2012).

Sheridan, J. and Butler, R. (2010) '"They're legal so they're safe, right?" What did the legal status of BZP-party pills mean to young people in New Zealand?', *International Journal of Drug Policy*, 21 (1): 77–81.

United Nations Office on Drugs and Crime (2010) *World Drug Report 2010*. New York: United Nations Publications.

Winstock, A.R., Mitcheson, L.R., Deluca, P., Davey, Z., Corazza, O. and Schifano, F. (2010) 'Mephedrone: new kid for the chop?', *Addiction*, 6 (1): 154–61.

19

The Gateway Hypothesis/ Stepping Stone Theory

The gateway hypothesis suggests that the use of 'soft' drugs, particularly cannabis, causes a progression to 'hard' drugs, such as opiates and cocaine. It is suggested that this progression is the result of either pharmacological changes in brain functioning leading to a desire for stronger drugs; or drug markets increasing opportunities to access a wider range of drugs. Critics contend that there can be associations between the use of different drugs without there being a necessary upward causal relationship and that there are many other reasons for drug use. Although most people that have used heroin have prior experience of cannabis, most people that have used cannabis do not go on to use heroin.

The gateway hypothesis, sometimes called the stepping stone theory, is an attempt to explain how people progress from legal to illegal drugs and from less harmful to more harmful drugs. The theory has had widespread popular appeal and retains an influence over policymaking despite there being little evidence to suggest that there is a pharmacological basis for the theory.

THE GATEWAY HYPOTHESIS

The gateway hypothesis or gateway theory, more accurately a concept than a theory, suggests that the use of 'soft' drugs such as cannabis predisposes individuals to subsequent use of 'harder' drugs such as opiates. First proposed by Kandel (1975, 2002), it is based on evidence of a sequence of initiation from non-use to alcohol and cigarette use, then moving on to 'soft' drugs such as cannabis earlier in illicit drug careers and 'hard' drugs later on. Thus cigarettes are considered to be a gateway or stepping stone to cannabis and cannabis is a gateway to heroin. The underlying concern is that the resulting progression towards 'hard' drugs, such as opiates and cocaine, results in a significant increase in risks of harm and dependency. This assumed gateway has been based on general population surveys, longitudinal studies, schools surveys and epidemiological studies of adolescent drug use and has had enormous political influence, guiding US drug policy since the 1950s.

There are three key characteristics to the gateway hypothesis: causation, pharmacology and markets. First, is the emphasis on causation. While most 'hard' drug users have initiated with 'soft' drugs and there is clearly a statistical association or correlation between earlier use of cannabis and later use of heroin, the distinction of gateway theory is that it proposes a *causal* relationship between the two, with earlier cannabis use being the reason for later heroin use. This causal relationship is supposedly based either on the pharmacological effects of the drug resulting in biological change, or on the operation of drug markets.

Regarding pharmacology, there is some research to suggest that a biological mechanism exists which may operate as a gateway in rats (for example, Ellgren et al., 2006). In humans, researchers identified a permanent loss of grey matter in the frontal lobe of chronic cocaine users which is associated with greater compulsivity to take cocaine (Ersche et al., 2011). However an increase in the brain's reward system was also identified by the researchers which predated cocaine use, which researchers argued indicates that certain individuals are vulnerable to developing cocaine dependency rather than the pharmacological effects of cocaine use cause dependency.

If there is minimal evidence to support a pharmacological causal relationship, more weight has been given to market-driven explanations for earlier initiation into 'soft' drugs leading to later use of 'hard' drugs. The market explanation suggests that a supplier might try to persuade a user to buy a different, stronger, more expensive or dependency-inducing drug to increase their business turnover or profit margins, and that a cannabis user might be more tempted to try 'hard' drugs because they are already in touch with a street dealer and therefore have that opportunity to experiment whereas a non-drug user would struggle to access 'hard'

key concepts in
drugs and society

drugs. A RAND study tested the cannabis gateway theory by modelling adolescent drug use and found that associations could be expected between cannabis and 'hard' drugs, with some people predisposed to try a range of drugs but that cannabis comes earlier in drug careers due to its easier access. Overall, however, the RAND technical report (Levitt et al., 2006: xiv) concluded that 'the gateway theory has little evidence to support it despite copious research'.

POLICY

In North America and some European countries an emphasis on adolescent prevention programmes have focused on delaying onset of alcohol and tobacco use in order to prevent use of illicit drugs. These programmes oversimplify the complexities of drug-taking behaviours, do not distinguish between experimental, recreational and problem use, and portray an inevitability in progression, despite research suggesting that only a minority of adolescents who experiment with drugs develop patterns of regular or problem use. Others have argued that instead of such abstinence messages, young people should be given accurate information about drugs, be taught decision-making and life skills, and learn to incorporate moderate and controlled use of legal substances such as alcohol into healthy and productive lifestyles.

Gateway theory has had a pivotal role in drug policy in the Netherlands, based on market-driven notions of gateway. Under the 1976 revision of the Dutch Opium Act, drugs were divided into two schedules: Schedule I drugs such as heroin were seen as having an unacceptable health risk, while Schedule II drugs such as cannabis were associated with a negligible health risk. These two Schedules were created in an attempt to separate the markets for 'hard' and 'soft' drugs with the aim of discouraging a move from 'soft' to 'hard' drug use. Consequently Dutch drug policy has tolerated the sale and use of cannabis in designated cannabis coffee shops since 1976 to break the perceived link between the sale of 'soft' drugs and 'hard' drugs. While this has been seen to be instrumental in lower prevalence of both 'soft' and 'hard' drug use in the Netherlands compared to their European counterparts, the 'honey pot' effect of drug tourism led to restrictions on the total number of cannabis coffee shops, along with proposed sales restricted only to Dutch residents.

CRITIQUE OF GATEWAY HYPOTHESIS

Statistically while most heroin users will have used cannabis prior to their first experience with heroin, most cannabis users do not progress to later use of heroin and therefore it is unconvincing to portray this temporal sequence as a causal relationship. Furthermore, trends in soft and hard drug use are not necessarily directly related: cannabis use increased in the UK and North America in the 1990s without a directly associated increase in hard drug use. However proponents of gateway theory counter this by arguing that cigarette smoking increases the *risk* of using cannabis and cannabis use increases the *risk* of subsequent hard drug use, if not resulting in use in each and every case.

Critics argue that while there are associations between the use of different drugs, proving a causal relationship is not possible due to the multitude of confounding variables. For example, reasons for drug use – such as personality, family background, peer influences, subcultural factors and socio-economic context – may result in associations between the use of different drugs, whereas reasons for early initiation with cannabis and later use of opiates and cocaine can relate to access and availability issues (see also **3 why do people take drugs?**). A report on cannabis by the Advisory Council on the Misuse of Drugs (the UK government drugs advisory body) concurs, concluding that proving any causal relationship between cannabis use and later use of 'hard' drugs was 'very difficult due to the many confounding factors that might also act as gateways' (2002: 9). Furthermore they note that 'even if the gateway theory is correct, it cannot be a very wide gate as the majority of cannabis users never move on to Class A drugs' (2002: 9).

Instead researchers have suggested that there are more complex patterns of drug use than simply 'soft' recreational drug use being the cause of 'hard' dependent drug use. For example, Hammersley et al.'s (2003) longitudinal study of persistent young offenders found little use of heroin or crack and little evidence of progression on to these drugs in later years. Instead they found frequent and heavy use of alcohol, cannabis and tobacco, and less frequent use of other drugs, with associated frequent low level offending. Of these users, 15 per cent were assessed as having substance abuse problems, despite most not using 'hard' drugs. Hammersley et al. concluded that their cohort 'could not be neatly divided into normal substance users without problems and "addicts" with problems' (2003: 70).

Secondary analysis of US data from the national household survey NHSDA and arrestee drug monitoring programme ADAM by Golub and Johnson (2002) suggests that few people in the general population in the USA become 'hard' drug users and increasingly their drug careers do not follow the traditional gateway sequence of initiation. Instead the reasons for hard drug use relate to social and economic problems such as poverty, unemployment, violence and family breakdown, and therefore it has been argued that prevention policies would be more effectively directed towards addressing these social problems rather than gateway theory which has little validity.

Regarding supply routes, Blakemore has dismissed the idea of market-driven gateway theory in the UK context when giving evidence to the House of Commons Science and Technology Committee. He argued that 'cannabis supply is, to a large extent, rather different from the supply of harder drugs' (HCSTC, 2006: 25). Research on UK cannabis supply has noted the importance of 'social supply' between friendship networks. Furthermore, Coomber's (2006) research with drug suppliers challenges market-driven gateway theory that suppliers might tempt users from soft, cheaper drugs towards hard dependency-inducing drugs through credit and 'freebies'.

SUMMARY

The gateway hypothesis suggests that the use of soft drugs, particularly cannabis, can cause a progression to the use of hard drugs, such as opiates and cocaine, which have increased risks of harm and dependency. This proposed progression can be the result of the pharmacological effects of the drug with a biological change in brain functioning causing a propensity to increased drug use, or the result of drug market characteristics which result in easier access to a wider range of street drugs. Critics suggest that while there are associations between the use of different drugs, there is no causal relationship. For example, reasons for a propensity towards (any) drug use can include personality, family background, peer influences and particularly social and economic problems, which may result in associations between use of different drugs, whereas reasons for patterns of initiation from earlier cannabis use to later use of opiates and cocaine can relate to access and availability issues.

REFERENCES

Advisory Council on the Misuse of Drugs (2002) *The Classification of Cannabis Under the Misuse of Drugs Act 1971*. London: Home Office.

Coomber, R. (2006) *Pusher Myths: Re-Situating the Drug Dealer*. London: Free Association Books.

Ellgren M., Spano S.M. and Hurd Y.L. (2006) 'Adolescent cannabis exposure alters opiate intake and opioid limbic neuronal populations in adult rats', *Journal of Neuropsychopharmacology*, 32: 607–15.

Ersche, K., Barnes, A., Jones, P., Morein-Zamir, S., Robbins, T. and Bullmore, E. (2011) 'Abnormal structure of frontostriatal brain systems is associated with aspects of impulsivity and compulsivity in cocaine dependence', *Brain*, 134 (7): 2013–24.

Golub, A. and Johnson, B. (2002) 'The misuse of the "Gateway Theory" in US policy on drug abuse control: a secondary analysis of the muddled deduction', *International Journal of Drug Policy*, 13 (1): 5–19.

House of Commons Science and Technology Committee (HCSTC) (2006) *Drug Classification: Making a Hash of it? Fifth Report of Session 2005–06, HC 1031*. London: The Stationery Office. Available at: http://www.publications.parliament.uk/pa/cm200506/cmselect/cmsctech/1031/103102.htm (accessed 1 August 2012).

Hammersley, R., Marsland, L. and Reid, M. (2003) *Substance Use by Young Offenders: The Impact of the Normalisation of Drug Use in the Early Years of the 21st Century*. Home Office Research Study 261. London: Home Office.

Kandel, D. (1975) 'Stages in adolescent involvement in drug use', *Science*, 190: 912–14.

Kandel, D. (ed.) (2002) *Stages and Pathways of Drug Involvement: Examining the Gateway Hypothesis*. Cambridge: Cambridge University Press.

Levitt, R., Nason, E. and Hallsworth, M. (2006) *The Evidence Base for the Classification of Drugs*. Technical report, prepared for the UK House of Commons Committee on Science and Technology. Santa Monica, CA: RAND. Available at: http://www.rand.org/pubs/technical_reports/TR362/ (accessed 1 August 2012).

> The concept of drug-related violence refers to the idea that particular drugs induce
> the user towards an aggressive or violent state. It also denotes a statistical associa-
> tion between drug use and/or selling and some kind of violent outcome.

There is a common assumption that alcohol and particular street drugs *make* people commit acts of violence. This is a view often reinforced by the regular reports
of alcohol-fuelled violence and of drug-crazed murderers in our popular mass
media and various statistics on crime showing strong links between the use of
alcohol and/or street drugs and violent outcomes. Broadly, although the actual
statistics differ, they provide a broadly similar picture in many countries. Illustrative
of this broader picture, Roizen (1997) has estimated that up to 86 per cent of
murders, 37 per cent of assaults, 60 per cent of sexual offences and 57 per cent of
(male on female) domestic violence offences are committed when the assailant is
under the influence of alcohol. Some research evidence also points towards a
significant relationship between the use of drugs, such as crack cocaine, amphetamines and barbiturates (Boles and Miotto, 2003), and violent action but figures
for these and other substances (such as PCP) are, in fact, fewer and far less reliable
(Collins, 1994). An array of more focused research, however, reveals a far more
complex picture than the statistics appear to present. Indeed, although alcohol and
other drugs may be highly *correlated* with violent crime, there is a range of evidence that, suggests that alcohol and other drugs do not *cause* such outcomes and
that, in fact, violence likely occurs for other reasons that can relate strongly to
either individual predisposition as well as other environmental or social (including
economic) factors. With all this in mind much of the rest of this chapter will focus
on alcohol (as it is by far and away the most linked substance as causing violence
and is also, of course, a drug itself).

CROSS-CULTURAL EVIDENCE

While it is true that alcohol does have fairly predictable effects (dependent on how
much is consumed) on certain motor functions –slowing reactions and affecting
coordination, for example – and on individual physiology, what we find when we
consider the effects of drinking in different societies is that alcohol does not have
uniform or predictable effects on *behaviour*.

In societies such as the USA, Australia and the UK, alcohol use is strongly linked
to aggressive, violent and anti-social behaviour whereas in many parts of South
America and the Mediterranean, drinking is far less associated with such behaviour

and in many cases is actually associated with peaceful and non-violent behaviour – despite, in some cases extreme levels of intoxication. The Camba of Bolivia in South America is one such group where most of the behaviours associated with drinking in Western industrial societies are, significantly, absent. Despite drinking locally produced alcohol, that in terms of strength is far more powerful than anything available in most other societies, and drinking heavily (a kind of ritualised 'binge' drinking that lasts until the alcohol runs out or participants fall asleep or unconscious), aggression or violence is not an outcome. Cross-cultural research of this kind (and there are numerous other examples showing a wide variety of behavioural outcomes) not only demonstrates that alcohol, even when consumed to excess, not only does not necessarily produce the stereotyped behaviour that we expect, but may in fact produce little variation in behaviour at all. Different relationships to alcohol and the evidence that it causes violence only in some cultures and not in others may relate to the *expectations* of the kinds of behaviour that surround it in different societies (WHO, 2004).

EXPECTATION

That expectation has a great deal to do with drug effects is a well-established fact. Numerous experiments with alcohol, various drugs and even placebos (substances that have no chemical effects but where the user thinks they do) have demonstrated that researchers can manipulate the behaviour of subjects involved in all manner of ways. Thus, in some experiments people have been fooled into believing that the drugs they have taken will increase aggressive or unusual behaviour (although they do not) and such behaviour often then emerges in the experimental subjects. In other experiments people have been told they are taking a particular drug and many then act according to what they think the drug's effects should be (for example, to make them feel drowsy or sleepy) even though the drug given does not have these effects. Clearly then, expectations of what a drug 'does' to a person appears to be a powerful factor in what a user then experiences and how they behave under the influence of a substance (or even a placebo). We might therefore imagine that for any substance where there is a strongly ingrained cultural belief that the substance causes aggression and violence (and as we have seen, not all do for, for example, alcohol) that separating out the cause of violence that subsequently results from belief or the substance is difficult.

SITUATIONAL VIOLENCE (COUPLED WITH EXPECTATION)

Understanding the *nature* of an alcohol-fuelled violent episode is important in further understanding the cross-cultural differences that can be observed. The picture of someone 'out of control' (the alcohol is seen to have either dismantled the normal inhibitory mechanisms which stop us all from being violent all the time or to have 'taken over' the individual) is common. The idea that the alcohol (or drugs) is to blame and there was nothing (once drunk) the drunken person could do about it is not uncommon. Such a perspective however is undermined by evidence that shows that drunken acts of violence, where people are seemingly out of control can be suddenly moderated when the assailant is confronted with choices about ending their violent behaviour – something that the idea that a person is 'taken over' by the substance involved struggles to deal with. Men that commit acts of 'out of control – the drink made me do it' domestic violence often stop if interrupted and also strategically injure their partners in places difficult for others to see – again hardly the act of uncontrolled violence. That violence appears to have very particular 'limits' within which the violence is effectively constrained – suggests that the degree of 'disinhibition' experienced is influenced by the context (and the considered norms of drunken behaviour) in which the drunken violence takes place. Consistent with this position, some of the more experimentally based research has shown that providing alcohol-intoxicated individuals with the choice to respond to aggression in a non-aggressive way (for example, where doing so does not involve 'losing face') in a potentially violent situation will often lead to a non-aggressive outcome (Gustafson, 1990; Kelly and Cherek, 1993).

DISINHIBITION AS 'TIME-OUT'

There is no doubt that many people *experience* alcohol- or drug-related behaviours as less inhibited but as we have seen the idea that disinhibition occurs as a predictable effect of alcohol or other substance use is not supported by the cross-cultural literature. The study of drug use in various tribal and other groups has shown that highly ritual-ised approaches to drug use – where, individuals/groups partake in a range of prepara-tions before drug use, carry out consistent behaviours (make-up, clothing, dance, chanting and so on) and have a common idea of the 'visions' they would like to see or the 'journey' they would like to travel when under the influence of drugs – can pro-duce predictable, desired outcomes (drug effects). This suggests that even with power-ful hallucinatory drugs the effects can be managed and brought under social control. The ritual is a powerful technique in managing both the drug-using environment and the required drug effect. In the West, ritualised drug use is much more muted but nonetheless very much present. Although ritual surrounding alcohol is varied, many do encourage drinking and/or the condemning of the abstinent: 'go on have another one'; 'what do you mean you're not drinking, just have one'. Not only do people want to drink but they want to do so with others and intoxication (to varying degrees) is a common aim. Indeed, it could be argued that the overwhelming objective to alcohol (and much drug) use is to relax or 'let go'. In other words not only is alcohol used to help relax but the user is self-consciously *aiming* at letting go of the stresses and strains of normal life. In such circumstances ritual can also be seen to include the preparation of getting dressed up and/or made-up to go out (and 'let go'); playing music to set the mood and relax; to talk to friends prior to the event, driving faster with loud music on the way. In other words even *before* we take that first drink we *expect* to become rela-tively disinhibited and partake in rituals to aid the success of that expectation. When this expectation is combined with the belief that alcohol (and other drugs) chemically aids this process *and* the physical experience of alcohol (and other drugs) affecting us physically (speech slurring and so on) we can see how the two become inextricably associated – to the point that one is believed to cause the other – at least in Western society.

ATTRIBUTION OF DRUG EFFECTS IN HISTORICAL PERSPECTIVE

Historically, different substances such as cannabis, tobacco, opium, heroin and cocaine – among others – have been attributed with the power to turn otherwise 'normal' people into 'immoral savages' stripped of the ability to think reasonably and made to act in unreasonable ways, often with violent outcomes. Many of these attributions however are now discredited: cannabis is no longer demonised as likely to drive a person to insane violence (as was propagated in 1940s and 1950s USA) and powder cocaine is no longer, as it once was, associated with giving the strength of ten men, the power to withstand small calibre bullets and to incite the rape of women (although nearly identical beliefs have now been transposed onto phencyclidine or 'PCP'). In other words, at different points in history and/or in different geographical locations, many substances have been believed to induce a range of behaviours – many of which are contradictory to beliefs at other times. Cannabis, for example, is now seen as a 'mellowing' drug and in some research is associated with less aggressiveness than even non-drug users whereas previously it was, as stated above, seen as likely to induce uncontrolled rage.

REAL DRUG-RELATED VIOLENCE

Statistics that report 'drug-related violence' relate for the most part, not to drug taking but to the distribution of illegal drugs – to drug dealing and trafficking. This is not a necessary relationship but one that comes about due to the illicit nature of the commodity involved, the high levels of demand and, consequently, the enormous sums of money the trade in drugs produces. The violence associated with the drug trade is mostly 'systemic', that is related to problems emerging in protecting trade or enforcing discipline within the market. It is not caused by the pharmacology of the drugs involved. Real drug-related violence thus appears to have more to do with the black market trading structures and the way they are policed than it has to do with drug effects. Alcohol-related violence of this kind also increased during US prohibition of alcohol (1920–1933).

MOST PEOPLE CONVICTED OF DRUG-RELATED VIOLENCE HAVE VIOLENT HISTORIES PRECEDING ANY DRUG USE

Although the research is far from comprehensive, there appears to be good evidence to suggest that many (perhaps most) of those committing drug-related violent crimes were already of a violent disposition before they were drug users and/or already had violent criminal records that preceded drug use. Indeed some cross-cultural research on PCP use – a drug commonly associated with violence in the USA – showed that in those groups with no history or tendency for aggression or violence none was produced as a result of PCP use whereas in the groups that did present greater levels of aggression and violence these were normal mechanisms for resolving conflict in those groups. Some research also suggests that certain individuals with a predisposition to aggression and violence may be more likely to choose substances they believe will enhance or complement that predisposition.

SUMMARY

While the belief that a range of substances – alcohol in particular – cause people to be aggressive and violent is a widespread and a popularly held one, as we have seen it is a view that is problematic in a number of significant ways. The cross-cultural evidence suggests that neither disinhibition, aggression nor violence is either a necessary or predictable outcome of alcohol or drug use and that expectations about what the drug 'does' to you are, along with the context in which use takes place, highly important factors. When combined with the knowledge that much drug-related violence is, in fact, related to drug markets and that many of those with drug-related criminal histories also had pre-drug use convictions for violence, we begin to see that the relationship of chemical substances to violence is not a simple one and one that largely sits outside of simple drug effects.

REFERENCES

Boles, S.M. and Miotto, K. (2003) 'Substance use and violence: a review of the literature', *Aggression and Violent Behaviour*, 8: 155–74.

Collins, J. (1994) 'Summary thoughts about drugs and violence', in R. Coomber (ed.), *Drugs and Drug Use in Society: A Critical Reader.* Dartford: Greenwich University Press. pp. 271–80.

Gustafson, R. (1990) 'Wine and male physical aggression', *Journal of Drug Issues*, 20 (1): 75–86.

Kelly, T.H. and Cherek, D.R. (1993) 'The effects of alcohol on free-operant aggressive behaviour', *Journal of Studies on Alcohol*, 11: 40–52.

Roizen, J. (1997) 'Epidemiological issues in alcohol-related violence', in M. Galanter (ed.), *Recent Developments in Alcoholism.* New York: Plenum Press. pp. 7–40.

World Health Organisation (WHO) (2004) *Global Status Report on Alcohol.* Geneva: WHO.

21
Drugs and Crime

The relationship between drugs and crime is a complex and disputed one, yet it is a cornerstone of drug policy in many countries. Four key types of drugs-crime relationship have been identified: that drugs cause crime, crime causes drugs, that a third variable causes both, and a bi-directional or reciprocal model. In terms of explaining why drugs cause crime, Goldstein's influential 'tripartite' framework proposed three explanations: psychopharmacology, economic compulsion and systemic.

A key focus for politicians, the media and the general public in relation to the 'problem' of drugs is the perceived relationship between drugs and crime. The view is widely held that controlled drugs are pharmacologically dangerous and can lead both directly to violent crime and indirectly to acquisitive crime in order to fund drug addiction. In turn this perceived relationship is used as a justification for banning certain drugs and criminalising and ostracising its users. However, while drug use has been shown to be associated with both a higher level of crime (prevalence) and a higher rate of offending (incidence) among those who are offending, the direct links between criminality and drugs are unclear and the idea of a causal relationship continues to be hotly contested owing to its political prominence.

The value of the global drug market has been estimated by the United Nations Office on Drugs and Crime to be US$400 billion, although the drug policy analyst Reuter has suggested that the global drug trade is probably closer to US$100 billion. In the 2005 World Drugs Report, the UNODC revised its estimate of the global drug trade to US$13 billion at production level, US$94 billion at wholesale level and US$332 billion at retail level. Estimates of the costs to society of drug-related crime range enormously depending on how the figure is calculated. Even with the development of international guidelines there is considerable variation, for example, one study estimated that the costs per capita of illicit drug use in Canada are US$38 per person and in the USA are US$384. In the UK, drug-related crime accounts for approximately 3 per cent of all recorded crime, yet the estimated cost of this drug-related crime is £14 billion, about three-quarters of the total cost of crime (£19 billion). The social and economic costs of Class A drug use in the UK were estimated to be £15.4 billion per annum in 2003/4, most of which (£14 billion) was crime. Of the costs of drug-related crime, 99 per cent are linked to problem drug users (see also **8 typologies of drug use**), estimated at over £44,000 per drug user per year.

DRUGS OFFENCES

Controlled substances tend to be classified into categories where the most harmful have the highest criminal sanctions, in the USA with the Comprehensive Drug Abuse Prevention and Control Act 1970 and in the UK with the Misuse of Drugs Act 1971. Aside from the costs of drug-related crime, the costs of enforcement account for the majority of expenditure in most jurisdictions. In the USA it is estimated that prison expenditure costs state governments approximately US$50 billion per year in total, with an additional US$5 billion spent by the federal government. Moreover, the very high level of incarceration for drug-related offences in the USA has steep personal as well as financial costs. More than 2 million children have a parent imprisoned for drug-related offences in the USA, and drugs offenders face a wide range of barriers to reintegration into society including obstacles to employment, withdrawal of welfare benefits and loss of educational loans.

There are four broad types of relationship between drugs and crime.

DRUGS CAUSE CRIME

First, there is the perspective that drugs cause crime. Within this 'drugs cause crime' relationship, Goldstein proposed an influential model which identified three key explanations, outlined below, although critics have argued that the three categories are not mutually exclusive and that the empirical research upon which Goldstein's model is based is flawed. Bearing in mind these caveats, the model is summarised here:

How drugs cause crime

Goldstein's (1985) 'tripartite framework' identified three key ways that drugs can cause crime, initially using New York homicides as the case study for his model, but subsequently applied by others to the drug–crime relationship more broadly.

Psychopharmacology

This explanation suggests that the direct acute pharmacological effects of the substance consumed will result in crime. Goldstein et al. (1992) classified 14 per cent of New York homicides as caused by psychopharmacology in 1988, linked to a range of legal and illegal, stimulant and depressant drugs. There is little evidence that the chemical effects of drugs directly lead to violent crime although a link between stimulants and aggression has been noted. Rather, it is the bio-chemical effects combined with psychology, socio-cultural context and situational factors (such as with alcohol, the crowded, hot and socially pressurised atmosphere of bars) that together can lead to an association, rather than causation, between alcohol and violence. Furthermore, at lower levels, use of drugs such as alcohol and MDMA could be considered socially functional rather than criminogenic.

Economic compulsive

More influential and more widely accepted are the perceived links between drug use and acquisitive crime, with drug dependency seen to lead to an economic compulsion to obtain 'earnings' from illegitimate if not legitimate means, in order to buy street drugs to fuel the necessity of consumption. This pattern of daily, dependent use (often injecting) of opioids (opiates such as heroin and their synthetic substitutes), crack cocaine or amphetamines is strongly associated with poverty, unemployment and social exclusion (see also **13 gender, ethnicity and social class**). Studies that drug-test people who are arrested for acquisitive crimes suggest that about two-thirds of arrestees test positive for drugs in their body when apprehended, and up to one-half of arrestees who have taken drugs in the past year say that their drug use is connected to their offending (Bennett and Holloway, 2005). It is this drugs-crime relationship which is the focus of public concern and political action.

Yet Goldstein et al. (1992) identified only 4 per cent of NYC homicides in 1988 as due to economic-compulsive drug-related crime. Furthermore the underlying premise that addiction causes offending to buy drugs would then imply that more severe dependency would lead to more compulsive drug seeking and a greater incidence of offending, whereas this is not the case – the heaviest drug users are not necessarily the heaviest offenders. Also price increases can lead to reduced consumption rather than a greater incidence of offending, suggesting that even dependent drug use is price sensitive and leads us to question the emphasis placed by the media, politicians and even some drug users on the power of pharmacological addiction and its motivation for crime (see also **4 addiction**).

Rather than there being a simple causal relationship whereby crime is caused by the need for (usually) opioids, a series of studies have highlighted the complexities of the relationship between potentially any drugs and crime. Through interviews with 151 Scottish offenders, Hammersley et al. (1989) found that there was a stronger association between non-opioid (poly)drug use and theft than opioid use and theft, and that alcohol was associated with fraud.

Systemic

Systemic crime is offending which arises out of the system of drug use and drug supply, the operation of the market and police enforcement, such as violence within drug markets or corruption within the police, which are associated with high levels of profit and risk within drug markets and the difficulties of accessing formal means of conflict resolution. Goldstein et al. (1992) estimated that 74 per cent of all NYC homicides in 1988 were systemic. Reiss and Roth (1993) identified four types of systemic crime: organisational crime (for example, territorial disputes over drug markets and distribution); transactional crime (for example, disputes between people buying and selling drugs); third-party crime (such as protection rackets, firearms and prostitution); and secondary crime (for example, money laundering). However, while organised crime, firearms and prostitution feature heavily in media reporting of drug-related crime, the prevalence of drug-related violence and firearms offences has been questioned in studies of drug suppliers and drug markets. For example the body of research by Coomber (2006) and by Pearson and Hobbs (2001) have emphasised the vested interests of drug suppliers in *not* engaging in violence that might draw unwanted attention from the police to their criminal activities, but instead how suppliers might cooperate and support each other's trade rather than actively engage in aggressive competition.

Crime causes drugs

In general, criminal careers precede drugs careers and therefore it has been suggested that some crimes may cause drug use. For example, drugs can be taken to cope with a chaotic or stressful criminal lifestyle, such as working in the sex trade; to improve criminal competence and alertness for burglars and those working in the 'grey' economy of the entertainment, leisure and sex industries; or to celebrate after successful criminal incidents.

Indirectly, crime may provide the disposable income to facilitate a lifestyle which includes (more) drug and alcohol use than the offender otherwise could not afford. While the initiation of a criminal career may have preceded experimentation with illicit drugs, the profits of crime can provide the resources to engage in drug taking. As a result, drug use may then develop into a primary motivation for continued involvement in crime rather than desistance.

A third factor causes both drugs and crime

It has been argued that the underlying cause of the drugs–crime relationship is neither drugs nor offending but the poverty, inequality and resulting desperation that drives people to become both dependent on drugs and motivated to commit crime. For example, the work of the influential Chicago School of urban sociology in 1920s America mapped the geographical distribution of residential areas with major social problems such as unemployment, poverty, poor housing conditions and drug problems within the city and identified a strong correlation between drugs, crime and poverty. In this instance, both offending and drug dependency are symptoms of deeper social problems and therefore policy is better directed at addressing the underlying cause of this clustering of associated problems within certain communities through urban planning and social intervention.

Alongside poverty, other factors have been identified as causing both drug use and crime. A study of persistent young offenders by Hammersley et al. (2003) suggested that stress and specifically bereavement can play a key part in the onset of drug problems among offenders, rather than there being a direct causal relationship between drugs and offending. Over one-half of drug-using offenders in their study had experienced bereavement within the previous two years. Furthermore, different drugs were linked to different offending careers: heroin and crack cocaine were more likely to be associated with acquisitive crime such as shop theft, whereas stimulants and polydrug use were related to theft of motor vehicles and assault.

A third reason for both drug careers and criminal careers might be wider socio-economic and cultural influences. For example, both may be a function of the pressures on young men to live a machismo and materialistic lifestyle which centres on licensed leisure venues where alcohol and drug use occur. Increased offending may lead to increased financial resources to fund drinking and drug use, and increased consumption may lead to further offending including possession and supply of drugs, as well as violent or disorderly behaviour and related crimes which disproportionately occur near licensed premises. By applying lifestyle theory to drugs and criminal careers, Walters (1994) argued that the primary motivating factor behind the development of a drug or criminal lifestyle was existential fear of uncertainty and a failure by individuals to cope with and adapt to change. Walters suggested that it was an individual's distance from the drug or criminal ideal rather than conformity to the stereotypical roles of such lifestyles, which defined a person's commitment to a drug or criminal lifestyle. Consequently Walters concluded that there was no direct causal link between drugs and crime but merely an 'interactive nexus'.

Bi-directional/reciprocal relationship

The fourth type of relationship between drugs and crime is that it is a reciprocal relationship whereby each can exacerbate the other, with a bi-directional association rather than a uni-directional causal relationship. An example of this would be drug-using sex workers leading chaotic lives which may also include minor offending, and the fines resulting from petty, persistent offending then adding to the financial incentive to engage in sex work.

DRUG USE DOES NOT CAUSE CRIME

Some researchers have argued that there is little evidence that drug use causes crime. There is so much variation between individuals, countries, socio-cultural and historical contexts, that we cannot say that there is a clear and simple causal relationship between the two. Drug use does not necessarily proceed after offending, or precede it, but rather develops independently. If drug use did cause crime then it would be expected to do so in all cases, with heavier drug use leading to heavier crime. Yet controlled use of potentially dependence-forming drugs such as opiates (for example, heroin) and crack cocaine has been noted by researchers (see also **15 drug effects**). McSweeney et al. (2006) estimated that no more than one-third of problem drug users in the UK finance their use of opiates and/or crack cocaine through crime or are significantly involved with the criminal justice system. Shewan and Dalgarno's (2005) study showed that it is possible to take heroin in a controlled way, with limited negative impact on the user or society, as did McSweeney and Turnbull's (2007) longitudinal study of non-problematic heroin users.

However, while there are small numbers who commit petty and persistent crimes to fund a lifestyle which includes drugs, most recreational drug users and even the majority of problem drug users (see also **8 typologies of drug use**) are not regular offenders and they appear to fund their drug use out of legitimate earnings. This then raises problems for the state because the most significant drug-related crime is the result of the criminal offence of drug possession which the government creates and enforces.

SUMMARY

While the variety of perspectives on the relationship between drugs and crime indicates its potential complexity, the priority given to the drugs–crime relationship in policy circles illustrates its symbolic and material impact on users and wider society. Furthermore, while there is a complex relationship between drugs and crime it is also important to note that much drug use can occur without criminal behaviour, just as offending also frequently occurs totally separate to the manufacture, trafficking or use of controlled drugs. Thus, given the sequence that criminal careers usually predate drugs careers, it could be argued that it is more likely that crime causes drug use or at least facilitates drug use rather than that drugs cause crime.

REFERENCES

Bennett, T. and Holloway, K. (2005) *Understanding Drugs, Alcohol and Crime*. Maidenhead: Open University Press.

Coomber, R. (2006) *Pusher Myths: Re-Situating the Drug Dealer*. London: Free Association Books.

Goldstein, P. (1985) 'The drugs-violence nexus: a tripartite framework', *Journal of Drug Issues*, Fall: 493–506.

Goldstein, P., Brownstein, H. and Ryan, P. (1992) 'Drug related homicide in New York City 1984 and 1988', *Crime and Delinquency*, 38: 459–76.

Hammersley, R., Forsyth, A., Morrison, V. and Davies, J. (1989) 'The relationship between crime and opioid use', *British Journal of Addiction*, 84 (9): 1029–43.

Hammersley, R., Marsland, L. and Reid, M. (2003) *Substance Use by Young Offenders: The Impact of the Normalisation of Drug Use in the Early Years of the 21st Century, Home Office Research Study 261*. London: Home Office.

McSweeney, T. and Turnbull, P. (2007) *Exploring User Perceptions of Occasional and Controlled Heroin Use: A Follow-Up Study*. York: Joseph Rowntree Foundation.

McSweeney, T., Stevens, A., Hunt, N. and Turnbull, P. (2006) 'Twisting arms or a helping hand? Assessing the impact of "coerced" and comparable "voluntary" drug treatment options', *British Journal of Criminology*, 47 (3): 470–90.

Pearson, G. and Hobbs, D. (2001) *Middle Market Drug Distribution*. Home Office Research Study No. 227. London: Home Office Research, Development and Statistics Directorate.

Reiss, A. and Roth, J. (eds) (1993) *Understanding and Preventing Violence*. Washington, DC: National Academy Press.

Shewan, D. and Dalgarno, P. (2005) 'Evidence for controlled heroin use? Low levels of negative health and social outcomes among non-treatment heroin users in Glasgow (Scotland)', *British Journal of Health Psychology*, 10 (1): 33–48.

Walters, G. (1994) *Drugs and Crime in Lifestyle Perspective*. Thousand Oaks, CA: Sage.

22

Drug Risks and Health Harms

> *Drug risks refer to behaviours that are likely to produce drug-related harm. Psychoactive drugs can contribute to health harms that affect an individual's physical and psychological well-being.*

Individuals assess and negotiate risk as part of everyday life. Research into various social problems, for example, teen pregnancy, poverty, school drop out and crime, has described individuals or groups who are 'at risk' or at 'high risk' for harm. Individual actions are characterised as 'risky', or as 'risk behaviours', although at times these concepts are not clearly defined. Moreover, engaging in risk taking is not the same as being 'at risk'. Scholarly work as well as social policy has focused on risk as it applies to and affects young people in particular. Youth are often perceived as irrational decision makers, that is, they risk inappropriately or for the wrong reasons. Other scholars have suggested that risk taking can serve important functions for youth, that is, youth have little power in society, and the use of psychoactive substances helps young people to 'defy their demeaned status' (Skager, 2009: 576). Although adults and youth can perceive drug-related risk in different ways, risk taking and experimentation can be important for shaping youth identities.

RISK AND DRUG-RELATED HARM

The underlying assumption of the 'abstinence only' perspective is that all psychoactive drug use is harmful. However, there are degrees of harm and many individuals who consume drugs subsequently desist without ever experiencing drug-related health, social or legal problems. Nutt et al. (2007) offered a useful method for categorising drug-related harm. They suggested that these harms can be broadly classified as: (1) physical harm; (2) dependence; and (3) social harm. Drug-related *physical harm* refers to outcomes that can affect people's physical well-being. These outcomes include fatal or non-fatal overdose, injury and accidents, damage to nasal passages, throat, skin and vital organs, hangovers, effects from ingesting adulterated substances that contain harmful ingredients, and polydrug combinations that can amplify the pharmacological effects of drugs. *Dependence* includes physical dependence and psychological addiction (see also **4 addiction**). Harms associated with drug dependence include tolerance, cravings and withdrawal. *Social harm* refers to the ways in which drug use can affect 'families, communities and society' (Nutt et al., 2007: 1047). These harms include stigma and marginalisation, problems associated with social relationships, work difficulties, involvement with the legal system, and costs that are associated with drug-related health problems.

Although this classification method is useful for understanding harm that can result from drug use, some drug-related harms do not fit within the three-tiered system. For example, drugs can produce psychoactive effects that were not intended by their pharmaceutical make-up. Drug taking can contribute to paranoia that can be psychologically but not physically induced. Paranoia can be brought on initially by the social setting in which drugs are consumed; Zinberg (1984) observed that 'set' and 'setting' (as well as the pharmaceutical effects of a drug) can contribute to drug experiences (see also, **15 drug effects**). At times, this drug-related harm can extend well beyond the timeframe of the drug episode.

Risk taking can create and amplify drug-related harm. Traditionally, risk taking was viewed in terms of individual decision making and action. This perspective fails to consider the wider structural factors that can exacerbate risk taking, and in turn drug-related harm (Rhodes, 1997).

PERCEPTION OF RISK

Drugs are generally consumed because individuals wish to alter the way they think – even if the effect is temporary. Many young people engage in drug use for pleasure, although Skager (2009) observed that scholarly work often fails to acknowledge this motivating factor. The perception of drug-related risk refers to how individuals perceive the risk of using particular substances. Drug-related risk as interpreted by government policy can differ substantially from how individuals perceive risk. For example, cannabis products are illegal in most industrialised nations, however, vast numbers of people have used and continue to use cannabis or marijuana. Attitudinal surveys conducted in various countries have shown that moderate to large percentages of people are in favour of decriminalisation or legalisation of cannabis (see also **40 decriminalisation, legalisation and legal regulation**). In the USA, a survey of adolescents who self-reported marijuana use during the past month found that only 1.4 per cent of young people believed that smoking the drug once a month produced *great risk* for physical and other harm (Substance Abuse and Mental Health Services Administration, 2009). Users of other drugs often share these views. In other words, governments and individuals often differ in how they perceive the extent of risk that might be associated with drug taking.

Perceptions of risk can change in response to new experiences and different settings. In a follow-up study of youth in Ireland, Mayock observed that 'drugs previously deemed dangerous moved gradually to a position of greater acceptance' (2005: 37). Other individuals reduce their drug use as they age and take on more responsibility relating to family or employment. Thus, perceptions of risk can be reduced or enhanced over time. Perceptions of risk can also be affected by the legal status of psychoactive substances. Alcohol and products known collectively as 'legal highs' generally are perceived as less risky to health, simply because they are legal (see also **5 legal drugs** and **18 novel psychoactive substances**).

Equally important is that the perception of risk is not necessarily related to risk taking. For example, people who inject drugs may be aware that certain injecting behaviours increase the likelihood of transmission of infectious disease, yet some continue to engage in these behaviours. Similarly, many individuals who smoke cigarettes are aware of the link between smoking and lung cancer, yet they continue to engage in the behaviour. Still others might understand the risk of driving while intoxicated but in certain contexts might engage in this behaviour or allow another intoxicated person to drive them.

THE 'EXPERT' VIEW

Definitions and assumptions of risk taking are socially constructed. 'Experts', that is, individuals with specialist knowledge often provide advice regarding the level of risk associated with particular behaviours. However, disagreements among experts can create uncertainty or doubt among laypersons (Giddens, 1991), and expert views can vary across countries and change over time. Still, expert opinion can influence the formation of drug policies. In a critical review of Australian's drug strategy, Duff (2003) suggested that drug policy has neglected the opinions and experiences of people who take drugs, and relied greatly on expert opinion. Consumers of psychoactive drugs are rarely looked upon as having credible knowledge about the substances.

Government policy that labels all drugs as risky can lead to distrust among drug takers, many of whom have not experienced significant drug-related harms. Further, there is little evidence that negative or alarmist information about drugs can contribute to a decline in substance use among individuals (Skager, 2009).

Although ecstasy users might be familiar with media stories and research findings that describe long-term effects of the drug (for example, research claims about the link between ecstasy and neurotoxicity), they generally do not personally know individuals who have experienced lasting negative effects that they attribute to ecstasy. Similarly, cannabis and marijuana users may be familiar with expert claims that link those substances to psychosis, however, they often fail to internalise the information because they have no personal experience with the potential harms. In other words, the personal experiences of users and the experiences of others known to them, are often strikingly different than messages portrayed by the official line. These conflicting bases of knowledge can lead to the perception that government advice about drugs (particularly information that advocates abstinence) lacks credibility.

MANAGING RISKS

Over time, many people who use drugs learn to manage or reduce the likelihood of drug-related harm. For instance, some individuals will carefully monitor dosage and frequency of use, obtain drugs from suppliers whom they perceive as trustworthy and only consume drugs in the company of people they know. Peer groups can be important for reducing risks among group members. For example, group norms and informal social control within peer groups have been found to contribute to risk reduction associated with ecstasy use (Panagopoulos and Ricciardelli, 2005). Those authors noted that in-group norms took the form of judgments surrounding excessive use, requiring members to be sober while driving, and monitoring group members who were experiencing adverse effects of the drug. In several studies, however, the use of polydrug use during the same drug episode amplifies rather than minimises drug-related harm (see also **6 polydrug use/polysubstance use**). Findings from those studies suggest the need for more appropriate risk management among people who use drugs. Managing risk is not specific to particular drugs of choice; rather, proactive efforts to reduce drug-related harm can be practiced among individuals who use various drugs, including heroin.

SUMMARY

Drug-related risks are culturally situated and vary across individuals, time and space. Concerns about drug-related risk are often raised by government officials as well as health, social welfare and education professionals. However, these concerns are more focused on the *potential* for harm, rather than the risk itself. Individuals who use psychoactive drugs perceive risk according to their own experiences and the experiences of people they know. Negative health information is unlikely to affect their drug-taking behaviour to any great extent.

Although certain behaviours can create or increase the probability of drug-related harm, other behaviours can reduce the likelihood of harm. Some drug users actively engage in harm reduction practices whereas others actively participate in drug-related risk. There is a need for effective interventions that can further reduce harms associated with drug taking.

REFERENCES

Duff, D. (2003) 'The importance of culture and context: rethinking risk and risk management in young drug using populations', *Health, Risk and Society*, 5 (3): 285–99.

Giddens, A. (1991) *Modernity and Self-Identity: Self and Society in the Late Modern Age*. Cambridge: Polity.

Mayock, P. (2005) '"Scripting" risk: young people and the construction of drug journeys', *Drugs Education, Prevention & Policy*, 12 (5): 349–68.

Nutt, D., King, L.A., Saulsbury, W. and Blakemore, C. (2007) 'Development of a rational scale to assess the harm of drugs of potential misuse', *The Lancet*, 369 (9566): 1047–53.

Panagopoulosa, I. and Ricciardelli, L.A. (2005) 'Harm reduction and decision making among recreational ecstasy users', *International Journal of Drug Policy*, 16: 54–64.

Rhodes, T. (1997) 'Risk theory in epidemic times: sex, drugs and the social organization of "risk behaviour"', *Sociology of Health and Illness*, 19 (2): 208–27.

Skager, R. (2009) 'Having fun and defying adults: speculations on why most young people ignore negative information on the dangers of drinking alcohol', *Addiction*, 104 (4): 576–77.

Substance Abuse and Mental Health Services Administration (2009) *The NSDUH Report: Marijuana Use and Perceived Risk of Use among Adolescents: 2002 to 2007*. Rockville, MD: Substance Abuse and Mental Health Services Administration.

Zinberg, N.E. (1984) *Drug, Set and Setting: The Basis For Controlled Intoxicant Use*. New Haven, CT: Yale University Press.

23
Injecting Drug Use

> *Psychoactive drugs can be consumed in different ways, including swallowing, smoking, snorting/sniffing, inhaling vapours and injecting. The various ways that people take drugs are collectively known as routes or methods of administering drugs. Injecting drug use (IDU) is the process whereby drugs are injected into a vein (intravenous), muscle (intramuscular) or beneath the skin (subcutaneous; 'skin popping').*

The hypodermic syringe was invented in Edinburgh in 1853 as a means to facilitate pain relief; injecting a drug generally reaches the brain more quickly than other methods of administration. Use of the hypodermic syringe spread to the USA and other countries shortly thereafter. The availability of medicinal morphine administered through injection led to large-scale addiction in some countries in the late 1800s. During this time and into the early 20th century, several patented and over-the-counter medicines were available to the general public. A high proportion of users included those from middle- and upper-income backgrounds, including large numbers of women. Syringe cases, containing a needle, syringe and other injecting paraphernalia became fashion accessories for the wealthy and in the USA were available for purchase from the Sears and Roebuck catalogue. Subsequently, sales of needles and syringes became available only through pharmacies, and possession without a prescription became a criminal offence in some countries.

key concepts in
drugs and society

CONTEMPORARY CONTEXT

The preferred route of administering drugs depends on cultural norms, individual factors and the method by which drugs are prepared and made available through drug markets. In an urban area of England, researchers have observed various social networks comprised of people who smoke heroin (David Best, pers. comm.). Members of these social networks live in relatively close proximity to groups of people who inject heroin, yet the smokers tend to continue the practice for years. In this context, cultural norms appear to discourage injecting among people who smoke. Similar observations have been noted in Ireland, where for three decades, injecting has been the preferred method of consuming heroin in the urban area of Dublin. In contrast, smoking heroin appears to be the preferred route in smaller east coast cities and towns in Ireland, where the practice can continue for several years as individuals often disdain injecting.

The different routes by which drugs are consumed are considered to be broad or general categories, and we know that the way that drugs are taken can differ across social networks, *within* these broad classifications. In several European countries, for example, hash is commonly mixed with tobacco in a rolled cigarette and then smoked. In contrast, hash is *not* generally combined with tobacco in the USA; rather, people are more likely to smoke hash using pipes, bongs and similar paraphernalia. Similarly, although several people in the USA who smoke marijuana do so in rolled joints, others prefer 'blunts' whereby the outer skin of a cigar is used to hold the marijuana. Although all these behaviours involve smoking as the route of administration, cultural and subcultural norms appear to influence the ways in which the drug is prepared for smoking (see, for instance, Johnson et al. 2006).

Individual factors can also affect people's preferred route of administration. Individuals who use cannabis or marijuana but who suffer from asthma may prefer to consume the drug through swallowing (for example, in baked food). People who have injected for several years may suffer from vein problems, and will switch their route of administering heroin from injecting to smoking. Some people who regularly inject a drug of choice subsequently will consume most other drugs in the same manner. That is, injection emerges as the individual preference for consuming drugs.

Certain drugs (for example, heroin, cocaine) are available in different forms, and the form in which the drug is obtained will often determine how it is consumed. For instance, heroin that is available in several cities on the east coast of the USA often differs from the type of heroin that is available in some states in the midwest and west, and this difference can affect how heroin is consumed. Drug market changes, such as the availability of high purity heroin, have also contributed to an increase in heroin sniffing (rather than injecting) in some areas of the USA. In comparison, sniffing low purity heroin will not generally produce the desired effects.

Several psychoactive drugs can be injected, and many people who inject drugs prefer to inject into a vein because the effects of drugs are said to be more powerful through intravenous compared to intramuscular injection. Users of anabolic steroids usually inject into a muscle although some will move to intravenous injection with the use of additional psychoactive drugs (see also **31 drugs in sport**).

INTERNATIONAL ESTIMATES

Global estimates of the number of people who inject illicit drugs are limited. IDU is often a stigmatised behaviour and people who inject drugs are considered to be a 'hidden population'. Estimates are often derived in whole or part from people presenting to drug services, and this contact is influenced by the availability of service provision, as well as individual and structural barriers. Mathers et al. (2008) noted the presence of IDU in 148 of 200 countries or territories, and concluded that approximately 16 million people were injecting drugs in 2007. The highest midpoint *prevalence* (that is, the number per population) was observed for Azerbaijan, a country in Eastern Europe. The largest *numbers* of IDUs were noted for China, the USA and Russia. In an earlier study, the global figure was approximately 13.2 million, with the majority of IDUs residing in developing and transitional nations (Aceijas et al. 2004).

LEARNING TO INJECT AND INJECTING SETTINGS

Research has focused on why people initiate drug injecting. In general, this practice is not often planned, but occurs because of a combination of curiosity, opportunity and being in the presence of an experienced injector (although cultural norms appear to deter some people from injecting even when these factors are present). Indeed some individuals who become regular injectors recall once having feared needles. Learning how to self-inject is most often learned through observation from the more experienced. Others inject drugs for years, yet never learn the process of self-injecting, instead relying on others to inject the drug for them. At times, 'injecting doctors' are paid with money or drugs for this service. Individuals often have preferences in terms of the social context of injecting. That is, some people nearly always inject with others, for example, a partner, friends or acquaintances. Others prefer to inject alone, which can decrease the probability of becoming exposed to blood-borne viruses (see below) but can increase the risk of fatal overdose.

HEALTH IMPLICATIONS

Injecting involves a series of behaviours that can pose risk for exposure to blood-borne viruses (see also **24 HIV, AIDS and other blood-borne viruses**) and other illnesses. A needle/syringe is designed to be used one time only, however, new needles and syringes are difficult to access in some countries. In these settings, people will often use the same needle several times and borrow from or loan injecting equipment to others. Some injectors have reported sharpening extremely blunt needles with sandpaper or the rough surface of matchboxes. Borrowing and loaning injecting equipment can contribute to the spread of HIV and hepatitis B and C viruses because of the risk of coming into contact with contaminated blood. Needle/syringe exchange schemes offer new injecting equipment which can help reduce the spread of blood-borne viruses. The schemes operate in various settings, including pharmacies, medical facilities, drug outreach and mobile units. Many schemes encourage clients to return their used needles/syringes in an effort to prevent used equipment from being discarded improperly. However, in some countries needle/syringe exchange schemes have become contentious political issues and as a result have not been implemented or have been closed down.

People who have injected drugs for several years can suffer from venous damage in the arms and other sites of the body. In some instances, abscesses can develop at damaged sites, and some individuals will inject into the groin area or neck because of venous damage to the arms and legs. There are other injecting behaviours which can negatively affect an individual's health. These include 'booting' (also known as flushing), front-loading and back-loading. These behaviours are engrained as ritual so that effective prevention efforts have been difficult to identify.

STIGMA

In many countries, IDU carries with it considerable stigma. Even regular and 'heavy' users of drugs who do not inject, often view injectors with disdain, referring to them as 'junkies' and other derogatory labels. This stigma might aid prevention efforts in that the perceptions can at times deter people from initiating injecting drug use. However, the stigma has real and negative implications for people who inject, who may avoid treatment and other interventions because of the fear that 'normals' will discover their injector identity. Many people who inject drugs attempt to conceal the behaviour by hiding the visible signs of injecting. For example, long-sleeve shirts are worn even in warm weather, and in some areas, special creams are available that conceal needle punctures.

SUMMARY

Drugs can be consumed through various routes, for example, swallowing, sniffing/ snorting, smoking, injecting. Several factors can contribute to the transition to injecting although cultural norms can deter some individuals from injecting. Behaviours associated with IDU can increase the risk for HIV and other blood-borne viruses. IDU is a highly stigmatised behaviour in several countries, which can reduce the likelihood that people will seek help for drug dependence and addiction.

REFERENCES

Aceijas, C., Stimson, G.V., Hickman, M. and Rhodes, T. (2004) 'Global overview of injecting drug use and HIV infection among injecting drug users', *AIDS*, 18 (17): 2295–303.

Johnson, B.D., Bardhi, F., Sifaneck, S.J. and Dunlap, E. (2006) 'Marijuana argot as subculture threads: social constructions by users in New York city', *British Journal of Criminology*, 46 (1): 46–77.

Mathers, B.M., Degenhardt, L., Phillips, B., Weissing, L., Hickman, M., Strathdee, S.A., Wodak, A., Panda, S., Tyndall, M., Toufik, A. and Mattick, R.P. (2008) 'Global epidemiology of injecting drug use and HIV among people who inject drugs: a systematic review', *The Lancet*, 372 (9651): 1733–45.

23 injecting drug use

24
HIV/AIDS and Other Blood-borne Viruses

> *Blood-borne viruses (BBV) refer to diseases that are spread through blood-to-blood contact. Human immunodeficiency virus (HIV) is a BBV that attacks the immune system. It is the virus that causes acquired immune deficiency syndrome (AIDS), a condition that impairs the immune system and leaves people substantially more vulnerable to opportunistic infection and illness.*

Within a span of three decades, HIV and AIDS have become major public health concerns. The initial spread of HIV was influenced by various social and political factors that shaped the nature of the pandemic. In 2007, an estimated 33 million people were living with HIV (UNAIDS/WHO, 2008), with the vast majority residing in the continent of Africa. In the same year, approximately 12 per cent of the population in South Africa were living with HIV. Vast regional differences exist across and within continents and countries in terms of the number of new cases of HIV and its prevalence, that is, the number of people per population who have tested positive for HIV antibodies. The availability of and access to treatment and other services also varies widely.

HIV is spread through contact with certain bodily fluids, namely blood, semen, vaginal secretions and breast milk. It is *not* spread through saliva, perspiration or urine. The methods by which HIV is spread are referred to as 'modes of transmission'. In several developed nations (for example, the USA, Canada, Australia), the primary mode of transmission is men who have sex with men. Heterosexual contact, namely unprotected sexual intercourse, is believed to be the most common form of transmission in several areas within sub-Saharan Africa. Behaviours associated with injecting drug use (IDU) also contribute to the spread of HIV. These behaviours include the loaning or borrowing of used injecting equipment, for example, needles/syringes, 'cookers', filters, spoons and water (see also **23 injecting drug use**). Estimates show that this form of transmission is most common in parts of Asia (for example, Vietnam, Malyasia) and Eastern Europe (for example, Russia, Ukraine). Behaviours associated with non-injecting drug use also can increase the likelihood of transmission. These behaviours include snorting, sniffing or smoking drugs whereby the virus can enter the bloodstream via open sores in the nasal membrane, mouth or lips. Moreover, sex-for-drug exchanges can serve as a conduit for infection.

Hepatitis B and C are blood-borne viruses that attack the liver and can lead to cirrhosis and liver failure. In some countries, viral hepatitis is the major cause of liver cancer. Spread primarily through contact with contaminated blood, hepatitis C virus (HCV) in particular is relatively common among people who inject drugs. In Canada, available data suggest that risk behaviours associated with IDU constitute the major source of transmission for HCV. The virus has been documented among people who use drugs but who have *never* injected (Scheinmann et al., 2007). Those authors reviewed 28 studies which found that rates of HCV among this group were higher than the general population, although the previous research did not specifically identify the reasons for this pattern. Although more research is needed in this area, HCV might be transmitted through paraphernalia that are used to smoke or inhale drugs. These implements include straws, rolled currency notes/bills and pipes.

ESTIMATES OF BLOOD-BORNE VIRUSES AMONG INJECTING DRUG USERS

Global estimates of the number of IDUs who are infected with BBV are limited, primarily because they are based on people who have presented for testing and because the effectiveness of monitoring differs substantially across countries. Moreover, HIV, HCV and hepatitis B virus (HBV) can be asymptomatic, particularly in the early stages of illness, and people are unlikely to present for testing when they are unaware of their infection. Despite being asymptomatic, people can still transmit these blood-borne viruses to other individuals. In some countries, epidemiological research has provided estimates of the number of IDUs who have tested positive for blood-borne viruses or the antibodies relating to these viruses. This research has provided local or national estimates of the prevalence and incidence of various BBV.

International estimates of the prevalence of BBV are often based on complex methodologies because monitoring systems differ across countries. These global estimates have been more likely to focus on HIV rather than other blood-borne viruses among IDUs. In an extensive review of data from various countries and territories, Mathers et al. (2008) provided mid-level estimates of the prevalence of HIV among people aged 15–64 years who inject drugs. Overall, the authors concluded that approximately 3 million people who inject drugs are likely to be infected with HIV. The lowest prevalence was estimated to be 0.01 per cent and this rate was documented for eight countries. The highest prevalence of HIV among IDUs was recorded for Estonia (72.1 per cent). The authors also noted that HIV among IDUs varied considerably within some countries. In Russia, for example, the prevalence varied from less than 1 per cent in Pskov to 74 per cent in Biysk.

FROM 'RISK GROUPS' TO RISK ENVIRONMENTS

In the early stages of the HIV pandemic, scholars and practitioners referred to 'risk groups', that is, groups of people who were at greater risk for HIV infection. However, the term 'risk group' is in many ways inappropriate because any one group can contain diverse cohorts, comprised of individuals whose behaviours can vary in degree and context from those within other cohorts of the same group. More recent work has described and focused on 'risk behaviours' and 'risk environments'. For instance, scholars have noted that the various environmental influences can increase the risk of transmission of BBV. Rhodes et al. (2005) suggest that these contributing factors include the social interactions between IDUs within social networks (micro-level), group dynamics such as acceptable practices and norms (meso-level), and wider policy initiatives (macro-level), for example, the availability and utilisation of needle/syringe exchange. The interaction of these factors, and in particular wider political and economic conditions, shape the risk environment and in turn can increase the probability of transmission.

INTERVENTIONS

Outreach and peer-led initiatives

Considerable efforts have focused on developing prevention initiatives to reduce the spread of BBV among IDUs. These efforts include community outreach and peer-based initiatives that (1) promote safer injecting practices, condom use and frequent testing for BBV, and (2) discourage the transition from sniffing or smoking to injecting drugs. Needle/syringe exchange schemes provide new needles and other injecting equipment that can help prevent or reduce the loaning and borrowing of used equipment. These schemes are available in Australia, Brazil, Canada, China, several European countries and elsewhere. However, political opposition has prevented the implementation or expansion of schemes in other countries, for example, the USA. The provision of new injecting equipment can be an important tool for reducing the spread of BBV. Further, needle/exchange schemes can serve as sources of referral for testing and treatment.

Regular testing

People who inject drugs can benefit from regular testing for BBV. The availability of anonymous and confidential testing varies across and within countries. Even if screening for BBV is widely available, stigma surrounding drug use and BBV can reduce the likelihood that people will present for testing. Additionally, the location and setting where testing occurs, as well as attitudes of health professionals can deter people from undergoing tests for BBV.

Treatment

There is no vaccine to prevent HIV or HCV infection. In many countries, however, a three-dose vaccine is available to prevent HBV. The doses are administered through intramuscular injection over a series of six months. Despite some availability of the vaccine, many people who inject drugs do not participate in HBV immunisation. Treatment is available for chronic HBV but not all individuals will benefit from treatment. HCV treatment can include a combination of interferon and ribavirin, which can boost the immune system. However, there are different strains of HCV and some strains respond better to treatment than others. Continued use of drugs can lower the effectiveness of interferon treatment. In some countries, people who inject drugs are not considered suitable candidates for interferon treatment. HIV can be treated with antiretroviral therapy which can slow the progress of HIV infection and its impact on the immune system. In other words, this intervention has the potential for improving wellness and extending longevity. Access to antiretroviral drugs is very limited in some countries. Further, support and counselling are often needed to assist people with treatment regimes.

Some IDUs are co-infected, that is, they have been diagnosed with two or more BBV. US data suggest that at least 50 per cent of IDUs who are HIV antibody positive also are infected with HCV (Centers for Disease Control and Prevention, n.d.). Co-infection can further weaken the immune system and can hinder the impact of treatment for BBV.

SUMMARY

A comprehensive approach is needed to prevent further spread of BBV among people who inject drugs. For example, people receiving treatment for blood-borne viruses often need substitute prescribing (see also **27 substitute prescribing**) and other drug services to assist them in recovery. However, substitute prescribing is not available in some regions, which can reduce the effectiveness of treatment for BBV. A comprehensive approach should also include frequent testing for BBV, the provision of needles, syringes and other injecting equipment, and support for the emotional impact of BBV.

REFERENCES

Centers for Disease Control and Prevention (n.d.) *Coinfection with HIV and Hepatitis C Virus.* Atlanta: Centers for Disease Control and Prevention.

Mathers, B.M., Degenhardt, L., Phillips, B., Wiessing, L., Hickman, M., Strathdee, S.A., Wodak, A., Panda, S., Tyndall, M., Toufik, A. and Mattick, R.P. for the 2007 Reference Group to the United Nations on HIV and Injecting Drug Use (2008) 'Global epidemiology of injecting drug use and HIV among people who inject drugs: a systematic review', *The Lancet*, 372 (9651): 1733–45.

Rhodes, T., Singer, M., Bourgois, P., Friedman, S.R. and Strathdee, S.A. (2005) 'The social structural production of HIV risk among injecting drug users', *Social Science and Medicine*, 61 (5): 1026–44.

Scheinmann, R., Hagan, H., Lelutiu-Weinberger, C., Stern, R., Des Jarlais, D.C., Flom, P.L. and Strauss, S. (2007) 'Non-injection drug use and hepatitis C virus: a systematic review', *Drug and Alcohol Dependence*, 89 (1): 1–12.

UNAIDS/WHO (2008) *Report on the Global AIDS Epidemic 2008: Executive Summary.* Geneva: Joint United Nations Programme on HIV/AIDS.

Section III

Drug Policy, Treatment and Perceptions of the Drug Problem

25
Drug Treatment and Quasi-compulsory Treatment

Drug treatment refers to various types of interventions that are provided to people who are addicted to or dependent on drugs. Quasi-compulsory treatment (QCT) refers to treatment interventions that are used under the guidance of the criminal justice system, in an effort to reduce substance misuse and criminal activity.

The availability of drug treatment and the way that treatment initiatives are implemented depend greatly on how drug use and addiction are interpreted by governments. Historically, either the criminal justice system or the medical profession gained control over 'what should be done' with individuals who use or are dependent on illicit drugs. In some countries, 'addicts' continue to be perceived as part of the 'criminal class' whose behaviours are addressed largely through punitive sanctions (Elovich and Drucker, 2008). In other nations, drug use and addiction are viewed as individual and public health issues, whereby drug treatment initiatives reflect the philosophy of harm reduction. Generally, the wider assumptions about addiction will determine how governments respond to it (see also, **4 addiction and 26 harm reduction**).

Drug treatment programmes vary considerably in terms of the underlying ideologies that guide treatment, and the nature and characteristics of interventions. In general, treatment programmes can be viewed from one of two broad philosophies. Some programmes are abstinence-based, whereby drug use is not tolerated and abstaining from all drugs is the primary treatment goal. The alternative philosophy draws on the principles of harm reduction, that is, treatment goals can include reducing the frequency of drug use, and reducing the harm associated with drug taking.

Types of drug treatment are often categorised or described as treatment modalities.[5] These modalities include short- and long-term *residential treatment* whereby 'residential' implies overnight stays in a closed environment. Therapeutic communities (TCs) represent one type of residential programme. Two common attributes of TCs include: (1) the involvement of treatment staff as well as people in recovery who combine efforts to help others who are engaged in treatment;

[5]Detoxification ('detox') is the process by which people withdraw from drugs, preferably in a safe environment. Detox is not considered to be a type of treatment, but rather a stage of treatment that is generally used for particular types of drug use, for example, dependency on opioids, benzodiazepines, and in some instances, alcohol.

and (2) an emphasis on group work and the interaction of group members. Non-residential treatment or *day programmes* offer one or more types of behavioural or motivational therapy. In the USA, these programmes are described as 'drug-free' outpatient programmes in that substitute medications are not usually permitted. *Substitute prescribing* (for example, methadone or high-dose buprenorphine maintenance) represents another type of treatment modality (see also **27 substitute prescribing**). This form of treatment tends to address opioid (for example, heroin) dependence. *Self-help groups* represent a fourth type of modality. Many of these programmes are designed with a 12-step approach, for example, Alcoholics Anonymous, Narcotics Anonymous, and are usually provided within community settings. Membership often requires abstinence. These modalities are not necessarily stand-alone; rather more than one type of service provision can be offered through the same programme. Other aspects of drug service provision do not constitute treatment but are important for people who are considering treatment. These provisions include the delivery of accurate advice and information about drugs (including how to use drugs safely). Additionally, people who complete treatment often return to the environment where they are reminded of their prior drug lifestyles. Aftercare services provide the support people need to reintegrate into their social environments, and are consistent with a continuum of care approach that is recommended as best practice. In many regions, however, aftercare is limited or lacking altogether, and importantly, the risk of relapse can increase without these supports.

Drug treatment is best viewed as a process that can occur over several years. Many people who participate in treatment programmes either prematurely leave or relapse (that is, use drugs again) after they complete a programme. Indeed, the lifestyles of some individuals are characterised by several cyclical stages of treatment attempts, followed by relapse. Some of the best programmes are characterised by a holistic approach to drug treatment. The assumption is that drug misuse is complex, and often associated with other problems and individual needs. These needs can include issues pertaining to accommodation, employment, education and training, relationships with family, children or partners, primary health care, mental illness and a host of other factors. A holistic approach addresses drug misuse as well as other individual needs. In many instances, this approach cannot be provided solely by treatment staff. Rather, the approach works through effective networking with other agencies which have the expertise available to address the particular problem.

DEMAND FOR AND EXPENDITURES ON DRUG TREATMENT

Ideally, drug treatment should be available for people who need it. In reality, the practice of *treatment on demand* rarely occurs. Treatment is often inaccessible because of limited resources. Waiting lists for certain types of treatment are common and various treatment modalities are not available in many countries. In some regions, drug treatment is largely privatised which excludes people who cannot afford to pay for treatment. Gender also contributes to treatment accessibility. For example, women with children are likely to avoid treatment that is accompanied by social service or social welfare involvement. Moreover, treatment agencies rarely provide on-site childcare. The demand for treatment varies by drug category; among new treatment admissions within the European Union, treatment for cocaine and cannabis nearly doubled from 2002 to 2006 (European Monitoring Centre for Drugs and Drug Addiction, 2009).

In many industrialised nations, government expenditures on drug treatment are well below the expenditures that are designated for targeting the supply of drugs (for example, policing). For example, US federal funds designated for drug treatment were approximately US$3 billion in 2002, which accounted for 19.1 per cent of all expenditures designated for that nation's drug war (Office of National Drug Control Policy, 2002).

EFFECTIVENESS OF DRUG TREATMENT

Research that investigates the effectiveness of drug treatment is often plagued with methodological problems, making it difficult to draw conclusions with regards to treatment outcomes. A major limitation concerns the challenges in locating appropriate control groups for comparison. Without these comparisons, we can never be certain whether the treatment was responsible for the outcome, or whether other factors contributed to the results. A second limitation focuses on *attrition*, that is, people who drop out of programmes. A potential consequence of high attrition is that people who drop out of treatment may differ a great deal from people who complete treatment, and this difference may bias the findings of a study.

Despite these caveats, considerable evidence has suggested that drug treatment is effective under certain conditions. The primary factors that appear to increase the likelihood of successful treatment outcomes include: (1) matching individual needs with the appropriate treatment; (2) longer lengths of stay in treatment; and (3) continuum of care approaches.

Drawing from scholarly evidence into treatment effectiveness, 'best practice' guidelines have been issued by a number of governments (Canada, New Zealand, the UK),[6] and international organisations (United Nations Office of Drugs and Crime, 2008). These guidelines generally offer advice with regards to how to treat various types of substance misuse among different types of populations.

QUASI-COMPULSORY TREATMENT

Links between drug use (including alcohol) and crime are widely recognised, although the nature of the relationship is less clear (see also **21 drugs and crime**). In several industrialised nations, large proportions of people processed by the criminal justice system have experienced drug-related problems or have a history of drug addiction or dependency. Internationally, drug offenders account for

---

[6]For the UK guidance, see http://www.nice.org.uk.

between 3.3 per cent (Romania) and 58 per cent (Thailand) of the total prison population (Bewley-Taylor et al., 2009). In the USA, arrests for drug-related offences have increased substantially over the last three decades, and in 2005 the figure approached 2 million.

Increases in the number of drug offenders as well as the revolving door of recidivism have led several countries to implement quasi-compulsory treatment initiatives as diversions from imprisonment. McSweeney et al. defined QCT as 'drug treatment that is motivated, ordered or supervised by the criminal justice system but which takes place outside prisons' (2007: 471). In other words, eligible offenders participate in some form of drug treatment, as a substitute for or as a condition of sentencing (see also **39 drug courts**). The goals of QCT are twofold, that is, to reduce both crime and substance misuse.

Much of the research into the effectiveness of QCT has been conducted by a team of researchers in England (for example, McSweeney et al. 2007). Their studies have revealed declines in drug use and criminal activity among people who complete QCT, and these reductions have been noted at 18-month follow-up (McSweeney et al., 2007). A study of 845 individuals (largely male) selected from 65 treatment sites across Europe compared participants in QCT and voluntary treatment across several European countries. The findings showed reductions in drug use and recidivism among individuals who had undergone either QCT or voluntary treatment. However, QCT participants were more likely than volunteers to be re-arrested or imprisoned during the follow-up period.

Analyses of the effectiveness of QCT tend to rely on self-reported behaviour relating to drug use or criminal activity. Although self-reports are characterised by a good degree of accuracy in various settings, under-reporting is a rational response when people anticipate penalties for illegal behaviours that they disclose. Similar to drug treatment programmes outside the gaze of the criminal justice system, QCT programmes have shown difficulties in retaining people in treatment. In one English study, just over one-half (54 per cent) of QCT clients were in treatment at six-month follow-up (McSweeney et al., 2007).

As described above, considerable literature has suggested that successful treatment outcomes depend in part on the appropriate match between an individual's needs and a particular drug treatment modality. QCT can be limited in terms of the types of treatment programmes that are available to offenders. In areas where treatment options are limited, offenders opt for the treatment that is available, regardless of whether the programme can meet their individual circumstances. This factor can contribute to drop-out, relapse and re-offending. As described above, however, research suggests that QCT can be effective in reducing drug use and criminal activity among some individuals.

SUMMARY

Although most people who misuse drugs may not require treatment, appropriate interventions can aid recovery for individuals who are involved in problem drug use. Treatment appears to reduce drug misuse among certain individuals, and factors such as programme characteristics can contribute to positive treatment outcomes. QCT shows promise and may be beneficial to individuals as well as the legal system. Research into the effectiveness of drug treatment is sometimes compromised by high attrition and an over-reliance on self-report data. Additionally, we know that some people recover from drug addiction and dependence without any treatment intervention at all (Granfield and Cloud, 1996). Considerably more research is needed on natural recovery to increase our understanding of recovery without treatment.

REFERENCES

Bewley-Taylor, D., Hallam, C. and Allen, R. (2009) *The Incarceration of Drug Offenders: An Overview.* Oxford: Beckley Foundation, Drug Policy Programme.

Elovich, R. and Drucker, E. (2008) 'On drug treatment and social control: Russian narcology's great leap backwards', *Harm Reduction Journal*, 5. Available at: www.harmreductionjournal.com/content/5/1/23 (accessed 16 October 2012).

European Monitoring Centre for Drugs and Drug Addiction (2009) *Statistical Bulletin, 2008. Demand for Treatment.* Lisbon: European Monitoring Centre for Drugs and Drug Addiction.

Granfield, R. and Cloud, W. (1996) 'The elephant that no one sees: natural recovery among middle-class addicts', *Journal of Drug Issues*, 26 (1): 45–61.

McSweeney, T., Stevens, A., Hunt, N. and Turnbull, P.J. (2007) 'Twisting arms or a helping hand? Assessing the impact of "coerced" and comparable "voluntary" drug treatment options', *British Journal of Criminology*, 47 (3): 470–90.

Office of National Drug Control Policy (2002) *National Drug Control Strategy: FY2003 Budget Summary.* Washington, DC: Executive Office of the President.

United Nations Office on Drugs and Crime (2008) *Drug Dependence Treatment: Community Based Treatment.* Vienna: United Nations.

26
Harm Reduction

Built on a public health approach to drug use, harm reduction involves undertaking initiatives to reduce possible harms associated with drug-taking practices in various risk environments. Harm reduction, unlike drug control/prohibition approaches, prioritises reducing harm from drug use rather than attempting to stop drug use altogether.

Harm reduction has been described as a principle, ideology, movement, policy, goal and set of interventions. Harm reduction applies both to illegal drugs such as heroin and crack cocaine, and legal drugs such as alcohol and tobacco. Harm reduction acknowledges that drug use can have damaging effects, but asserts that these need to be practically addressed rather than ignored or worsened. Harm reduction also acknowledges that some drug-using practices are safer than others and so seeks to promote such practices among users or potential users in the recognition that total abstinence from drugs may not necessarily be an appropriate, desirable or even feasible goal. This has led to criticisms from drug prohibition and abstention advocates, particularly in the USA. They accuse harm reductionists of condoning, encouraging and even facilitating drug use, which is perceived as inherently risky, socially unacceptable and morally bereft. Harm reductionists are also criticised for being implicitly supportive of drug legalisation (see also **40 decriminalisation, legalisation and legal regulation**). However, harm reduction may be pursued within a drug control/prohibition framework, where, for example, drug law enforcement practices operate alongside initiatives to reduce harmful injecting practices.

Historically it is difficult to locate the birth of contemporary harm reduction, although the development and implementation of the Mersey Harm Reduction Model (MHRM) in Liverpool, UK in the mid-1980s is seen as one of the harm reduction movement's principal starting points. The first International Conference on the Reduction of Drug Related Harm took place in 1990 in Liverpool, UK, and was influential in the subsequent exporting of the harm reduction concept to other locales, notably developing or transitional countries and regions. The conferences were vital in the establishment of the International Harm Reduction Association (IHRA), now known as Harm Reduction International; while the *Mersey Drugs Journal* launched by the Mersey Drug Training and Information Centre (MDTIC) became the *International Journal of Drug Policy* in 1989, a key academic publication in the drugs research field.

Key goals of harm reduction include the prevention of HIV/AIDS and hepatitis C Virus (HCV) through providing free and easy access to sterile needles for injecting drug users (IDUs); the prevention of drug-related deaths including drug overdoses; and the implementation of drug dependency treatment, through methadone maintenance programmes for example. It is estimated that IDUs now account for 1 in 10 new HIV infections worldwide. Since the early 1990s, one of the successes of harm reduction has been to help control the spread of HIV/AIDS among IDUs. However harm reduction implementation, notably in developing or transitional countries such China and Taiwan, has been slow and uneven, with for example less coverage in prison settings than in community settings.

HARM REDUCTION AND THE INTERNATIONAL COMMUNITY

Harm reduction approaches are endorsed by international organisations such as the Joint United Nation Programme on AIDS (UNAIDS), United Nations Office on Drugs and Crime (UNOCD), UNICEF, the World Health Organisation and the World Bank. Globally, harm reduction provision – predominately aimed at IDUs and including needle and syringe exchange services and opiate substitution therapies – are present in 82 countries to date, including the UK, the USA, Canada, Indonesia, Egypt and Poland. The majority of these countries also give explicit support to harm reduction in national policy documents. Despite this support there remain considerable nation-specific barriers to the implementation and success of harm reduction initiatives. In many countries domestic legislation prohibits the possession of drug-injecting equipment, undermining safe injecting practices. In Uzbekistan, peer, family and community-based harm reduction has been thwarted by a general suspicion of international non-governmental organisations and charities, alongside regular 'crackdowns' on drug users by the police.

HARM REDUCTION AND DRUG USER PARTICIPATION

The intertwined principles of public health and harm reduction include user involvement in, and user friendliness of, drug harm reduction services. Services need to be easy to access (that is, 'low-threshold') by some of the most marginalised, stigmatised and criminalised people in society (O'Hare et al., 1992). Evidence suggests that cities or countries which adopted interventions based on these principles have had most success in controlling, averting or reversing HIV and HCV epidemics. It is argued that harm reduction researchers and policymakers should research, enable and support user peer group harm reduction practices as well as 'formal' user-led organisations. Social network peer mentoring has been found to reduce HIV and HCV infection rates among IDUs. User involvement in services incorporates invaluable non-expert knowledge regarding risky, harmful, but also safer drug use practices which form part of drug-user cultures. A historical overview of public health and harm reduction practices among drug users in New York City, Rotterdam and Buenos Aires during the emergence of HIV/AIDS showed that as awareness of the risk of shared injecting equipment (or 'works') grew, users attempted to reduce likelihood of infection by buying or stealing parts for their own 'works' or setting up 'underground' needle exchange services well before official responses to the epidemic (Friedman et al., 2007).

NON-INJECTING DRUG USERS AND HARM REDUCTION

Although historically harm reduction has concentrated on IDUs, predominately as a result of HIV/AIDS and later HCV epidemics among this specific population, other drug-using groups have also been the focus of various harm reduction initiatives. One of the earliest examples of harm reduction campaign material predominately aimed at non-injecting 'recreational' drug users was the groundbreaking *Peanut Pete* series, which was developed, designed and distributed in the early 1990s by the charity Lifeline in the north-west of England as a response to the use of 'dance drugs' among young people attending raves and clubs.

Knowledge of emergent trends in drug use is vital to harm reduction initiatives being rapid response, pragmatic, community led and community based. British users of the 'club drug' ketamine typically limit their consumption to private spaces both to avoid making themselves vulnerable to accident or attack in public spaces and because intoxication in public was perceived to be socially unacceptable. By drawing on such lay knowledge and beliefs, harm reduction initiatives can be made more culturally and linguistically relevant to target populations, a point also pertinent to the development of drug education material aimed at young people.

BARRIERS TO HARM REDUCTION

There are a number of both ideological and practical barriers to the implementation of harm reduction initiatives, notably those aimed at the most vulnerable groups of drug users such as injecting opiate users. Those who inject drugs in developing and transitional countries tend to be worst affected by these barriers. Access to needle and syringe exchange provision (NSP) is hampered by poor service coverage and poor services with a lack or appropriate equipment, a lack of community-based outreach workers, restricted opening hours and a lack of client confidentiality.

Criminal justice responses to IDUs and NSP may involve repressive legislation which effectively criminalises NSP operations, resulting in the harassment of drug workers and the arrest of those using services. Drug law enforcement practices by the police such as confiscating injecting equipment from homeless IDUs in urban centres can destabilise harm reduction initiatives and lead to an increase in the practice of needle sharing. In some countries, supply-side drug policies have had particularly harmful effects on individuals and communities. Bastos et al. (2007) argue that in South America, particularly in Colombia and Brazil, poverty, structural violence, entrenched corruption, mutual distrust between communities and administrators – alongside human rights violations linked to illegal cocaine production and supply-side policies to disrupt illicit distribution – have severely undermined public health and education initiatives aimed at reducing harm among individuals and communities.

Resource shortages have also tended to hamper the expansion of harm reduction initiatives, particularly in developing or transitional countries or regions, despite such places often being the focus of international efforts to disrupt drug supply through crop eradication (see also **36 crop eradication, crop substitution and legal cultivation**). In Latin America, RELARD, a harm reduction network for IDUs, receives no funding from the international community and little regional funding, instead relying principally on charitable contributions from its members (Bastos et al., 2007). In the USA, a federal (national) ban on funding for NSP since 1988 has meant that monies tend to come from city, county and state governments, despite evidence that federal funding for NSP tends to result in larger numbers of syringes being exchanged and a greater variety of harm reduction services being offered.

Another difficult barrier to overcome is the continued stigma and direct and indirect discrimination faced by IDUs which further increases the risk of drug-related harms. This is because such stigma and discrimination may force IDUs 'underground' which in turn reduces their access to harm reduction services.

CRITICISMS OF HARM REDUCTION

There have been criticisms of harm reduction in terms of its over-reliance on changing individuals' modes of behaviour, rather than concentrating on the 'risk environments' in which people undertake possibly harmful practices. The call to move away from individualistic models of drug harm reduction towards a 'healthy environments' model suggests drug harm reduction become more closely allied to other non-drug and non-health interventions concerned with social justice and the reduction of vulnerability to tackle public health problems (Rhodes, 2002).

Another criticism of harm reduction models includes its muted and theoretically underdeveloped stance on morals, ethics, rights and values. This means that harm reduction advocates are sometimes reluctant to engage with opponents on the basis of anything other than scientific and medical evidence for the immediate benefits of drug harm reduction. Subsequently opponents to harm reduction are able to wage emotional, moralistic and often stigmatising media campaigns against 'controversial' initiatives such as safe injecting sites. Such campaigns can be hard for harm reduction proponents to counteract effectively. In response to such criticisms, advocates are more fully engaging with the moral issues and practical ethics of the harm reduction approach (Fry et al., 2008). For example, advocates have called for more honest and open critiques of the **37 war on drugs** in light of growing evidence that prohibitionist policies and practices have exacerbated harm to individuals, communities and nation states (Tammi and Hurne, 2007). However it is worth remembering that harm reduction approaches are inherently supportive neither of prohibition nor legalisation (Erickson, 1995), meaning that harm reduction traditionally encompasses a 'broad church' of positions towards drug control.

SUMMARY

Drug harm reduction can be defined as a set of practical, public health strategies designed to reduce the negative consequences of drug use and promote healthy individuals and communities. Harm reduction now spans a range of practices, including user service delivery; community development initiatives; harm reduction-orientated national government policies; research on the efficacy of harm reduction initiatives; and treatment services whereby abstinence from drugs is placed second to the health of users. The now global, if uneven, reach of drug harm reduction has led some to assert that harm reduction has 'come of age' (Stimson, 2007). However, there remains concern that harm reduction provision remains geographically patchy and that harm reduction is being undermined by the prohibitionist 'war on drugs'.

REFERENCES

Bastos, F.I., Caiaffa, W., Rossi, D., Vila, M. and Malta, M. (2007) 'The children of mama coca: coca, cocaine and the fate of harm reduction in South America', *International Journal of Drug Policy*, 18: 99–106.

Erickson, P. (1995) 'Harm reduction: what it is and is not', *Drug and Alcohol Review*, 14 (3): 283–5.

Friedman, S.R., de Jong, W., Rossi, D., Touzᴁ, G., Rockwell, R., Jarlais, D. and Elovich, R. (2007) 'Harm reduction theory: users' culture, micro-social indigenous harm reduction, and the self-organisation and outside-organising of users' groups', *International Journal of Drug Policy*, 18: 101–17.

Fry, C.L., Khoshnood, K., Power, R. and Sharma, M. (2008) 'Harm reduction ethics: acknowledging the values and beliefs behind our actions', *International Journal of Drug Policy*, 19 (1): 1–3.

O'Hare, P., Newcombe, R., Matthews, A., Buning, E.C. and Drucker, E. (1992) *The Reduction of Drug-Related Harm*. London: Routledge.

Rhodes, T. (2002) 'The "risk" environment: a framework for understanding and reducing drug-related harm', *International Journal of Drug Policy*, 13 (2): 85–94.

Stimson, G.V. (2007) 'Harm reduction – coming of age: a local movement with global impact', *International Journal of Drug Policy*, 18 (2): 67–69.

Tammi, T. and Hurne, T. (2007) 'How the harm reduction movement contrasts itself against punitive prohibition', *International Journal of Drug Policy*, 18 (2): 84–87.

27
Substitute Prescribing

> *Prescribed medicine used as a substitute for a drug that has produced dependence. Substitute prescribing generally refers to opioid substitution treatment or opioid substitution therapy whereby opioids are prescribed to people who are dependent on heroin or other opiates.*

Opiate drugs, for example, morphine and codeine, are sourced from the pod of the opium poppy and are used and prescribed for pain relief. Drugs that are derived from these natural opiates are referred to as *semi-synthetic* opiates and include heroin, oxycodone, hydrocodone and other substances. In contrast, *synthetic* drugs are not found in nature; rather they are manufactured from various chemical compounds. The term, *opioids*, includes opiates as well as synthetic substances that are designed to mirror the effects of morphine. Consistent use of opioids can result in drug dependence whereby individuals experience cravings for the drug, undergo withdrawal with cessation of opioid use and feel the need to experience the effects of the drug in order to function 'normally'. The onset and intensity of opioid dependency varies across individuals and social contexts.

Treating drug dependence with a substitute drug generally involves the prescribed use of a medicine that is chemically related to the drug that has produced the dependence. In most instances, the prescribed medicine is an opioid which works to reduce withdrawal symptoms and cravings among people dependent on heroin or other opiates. The primary opioids that are used in substitution treatment include methadone and high-dose buprenorphine. These types of interventions are referred to as methadone maintenance treatment (MMT) and high-dose buprenorphine maintenance treatment (HDB) whereby the use of the word *maintenance* implies long-term treatment, for example, 3 months or longer.

People who are dependent on heroin or other opioids develop tolerance so that increasingly higher doses of the drug are needed to experience the effects. Once dependent, abstaining from opioids will bring about withdrawal symptoms, for example, nausea, vomiting, cramps, restlessness. Generally people do not die from opioid withdrawal, although withdrawal symptoms can be psychologically and physically incapacitating. Withdrawal symptoms disappear quickly when opioids are consumed. Methadone maintenance involves a single daily dose of methadone, which usually is consumed orally. Buprenorphine treatment is consumed sublingually (beneath the tongue) and often administered on alternative days. Withdrawal and cravings for other opioids, for example, heroin, are usually reduced considerably when the dosage of the substitute drug is sufficient.

Substitute prescribing for opioid dependency has its roots in the late 19th and early 20th centuries when heroin was used to treat morphine dependency and alcoholism. Methadone emerged several years later. First manufactured under the trade name Dolantin® by German chemists in 1939, the generic name, methadone, was coined by the American Medical Association in 1947 (Gerlach, 2004). In the 1960s, Robert Halliday (Canada), and Vincent Dole and Marie Nyswander (USA) were among the first to argue the benefits of methadone maintenance as a treatment for heroin dependency. Beginning in the 1990s, high-dose buprenorphine emerged as an alternative treatment to methadone for opioid dependence. Injectable diamorphine (pharmaceutical heroin) for the treatment of heroin dependence has been available since the 1920s in selected regions within the UK, although this intervention has declined over time and is generally used only when other treatment initiatives have failed. Codeine-based products (for example, dyhydrocodeine) and benzodiazepines have also been prescribed for opioid dependence, although in many countries, these initiatives are not considered to be clinically appropriate for opioid dependence.[7]

EXTENT AND NATURE OF PROVISION

Opioid substitution treatment is available in several countries or in selected regions within countries. Elsewhere the treatment is banned entirely. Most European countries, New Zealand, Australia, Canada, Thailand, India, Iran, China and the USA offer some provision of MMT and/or HDB. The availability of heroin-assisted treatment is less extensive although a few European countries offer this provision, and pilot studies are occurring elsewhere, including Canada. Globally methadone maintenance is the most common form of opioid substitution treatment. However, a few countries (for example, France) have considerably higher utilisation rates of HDB than MMT. In the USA, methadone maintenance has been available for a number of years, but only through licensed clinics where provision is very limited. Moreover, methadone maintenance is prohibited in some states

---

[7]Substitution treatment has also been used with non-opioid drugs. For example, dexamphetamine (in the form of syrup or tablets) has been prescribed to people addicted to amphetamines. At this writing, evidence is lacking with regards to the effectiveness of this type of intervention.

within the US. The US government approved HDB as a treatment for opioid dependence in 2002, and the substitute drug can be prescribed by licensed physicians and dispensed in community settings.

Strict guidelines regarding substitute prescribing policies have been introduced by several governments. Globally, these policies vary considerably and have been debated widely by scholars and practitioners. In some regions, general practitioners are actively involved with clients and work in conjunction with other professionals who have expertise in addiction and drug dependency. This mode of delivery is known as 'shared care'. Elsewhere, either treatment clinics or general practitioners have sole responsibility for providing substitute prescribing. Policies also differ with respect to how the substitute drug is dispensed. For example, some programmes require 'supervised consumption' whereby pharmacists or treatment providers are required to observe clients who consume the prescribed medicine. Other programmes provide 'take home' doses when clients are stabilised. Treatment ideology also differs across programmes. Some programmes encourage clients to reduce methadone or buprenorphine dosage levels at various stages, with abstinence viewed as the primary treatment goal. Alternatively, other programmes highlight treatment retention and stabilisation as the main treatment goals.

BARRIERS TO TREATMENT

Despite what appears to be fairly extensive provision of opioid substitution in several regions of the world, accessibility to and utilisation of this treatment are limited. Of an estimated 16 million people globally who use opioids and 12 million who use heroin (United Nations Office on Drugs and Crime, 2008) fewer than 650,000 receive substitute treatment (Chatterjee, 2008). In some countries, opioid substitution is illegal and in other countries, treatment space is extremely limited and waiting lists are extensive. Additionally, several individual and structural factors serve as barriers to treatment. For example, substitute prescribing appears to work best for individuals who are motivated to reduce or abstain from using opioids. Sometimes it takes several years before people experience major problems with health or social functioning as a result of opioid dependence. Treatment entry is often delayed until individuals experience serious problems associated with drug dependency. Structural barriers also can affect accessibility and utilisation of opioid substitution treatment. For example, admission criteria (for example, abstinence from all drug use) are at times perceived as too stringent by potential treatment clients. Others are deterred from seeking treatment because of real or perceived stigma associated with substitute prescribing. For example, women with children may avoid treatment because they anticipate community disapproval and intervention with regard to their parenting capabilities. Additionally, some individuals drop out of treatment because they find it difficult to comply with programme regulations. For example, clients who are employed often face difficulties collecting prescribed medicine several days per week and at specified times.

BENEFITS OF SUBSTITUTE PRESCRIBING

Several studies have shown that MMT is effective in reducing opioid use (Simoens et al., 2005), drug-related crime (Lind et al., 2005) and risk behaviours associated with HIV (Corsi et al., 2009). Although the time spent in treatment, dosage levels and various programme components can affect the outcome of MMT, clearly most of the research evidence indicates that MMT can be beneficial to the individual as well as society. Other research is more critical, and some scholars have argued that previous research into the effectiveness of MMT is plagued by methodological limitations (Fischer et al., 2005). Less is known about the effectiveness of HDB, although recent studies have shown favourable outcomes.

CHALLENGES TO CURRENT PROVISION

Substitute prescribing has its limitations. First, drug treatment should be designed to meet the needs of the individual and substitute prescribing is not effective for all clients. Some individuals benefit more from other forms of drug treatment and others require no treatment at all. Treatment approaches that are based on the assumption that 'one size, fits all' are bound to demonstrate unfavourable outcomes for several clients. Second, substitute prescribing is not intended to be used as a 'standalone' treatment initiative. Rather, early proponents of methadone maintenance emphasised the importance of a holistic approach to treating drug dependency – one that focused on improving an individual's self-worth through social rehabilitation gained from valuable work, a stake in the community and other factors. Although some programmes do combine substitute prescribing with other modalities, for example, counselling, or attempt to address problems such as inadequate housing and unemployment, many programmes focus on prescribing and monitoring only. Similarly, a comprehensive approach to drug treatment requires an aftercare component. Individuals who complete maintenance programmes often need continued support in the form of aftercare in the community. Resources for this provision are often limited which can contribute to the risk of relapse.

Third, in many regions, substitute prescribing policies are organised under the assumption of distrust. For example, some programmes require physicians and pharmacists to use written contracts to ensure that clients act responsibly. The substitute medicine often must be consumed in the presence of a pharmacist or other provider, a policy that is not utilised with other prescribed medicine. The reasoning behind supervised consumption is to prevent the substitute drug from being distributed illegally by the client, a transaction known as *diversion*. However, it is erroneous to assume that all or the majority of clients will engage in diversion of the substitute medicine. Distrust is also reflected in programme regulations that require urine samples in which the presence of illegal drugs can result in penalties (for example, terminating treatment participation, reducing dosage). Such policies assume that clients are deviant and may hinder treatment progress. Alternatively, urine samples are beneficial when used for clinical decision-making, for example, alerting treatment providers to the possibility of overdose.

Fourth, favourable treatment outcomes depend in part on the right dosage of the substitute medicine. Dosage levels that are too low increase the probability of relapse and reduce treatment retention. Dosage levels need to be tailored to meet the needs of the individual, and must be sufficiently high so that withdrawal symptoms and cravings are minimised. Some clients continue to use heroin while participating in a programme of substitute prescribing, and inadequate dosage levels appear to be one factor that contributes to continued use of heroin or relapse. Fifth, some clients continue to use other drugs, for example, benzodiazepine, alcohol, which can contribute to fatal and non-fatal overdose, particularly when combined with methadone. These issues present real challenges to treatment providers as well as clients.

SUMMARY

Methadone and high-dose buprenorphine maintenance treatment are two of the most common methods of substitute prescribing currently available. Service provision varies across and within countries, and in some regions, substitute prescribing is not an option. Studies have shown that MMT in particular can be beneficial for individuals as well as the wider community. However, several barriers to treatment can deter potential clients from participating in substitute-prescribing programmes.

REFERENCES

Chatterjee, P. (2008) 'The methadone fix', *Bulletin of the World Health Organization*, 86 (3): 164–5.

Corsi, K.F., Lehman, W.K. and Booth, R.E. (2009) 'The effect of methadone maintenance on positive outcomes for opiate injection drug users', *Journal of Substance Abuse Treatment*, 37: 120–6.

Fischer, B., Rehm, J., Kim, G. and Kirst, M. (2005) 'Eyes wide shut? – a conceptual and empirical critique of methadone maintenance treatment', *European Addiction Research*, 11 (1): 1–14.

Gerlach, R. (2004) *A Brief Overview on the Discovery of Methadone*. Münster: INDRO e. V.

Lind, B., Chen, S., Weatherburn, D. and Mattick, R. (2005) 'The effectiveness of methadone maintenance treatment in controlling crime', *British Journal of Criminology*, 45 (2): 201–11.

Simoens, S., Matheson, C., Bond, C., Inkster, K. and Ludbrook, A. (2005) 'The effectiveness of community maintenance with methadone or buprenorphine for treating opiate dependence', *British Journal of General Practice*, 55 (511): 139–46.

United Nations Office on Drugs and Crime (2008) *2008 World Drug Report*. Vienna: United Nations.

28

The New Recovery Approach

Recovery from addiction has long been a goal of treatment. How best to help people addicted to drugs and/or alcohol is a key issue. Some advocate complete abstinence as the only appropriate way for people to be treated while others argue that 'recovery' can be defined far less narrowly and that abstinence is but one form of recovery.

In recent years a new impetus has been achieved by abstinence orientated recovery that has challenged anew traditional forms of treatment such as substitute prescribing and harm reduction approaches.

Building on the foundations of the 1960s anti-psychiatry movement and 1970s anti-discrimination legislation alongside a growth in health consumerism and the empowered 'expert patient' in the USA, the UK, Australia and New Zealand, concern with 'recovery' initially emerged among those with personal experience of mental health difficulties and has since developed into what has been called the 'recovery movement'. In relation to substance use, the new recovery approach maintains that there should be an explicit emphasis on recovery from alcohol and/or drug dependence and that abstinence or sobriety for a sustained period, preferably for life, is the goal to which all those working in addiction services, including service users, should be orientated.

Although the new recovery approach can be distinguished from the 12-step recovery programmes as developed by Alcoholics Anonymous and Narcotics Anonymous that remain dominant in the USA, it does have similarities with them, in particular it's emphasis on 'stages' of recovery (which may include being 'in recovery' but not yet 'recovered'); on sobriety and/or being 'drug-free'; on peer support delivered in group settings; and on social inclusion or reintegration into 'mainstream' society.

An emphasis on recovery and in particular abstinence from all illicit drugs as a suitable and measurable outcome for those entering drug treatment has found recent favour with national governments working within a broadly prohibitionist framework who tend to take a 'tough on drugs' stance. 'Supporting people to live a drug-free life' is for example explicitly stated as the principal aim of the current UK coalition government's drug strategy 'instead of focusing primarily on reducing the harms caused by drug misuse' (Home Office, 2010: 2) (also see **26 harm reduction**).

DEFINITIONS OF RECOVERY

'Recovery' in its broadest sense however remains an ill-defined and contested concept which has been used to indicate an approach, a model, a philosophy, a paradigm, a movement, a vision and most sceptically, a myth (Roberts and Wolfson, 2004). Particular definitions of recovery from alcohol and drug addiction are not only wide-ranging but also sometimes conflicting. In this regard William White (2007), a key US-based advocate of the new recovery approach, has argued that it is important that consensus is achieved on both a working definition of recovery as well as the conceptual boundaries of what 'addiction recovery' constitutes if recovery-orientated interventions are to be successful. From a five-year review of peer-reviewed journal articles, Laudet (2007) notes that most US researchers and addiction professionals implicitly define recovery in terms of recovery from substance use alone and most often as total abstinence from alcohol and all drugs, or at the very least from an individual's main problem drug. This latter notion of recovery from use of a 'main problem drug' has however been criticised by those pointing to addiction service-users' propensity to have concurrent or sequential problems with multiple substances, including alcohol and the need to have a person focused approach to recovery rather than a narrow substance focused one (White, 2007).

Narrowing down definitions can be notoriously difficult however. The renowned Betty Ford Institute Consensus Panel's report has been influential in the USA in setting out an initial definition of recovery from addiction (also see **4 addiction**) as a 'voluntarily maintained lifestyle' consisting of 'sobriety, personal health and citizenship' which is assumed to be more 'productive' than a lifestyle dominated by 'substance-dependence' (2007: 221). From this particular definition, however, we can see that recovery-orientated discourse, policy and practice can involve normative judgments about what being a 'good citizen' is or should be. In the UK and other countries the disease model of addiction has far less credibility among addiction professionals and experts, is seen as linked to 'moral education' as much as abstinence and as such will struggle to garner broad support for such a definition internationally.

ISSUES WITH 'ADDICTION RECOVERY'

Calls for a re-orientation towards recovery within addiction services, particularly in the UK where medium- to long-term methadone maintenance is the norm for opiate users, have been made in a context whereby client outcomes towards abstinence were rarely measured by services, or where they were, have been seen as disappointing for those wishing to see clients end up 'drug-free'. In the UK, one study by Neil McKeganey et al. (2004) has been used by advocates of the new recovery approach to maintain that *total abstinence* or being 'drug-free' is the principal goal of drug users themselves and therefore that drug services should be wholly abstinence-oriented. In this version of addiction recovery there is no place for **26 harm reduction** strategies or 'medicated recovery' such as aforementioned methadone maintenance programmes that evidence suggests reduces harm to injecting street heroin users. Instead because harm reduction aims to reduce harm from drug use but not necessarily drug use per se, it is represented by some as being a negative approach that runs in direct opposition to abstinent recovery. This debate between harm reductionists and the 'new abstentionists' has become increasingly and unhelpfully polarised and politicised in recent times, particularly in the UK and Australia (Best et al., 2010).

There have been criticisms of the McKeganey et al. (2004) study in that it reiterates a historic, ideological but potentially unhelpful dichotomy between harm reduction on the one hand and abstinence on the other, where a 'harm reduction abstinence continuum' (where, for example, reducing immediate and medium-term harm through medication may be seen as beneficial initially with a concern to facilitate a move to abstinence when the client is ready or able) and the move to abstinence may be more indicative of drug service clients' many and varied needs and aspirations (Martin, 2005). There have also been criticisms of the McKeganey et al. (2004) study – which much of the UK and some other countries' recovery momentum was gained from – on the grounds that its methodological approach produced an overly simple and decontextualised concept of 'abstinence' focused 'treatment' by asking what the aim of treatment was for those addicted. It didn't engage with a concept of recovery that could understand treatment towards abstinence as involving different forms of appropriate intervention beyond abstinence. Countering this, Neale et al.'s (2011) in-depth qualitative research points instead to a more nuanced notion of 'abstinence' and 'recovery' which captures those drug users who wish to be abstinent from their main problem drug but not necessarily from all drugs for all time, including alcohol. Other drug service users highlight that abstinence from drugs is but one aspiration among many which include better mental and physical health, enhanced family relations and an improvement in financial circumstances (Neale et al., 2011).

It is also the case that while there is a considerable historic evidence base for the efficacy for opiate substitution as a means to reduce various harms to treatment populations (helping stabilise lifestyles, reducing drug use, decreasing involvement in crime), there is not an equivalent evidence base for 'abstinence-orientated treatments', particularly in the UK. However for Best et al. (2010) this reflects the dominance of medical treatment options (as opposed to holistic and/or service-user led services, for example) and the dominance of quantitative research methods such as randomised control trials which do not capture often complicated, multidimensional and long-term recovery processes at work in people's drug careers. White (2007) has shown that recovery *is* possible and sustainable over a longer period of time through *both* engagement *and* non-engagement in substance treatment programmes. The latter, referred to as 'natural recovery' (see also **25 drug treatment and quasi-compulsory treatment**), suggests that some people experiencing problems with alcohol and drugs may simply 'mature out' of their problems as they get older. In addition a substantial body of literature has built up over the last 30 years on the efficacy of therapeutic communities (TCs) – imported from the USA in the 1960s to Europe and the UK in the 1970s – which has fed into the contemporary concept of peer-based recovery support or 'recovery communities' for dependent alcohol and drug users (White, 2009). Hence the increasing focus on recovery, sobriety and being drug-free in contemporary alcohol and drug services is not as novel as it may first appear. Finally there is some concern that a blanket re-orientation of alcohol and in particular drug services to recovery risks excluding potential service-users, such as binge-drinkers or recreational drug users, who do not fall under traditional definitions of 'alcoholic' or 'problem drug user', and for whom recovery may have little meaning or relevance to their use patterns.

REFERENCES

Best, D., Bamber, S., Battersby, A., Gilman, M., Groshkova, T., Honor, S., McCartney, D., Yates, R. and White, W. (2010) 'Recovery and straw men: an analysis of the objections raised to the transition to a recovery model in UK addiction services', *Journal of Groups in Addiction and Recovery*, 5: 264–88.

Betty Ford Institute Consensus Panel (2007) 'What is recovery? A working definition from the Betty Ford Institute', *Journal of Substance Abuse Treatment*, 33: 221–8.

Home Office (2010) *Drug Strategy 2010: Reducing Demand, Restricting Supply, Building Recovery: Supporting People to Live a Drug Free Life*. London: Home Office.

Laudet, A. (2007) 'What does recovery mean to you? Lessons from the recovery experience for research and practice', *Journal of Substance Abuse Treatment*, 33: 243–56.

Martin, P. (2005) 'Critique of "What are drug users looking for when they contact drug services: Abstinence or harm reduction?" by Neil McKeganey, Zoᐁ Morris, Joanne Neil and Michele Robertson', *Drugs: Education, Prevention and Policy*, 12 (4): 257–259.

McKeganey, N., Morris, Z., Neale, J. and Robertson, M. (2004) 'What are drug users looking for when they contact drug services: abstinence or harm reduction?', *Drugs: Education, Prevention and Policy*, 11: 423–35.

Neale, J., Nettleton, S. and Pickering, L. (2011) 'What is the role of harm reduction when drug users say they want abstinence?', *International Journal of Drug Policy*, 22: 189–93.

Roberts, G. and Wolfson, P. (2004) 'The rediscovery of recovery: open to all', *Advances in Psychiatric Treatment*, 10: 37–49.

White, W. (2007) 'Addiction recovery: its definition and conceptual boundaries', *Journal of Substance Abuse Treatment*, 33 (3): 229–41.

White, W. (2009) *Peer-Based Addiction Recovery Support: History, Theory, Practise and Scientific Evaluation*. Chicago, IL: Great Lakes Addiction Technology Transfer Center.

29

Prevention: Primary, Secondary and Tertiary

Primary/secondary/tertiary prevention refers to a broad range of interventions that aim to prevent people from starting to use drugs, encourages drug users to stop, or aims to reduce harm once drug use has started.

Primary drug prevention aims to discourage people, particularly children and young adults, from starting to use drugs. Secondary drug prevention chiefly aims to encourage those already using drugs to stop, to reduce their use, or to use more safely (see also **26 harm reduction**). Tertiary drug prevention involves the treatment of the drug user, usually with the eventual goal of user abstinence, although interventions may also aim to reduce the negative impact of dependent drug use. Prevention differs from drug enforcement activities such as police or military action. However, prevention activities such as drug education programmes are typically undertaken alongside enforcement activities. Primary, secondary and tertiary prevention initiatives are not mutually exclusive and there may be considerable overlap between the interventions any one individual or group experiences.

key concepts in
drugs and society

The aims of drug prevention interventions are located within the goal of national and international drug control policy, namely the reduction or elimination of illicit drug use. For legal drugs a number of regulatory interventions such as price controls are used to prevent or reduce use. Regulatory interventions may be general, such as minimal alcohol unit pricing, or targeted at specific groups, such as age limits for tobacco and alcohol purchases.

PRIMARY PREVENTION

Primary prevention interventions aimed at illegal drug use are many and varied, although broadly speaking they focus on increasing people's knowledge about drug risks and harms to discourage use or delay the onset of first use. Age of initiation into drug use (including tobacco and alcohol) is crucial as use of specific substances early in life increases the risk of progression to more frequent and problematic use later on in life.

Large-scale anti-drugs campaigns or public information campaigns, often undertaken via the radio, television or increasingly the Internet are aimed at a universal audience. In the UK, the Talk to Frank campaign is 'multiplatform', meaning that anti-drug messages are distributed via various media channels, including the social networking site Facebook. Typically large-scale universal prevention campaigns use variations on abstinence or 'Just Say No' messages to discourage people from drug use, emphasising the risk of serious injury or death from drug use.

It is often assumed that public information campaigns prevent drug use. However, there is a dearth of meaningful evaluations of such campaigns. Those evaluations that have been undertaken have found that large-scale drug prevention programmes, particularly those that take a fear/scare based approach, frequently have little or no impact on drug use, or may even be counterproductive. One such example was the National Youth Anti-Drug Media Campaign, a large-scale American prevention programme aimed at preventing marijuana/cannabis use. In the evaluation of the campaign, around 80 per cent of young people indicated that they had repeatedly seen the campaign's anti-drug messages, many on a weekly basis. However, the only statistically significant results in the evaluation were that some youths reported an increase in marijuana/cannabis use upon increased exposure to the campaign (Orwin et al., 2004). This highlights the weak evidence base for public information campaigns or universal primary prevention initiatives. There are various problems with assessing the 'impact' of campaign messages as showing an awareness of particular campaign messages (such as knowing about drug risks) does not necessarily translate into less or discontinued use.

Primary prevention includes school-based interventions aimed at all pupils. Age-specific interventions are the norm. Such interventions may involve an emphasis on pupils developing interpersonal skills in order to resist 'peer pressure' to take drugs. Self-reported drug use is used as a principal measure of the success of such interventions, although an increase in negative attitudes to drug use may also be used as a measure of success. However, there are problems with measuring the success of interventions more generally. It is unclear for example the period over which abstinence from drugs or reduced alcohol consumption would need to occur before any prevention programme is deemed successful. Reviewing evaluations of programmes aimed at reducing alcohol consumption, Foxcroft et al. (2003) found nearly half of psychosocial and education interventions for under-25s (mostly undertaken in the USA) were ineffectual in terms of reducing self-reported alcohol consumption in the short-term (up to 1 year), with even fewer studies reporting medium (1–3 years) or longer-term (>3 years) effectiveness.

Social norms interventions as prevention

An ever more popular prevention approach, developed primarily in the USA for use in the American college system, is called 'social norms' or 'social norms marketing' (for an overview, see Perkins, 2003). Social norms is an alternative to the traditional 'fear-based' approaches to health education, emerging in light of growing evidence that traditional prevention interventions are largely ineffectual (Reuter and Stevens, 2007). Social norms has focused on a broad range of health behaviours, including preventing tobacco, alcohol and illegal drug use as well as promoting healthy behaviours such as participation in sport among young people.

Social norms initiatives are based on evidence that individuals tend to incorrectly perceive the attitudes and/or behaviours of their peers and other community members to be different to their own, when in fact they are not. Assuming peers have already initiated drug use when they have not is one example. It is suggested that such misperceptions lead to increased 'peer pressure' or peer influence, whereby (young) people end up consuming drugs because they think everyone else has. In turn this can result in the misinformed individual rationalising their drug-using behaviour, that is, 'Everyone's doing it, why shouldn't I?' and even suppressing healthy behaviours, that is, 'No-one else exercises, why should I'? Social norms interventions involve correcting individuals' misperceptions about their peer groups (and/or about the wider population) by revealing the healthier norm (that is, drug use is less common than they might think). The individual is then expected to not start or else reduce their participation in non-normative unhealthy behaviours and begin or else increase their participation in normative healthy behaviours. One issue with social norms interventions is that abstainers from tobacco, alcohol and drug use, or those who have lower than 'normal' use patterns, may start or increase their use when they are told they are not the norm. This is known as the 'boomerang effect'.

Social norms is increasingly being taken up in countries other than the USA, including Canada, Australia and the UK, although it is unclear how the approach translates into community settings and different cultures (McAlaney et al., 2011). Even in the USA, where 'social-norms marketing' has been taken up with great enthusiasm, evaluations of such programmes are mixed. Although some programme evaluations have highlighted positive outcomes in terms of reductions in unhealthy behaviours, others have either failed to show any change in behaviour or have increased the very behaviours and misperceptions they set out to decrease.

SECONDARY PREVENTION

Secondary prevention interventions tend to focus on specific groups thought to be 'at risk' of drug use such as vulnerable and disadvantaged young people or on current drug users. An example of a secondary prevention intervention would be a drugs education workshop with young people in local authority care, school truants or those who have been excluded from school, all of whom are more at risk of developing dependent patterns of drug use than the general population (Reuter and Stevens, 2007). Another example would be a combination of early screening of adolescent substance use alongside targeted interventions such as motivational interviewing aiming to encourage behaviour change, either towards abstinence or towards less harmful consumption practices (Tait and Hulse, 2003). Indeed programmes that have shown a small demonstrated effect on patterns of drug use share these characteristics of intense, focused and repeated sessions carefully tailored to specific groups. However such programmes are costly and difficult to replicate across entire school systems, with most being inappropriate for broader audiences (Gottfredson and Gottfredson, 2002).

TERTIARY PREVENTION

Tertiary prevention is concentrated on the provision of treatment for alcohol and drug users (for a more detailed discussion, see also **25 drug treatment and quasi-compulsory treatment**). Tertiary prevention or treatment aligns with broader national and international drug control policy aims in terms of reducing the number of people dependent on drugs and reducing the harms associated with dependence. There are four main forms of tertiary prevention or modes of treatment for those dependent on alcohol and drugs: rehabilitation programmes in residential settings; rehabilitation programmes in community settings; in-patient units where medical detoxification takes place; and methadone maintenance or methadone reduction programmes for those dependent on opiates. Individual users may experience one or a combination of these modes of treatment, with varying degrees of success.

REFERENCES

Foxcroft, D.R., Ireland, D., Lister-Shart, D.J., Lowe, G. and Breen, R. (2003) 'Longer-term primary prevention for alcohol misuse in young people: a systematic review', *Addiction*, 98: 397–411.

Gottfredson, D.C. and Gottfredson, G.D. (2002) 'Quality of school-based prevention programs: results from a national survey', *Journal of Research in Crime and Delinquency*, 39 (1): 3–35.

McAlaney, J., Bewick, B. and Hughes, C. (2011) 'The international development of the "social norms" approach to drug education and prevention', *Drugs: Education, Prevention and Policy*, 18 (2): 81–9.

Orwin, R., Cadell, D., Chu, A., Kalton, G., Maklan, D., Morin, C., Piesse, A., Sanjeev, S., Steele, D., Taylor, K. and Tracy, E. (2004) *Evaluation of the National Youth Anti-Drug Media Campaign*. Washington, DC: National Institute of Drug Abuse (NIDA). Available from: http://www.nida.nih.gov/DESPR/Westat/NSPY2004Report/NSPY2004Report.zip (accessed 25 July 2012).

Perkins, H.W. (ed.) (2003) *The Social Norms Approach To Preventing School And College Age Substance Abuse: A Handbook For Educators, Counsellors and Clinicians*. San Francisco, CA: Jossey-Bass

Reuter, P. and Stevens, A. (2007) *An Analysis of UK Drug Policy: A Monograph Prepared for the UK Drug Policy Commission (UKDPC)*. London: UKDPC.

Tait, R.J. and Hulse, G.K. (2003) 'A systematic review of the effectiveness of brief interventions with substance using adolescents by type of drug', *Drug and Alcohol Review*, 22: 337–46.

30
International Drug Control History/Prohibition

> International drug control history charts the development of the current dominant approach – that of prohibition – to the global cultivation, production, distribution and consumption of particular intoxicating substances.

It is easy to forget in the contemporary climate of 'drug control' that global prohibition has not always been the dominant approach to human consumption of intoxicating substances. People have always taken what we now call 'drugs'. There is a long tradition of cultivation, production and trading of intoxicating substances, with use not always having been considered problematic for individuals or societies. Our current international drug control system, with its global conventions, international strategies, national laws and domestic policies supervised by the United Nations (UN), has a much shorter history. This system of drug control via global prohibition has evolved over the last 100 years during which the USA has extended and consolidated its influence over international matters (McAllister, 2000). In particular, consuming substances for relaxation, recreation, pleasure and experimentation – essentially 'non-medical' use of drugs – has been the focus of prohibition advocates. Notions of **4 addiction**, compulsion, individual pathology and moral degeneracy have formed the basis for assertions about the need to control certain drugs by prohibiting or 'banning' them. The desire to strengthen professional power among medical and pharmaceutical practitioners, alongside exaggerated and misinformed understandings of drugs and their users, have also played a crucial role in the development of prohibition.

Currently every nation in the world is either a signatory or has laws which are in accordance with at least one of the relevant UN conventions, with prohibition enforced by nation states' police and military forces. The production and sale of cannabis, cocaine and opiates is globally prohibited (except for limited medical use in some settings) while the possession of these substances is also criminalised in

key concepts in
drugs and society

the vast majority of countries, although recently some Latin American countries such as Argentina have moved towards the decriminalisation of possession of small amounts of cannabis, cocaine and heroin (see also **40 decriminalisation, legalisation and legal regulation**). A wide range of amphetamine-type substances (ATS) are also globally prohibited. However, despite commonalities between nation states and evidence of convergence in the drug laws of members of the European Union, prohibition is best seen as a continuum of activities, with the most decriminalised and regulated forms of prohibition at one end (for example, the Netherlands' cannabis policy of the 1980s and 1990s) and the most punitive and criminalising forms of prohibition at the other (for example, the USA's policy towards crack cocaine users/dealers) (Levine, 2003). The question remains, how did global drug prohibition come to be the dominant drug control system in recent history?

PROHIBITION PREVAILS: THE DEVELOPMENT OF AN INTERNATIONAL DRUG CONTROL SYSTEM

Since the beginning of civilisation people have cultivated and ingested naturally occurring intoxicating substances, with the opium poppy (*Papaver somniferumm*), coca leaves (*Erythroxylum*) and cannabis plant (*Cannabis sativa*) thought to be the most widely used. Coca leaves for example were consumed for physical stimulation by labourers, and for bartering and sale along early trade routes. The colonial ambitions of Western powers in part drove changes to the cultivation, production and use of opium and coca leaves. British success in the two 'opium wars' of 1839 and 1857 meant the Chinese were eventually forced to legalise the opium trade. A similar pattern of the establishment of trade monopolies and the use of military force by British and Dutch colonial powers in South America underpinned the move from native cultivation of coca leaves to commercial production of cocaine for a lucrative global market.

The global commercial trade in opium, coca and cannabis and its links to Western colonialism sets the scene for the USA's entry into emergent drug debates in the mid-19th century. After years of prohibition campaigning in the UK and India, the USA was forced to address the emergent 'opium question'. Following the recommendations of the Philippines Opium Commission of 1903, the US federal government, to the delight of US Christian missionaries, banned the (non-medical) use of opium owing to the perceived deleterious physical and moral effects the substance was said to have on its users. American Christian missionaries were also influential in the setting up of the Shanghai Opium Conference convened by the USA and a follow-up conference in The Hague in 1911, which resulted in the 1912 International Opium Convention (IOC). Prohibition remained a minority stance held by the USA against the dominant position of opium trade regulation held by other conference participants such as the British and the Dutch. However the 1912 IOC established a broad principle of intervention in the non-medical use of substances via the argument that governments had a moral duty to protect people from 'dangerous drugs'. In the USA, the acceptance of this principle rested on the use of racist language and imagery about the 'threat' of 'Negro cocaine fiends' and 'Chinese opium devils' to white American society. Drug prohibition then has profoundly racist origins; origins which still shape the way in which the 'drug problem' is framed in contemporary times. Some of the earliest prohibition-ist drug laws in the USA were introduced at state level specifically against the use of opium by Chinese immigrants. Moral crusaders disseminated drug propaganda which played upon America's profound racism, xenophobia and fear of 'the Other'. Such propaganda represented drugs as being able to completely strip users of any free will and moral sensibilities while lending them 'superhuman' physical powers, with for example a 1913 article in the *New York Times* called 'Negro Cocaine Fiends Are a New Southern Menace' telling how 'southern sheriffs had switched from 0.32-calibre guns to 0.38-calibre pistols to protect themselves from drug-empowered blacks' (see also **32 drug scares and moral panics**).

By the early 1930s, the widespread violation of alcohol prohibition in the con-text of the Great Depression effectively ended national prohibition in the USA. However, by this time domestic drug prohibition had already been separated from alcohol prohibition via the creation of the Federal Bureau of Narcotics under the leadership of campaigner Harry J. Anslinger (Musto, 1999). Over the next 30 years, with Anslinger at its helm, the Bureau played a key role in dis-seminating US anti-drug propaganda and acculturating Americans to new anti-drug laws through a potent mix of hysteria and racism. The internationalisation of the US approach saw other countries using the same demonisation of drug users to justify the adoption of national legislation such as the Dutch Opium Act 1919 and the UK Dangerous Drugs Act 1920.

The establishment of the League of Nations following the First World War and the growth of the USA as a 'super-power' marked the further development of the international drug control regime through specialised support bodies within the League of Nations, such as the Opium Advisory Committee (OAC). The process of building a prohibition-based international drug control system continued with the 1928 Geneva Convention and the 1931 Convention for Limiting the Manu-facture and Regulating the Distribution of Narcotic Drugs. During the inter-war years more substances, including cannabis, became subject to control, with a schedule created to classify substances ostensibly according to their scientific value and potential for harm. As Convention signatories, nation states were required to implement domestic drug laws to ensure they complied with international obliga-tions. Yet few signatories had many users of the drugs brought under control by the Convention. This belies the fact that the international drug control system has been built predominately around racist and moral crusades based on spurious claims about drug effects on particular populations such as the working classes and non-whites by middle-class medics, scientists and politicians seeking to consolidate and extend their professional power.

The Second World War enabled the USA to consolidate its position as the leader of an increasingly extensive drug control regime (McAllister, 2000). The immedi-ate post-1945 era saw the consolidation of international prohibition with its own bureaucracy, ideology and mechanisms for enforcement via the newly established UN Economic and Social Council (UN ECOSOC), supported by the Commission on Narcotic Drugs (CND). Drug prohibition became one of the key priorities of the newly formed UN as the 1961 UN Single Convention on Narcotic Drugs combined and consolidated the nine drug conventions introduced since the 1911 Hague conference (Levine, 2003). The 1961 UN Single Convention was a major success for the USA via the extension of the international system of licensing, reporting and certifying raw 'narcotic' transactions, including those in cannabis and coca leaves, overseen by the International Narcotic Control Board (INCB). The 1971 Convention on Psychotropic Substances supported by domestic policies of signatory nations extended global prohibition to barbiturates, hallucinogens and amphetamines not previously covered by the 1961 Single Convention. In the USA the Nixon administration launched its **37 war on drugs** with the 1970 Controlled Substance Act (CSA) and the creation of the Drug Enforcement Agency (DEA). Subsequent US administrations escalated the war with increasingly punitive national policies put in place during the Reagan and Bush eras and supported by anti-drug foreign policies aimed at for example crop eradication in producer countries (see also **36 crop eradication, crop substitution and legal cultivation**). The DEA remains a key US and crucially international drug law enforcer, with over 5000 special agents and 87 foreign offices in over 60 countries.

THE FUTURE OF GLOBAL DRUG CONTROL/PROHIBITION

Until relatively recently the term 'drug prohibition' was rarely deployed in the public domain, with the terms 'narcotic control' or 'drug control' more commonly used (Levine, 2003). Instead 'prohibition' has been used to signify the USA's failed alcohol prohibition policies of the early 20th century. The slippage between the concepts of 'drug control' and 'prohibition' is problematic as it is unclear whether prohibition amounts to a drug *control* framework *or* actually signifies a *loss of control* over the regulation of banned substances whose production and distribution is in fact controlled by those operating illegal drug markets. Historically the successes of the international drug control system lie more in the control of legal markets in (psychoactive) medications such as barbiturates, achieved through a license system that restricts provision and authorisation of sales to specific (medical) professions or licensees.

As global drug prohibition and particularly the **37 war on drugs** becomes more openly debated, it may lose some of its ideological and political power (Levine, 2003). There are tensions for example between member states of the European Union who favour more tolerant (that is, the Netherlands in 1980s and 1990s; Portugal) or more punitive (that is, Sweden) drug control regimes (Chatwin, 2003). However being 'tough on drugs' at a local level remains a vote-winner for most nations' political parties (for example, Australia's conservative Liberal party). Strong drug prohibition stances remain entrenched in nations powerful on the international stage, including the USA, Russia and China. Political and financial vested interests have further entrenched the prohibition regime. In many countries including the UK, the USA and Australia, anti-drug police and military operations receive extensive government funding and support, while both publicly and privately run prisons hold hundreds of thousands of non-violent drug offenders. Echoing anti-drug, pro-prohibition debates of 100 years earlier, certain substances are still routinely described as inherently 'evil' and their users immoral (Szasz, 1987). Despite ongoing challenges to the efficacy of our contemporary international drug control system, most notably by the international harm reduction community, global drug prohibition looks set to continue, albeit increasingly undermined and beleaguered by evidence-based critiques.

REFERENCES

Chatwin, C. (2003) 'Drug policy developments within the European Union: the destabilising effects of Dutch and Swedish drug policies', *British Journal of Criminology*, 43 (3): 567–82.

Levine. H. (2003) 'Global drug prohibition: its uses and crises', *International Journal of Drug Policy*, 14 (2): 145–53.

McAllister, W.B. (2000) *Drug Diplomacy in the Twentieth Century: An International History*. London: Routledge.

Musto (1999) *The American Disease: Origins of Narcotics Control*, 3rd edn. New York: Oxford University Press.

31
Drugs in Sport

Performance-enhancing drugs (PEDs) are any substance considered by the World Anti-Doping Agency to unfairly enhance sporting performance. Concerns over the use of PEDs in the sporting arena tend to focus publically on two main issues: concerns over cheating and gaining an unfair advantage, and concerns to protect the health of the sports participant. However a broader, social analysis of concerns over the use of drugs in sport suggests that such issues are better understood as part and parcel of those concerns about drugs in the non-sporting world and the sporting world should in part be read off as 'mirroring' how the drug problem has been presented there. Further analysis also indicates that much that is assumed about controls over PEDs is unproven and even contradictory

Today the condemnation of using various banned substances to gain an advantage is so ingrained in the popular psyche as the right and proper approach to the issue that it would be easy to see it as a simple issue needing no contextualisation. However, just as the use of currently illicit drugs in the non-sporting world has not always been condemned it is also not the case that society or sport-controlling bodies have always frowned upon or legislated against the kind of substances now banned in the sporting arena.

Records of the earliest Olympics in ancient Greece refer to the use of various plants and intoxicants to aid endurance and performance but perhaps more intuitively we can accept that this was because plants and other substances were used to help people work, endure pain and relieve stress in all areas of life. Using substances in sporting activity was thus an extension not exception to the norm. Even today in rural India we see examples of this where opium is consumed to enable peasant farmers to endure long days in the field and to help them work (Ganguly, 2004). In comparatively modern times (1904) athletes were injecting themselves with strychnine and drinking brandy to win the Olympic marathon and up to the 1950s Tour de France champions were openly using PEDs and their records are not considered tarnished. Early examples of sporting performance is often therefore, *unremarkably* linked to the pursuit of improvement by ingesting (and even injecting) substances of various kinds. Related to this is the fact that certain 'cultures of acceptance' of the use of performance-enhancing activities within some sports – such as cycling – has meant that PEDs were previously accepted by both the sporting authorities and those competing as relatively legitimate. In cycling such a culture has persisted to some extent in spite of the overwhelming condemnation from outside the sport and attempts by the sport's administrators to 'clean it up'. The result – at present – is a sport relatively awash with attempts to artificially enhance performance while constantly at war with itself in an effort to rid itself of such practices.

A combination of events has led to the almost universal condemnation of PED use to aid performance that we are familiar with today – the rationality behind those events however is not simply related to a concern for competitors' health and protection of sporting virtue and fair play. Briefly, the Olympic ideal originally nurtured in the public (that is, private/privileged) schools of the UK and transposed onto the worldwide sporting arena by one of the key instigators of the modern Olympics, Pierre de Coubertin, places fair play and the moral leadership that sport can play at its forefront. As has already been stated however, the use of PEDs has not always been seen as not in the spirit of fair play but part and parcel of sport itself. This changed when the systematic introduction of anabolic steroids in the old Soviet Union and other Eastern European (Communist) countries appeared to produce rapid improvements in physique and performance especially in the strength events, such as weightlifting. Although the use of steroids spread to the USA and other countries there seems little doubt that concerns around PEDs in the sporting world were becoming mixed up with growing concerns about the use of illicit drugs in the non-sporting world as well as association with political regimes seen as morally corrupt (Coomber, 1998; Beamish and Richie, 2005). Since the 1980s renewed drug scares in the non-sporting world have had (albeit often unacknowledged) a symbiotic effect on how PED use is viewed within the sporting world mirroring exaggerated claims about health risks and the power of the drugs taken.

PERFORMANCE-ENHANCING DRUGS – THE SUBSTANCES

Most people will associate PEDs with anabolic steroids and derivations of them. Anabolic steroids provide the user with higher levels of the 'male' hormone testosterone, a substance that occurs naturally in mammals and promotes cell growth.

In general men have much greater natural levels of testosterone than women. Anabolic steroids are associated ergonomically (that is, in terms of performance enhancement) with muscle growth; increases in strength but also of masculine characteristics such as facial hair and a deepening of the voice.

PEDs have a number of broad categories under which they are listed which characterise the action they have on the body. Substances such as anabolic steroids (AS) and human growth hormone (HGH) are substances that promote growth of musculature and physique and it is widely assumed, with appropriate exercise and diet, performance. ASs and HGH are associated with strength or power sports (weightlifting; boxing; American football) whereas other substances such as amphetamine or caffeine, 'stimulants' that provide the body with 'extra energy' are associated with performance gains where alertness, 'speed' and endurance is enhanced. Other major forms of PEDs are those that mimic the effects of altitude training (mostly endurance/fitness gains) by increasing the amount of white blood cells in the body. Numerous other substances ranging from those found in inhalers for asthma sufferers to ginseng drinks bought in local shops have potential – according to the World Anti-Doping Agency – to enhance performance and are thus included in the list of banned substances.

LEGAL STATUS

In many countries around the world substances such as ASs are not illegal and in some countries, like the UK, Canada and Australia they are 'controlled' substances but not to the same degree as in the USA where penalties for supply (up to 20 years imprisonment) *and* possession for use (up to five years imprisonment) are generally higher than elsewhere. The inclusion of certain PEDs into control legislation, despite there being little by way of a 'drug problem' associated with them is consistent with the way that drug controls (see also **30 international drug control history/prohibition**) in contemporary society tend to grow and become increasingly inclusive rather than be judged individually on their specific levels of riskiness or problem posed to society.

DRUG USE IN SPORT – PREVALENCE

Exactly what proportion of sportsmen and sportswomen use performance-enhancing drugs is unknown and is the subject of some considerable debate. Over the years numerous sporting heroes and retiring anti-doping administrators have suggested that the use of PEDs in professional sport is widespread – with figures of up to 80 per cent being mentioned – while others, usually those whose job it is to prevent the use of PEDs in sport, claiming that use is minimal (less than 1 per cent test positive for PEDs at major sporting events such as the Olympics) and that prevention activities are thus working. The trouble is, actually detecting the use of PEDs is not very easy and the fact that few sportsmen and sportswomen actually test positive is not necessarily an indication that the use of PEDs is itself negligible. A number of retired testing officials have in fact declared that the only ones they catch are the stupid ones.

HEALTH RISKS

There are numerous health risks associated with PED use. Drug 'fact sheets', such as the one reproduced below, dealing with anabolic steroids relate a whole string of potential side-effects as follows:

Damage caused by long-term use

Steroids can produce many unpleasant and often permanent side effects, including:

- damage to the gonads (testicles or ovaries);
- liver diseases;
- malfunctions of the kidneys or heart;
- 'roid rage', which is characterised by uncontrollable outbursts of psychotic aggression;
- paranoia;
- mood swings, including deep depression;
- severe acne;
- high blood cholesterol levels;
- high blood pressure;
- injuries to tendons that cannot keep up with the increased muscle strength;
- delusional feelings of being superhuman or invincible;
- fluid retention;
- trembling and muscle tremors;
- stunted bone growth in adolescents.

Gender-related side effects

For men – testicle and penis shrinkage, reduced sperm count, impotence, prostate problems, gynaecomastia (breast development) and baldness.

For women – loss of the menstrual cycle (amenorrhea), shrunken breasts, deepened voice, facial and body hair, and abnormal growth of the clitoris.

Source: Steroids Fact Sheet. 2010. State of Victoria. Better Health Channel in collaboration with the Australian Drug Foundation. http://www.betterhealth.vic.gov.au/bhcv2/bhcpdf.nsf/ByPDF/Steroids/$File/Steroids.pdf

---

In the 1970s and 1980s there was a particular anabolic steroid (now off the market) that caused extensive liver damage and numerous deaths. Overall however, as in the non-sporting world the risks attached to PEDs – while real – tend to be exaggerated, overplayed and used to bolster drug scares and support policy shifts towards greater penalties – and potential side-effects are often read off as 'likely' side-effects as opposed to potential ones (Coomber, 1998).

HOW EFFECTIVE ARE PEDS?

This is one of the key issues around PEDs and yet it goes largely unquestioned. The overriding assumption of nearly all sportspeople, sports administrators, policymakers, the media and the lay public is that not only do they work but they produce huge gains in performance. Unfortunately the scientific evidence to back either of these statements up is moderate at best for the former and almost completely absent for the latter. Experiments to prove the efficacy of PEDs are difficult to undertake because the process of comparing athletes that take steroids with a group not taking steroids under controlled conditions has proven to be difficult. To measure the effect of steroids on athletes we have to know (as with all medicines/drugs) how much is the result of placebo and how much the result of the drug. For all drugs being tested there is an 'experimenter effect' as well as a placebo effect. For athletes this would work something like this: the athlete knows they are being observed, they are paid attention to, they respond to this by wanting to perform for the experimenter and they try as hard as they can, their results improve, this increases their confidence and their results improve further. Add in to this the belief they are taking a substance that will improve their performance they are bolstered further and this further improves performance. Experiments trying to measure this have tended to try to compare two groups – those being prescribed steroids and those being prescribed a placebo (neither group knows if they are being given steroids or not). If, after testing, the steroid-using group significantly outperforms the non-steroid-using group the effectiveness of the PED is proven. Results to date, however, have been mixed (Donohoe and Johnson, 1988; Doyle-Baker et al., 1998). Some results show little or no difference between the groups, some have seen the placebo group outperform the steroid group and in others the steroid group has outperformed the non-steroid group. Despite best efforts however it has often proven difficult, because of the side effects of steroids, to hide from the groups those who have and have not been given steroids and thus, to some degree, distorting the experiment. Gains made however, from all the experiments, regardless of steroid use were not exceptional and are the kind of gains possible from hard work, specialised training regimes and confidence alone. Moreover, it is undoubtedly the case that some 'clean' athletes have made large performance improvements that have taken them to the top of their sport that many think only possible through drug use.

PED users argue that experiments will never show the effects they *know* are produced because experiments are always conducted with too low a dosage and that it is only with the kinds of dose used 'on the street' that effects will be seen.

Whatever the real picture it is clear that PEDs do not have the huge effects on performance that they are often credited with in the media and as assumed by the general public.

DOES MAKING PEDS PROHIBITED ENSURE A LEVEL PLAYING FIELD?

There is an illusion that is perpetuated by anti-doping bodies in the war against PEDs that a non-drug-using forum ensures a level playing field yet inequality in sporting activity is everywhere. Natural differences between athletes/sportspersons (look at the physical advantages that runner Usain Bolt, and swimmer Michael Phelps have) are highly meaningful and some sports try to reduce this inequality by having for example, different categories (such as weight bands: boxing; weightlifting; judo) but others that could choose not to (the high jump could have height categories; the shot put could have weight categories). Essentially however it is wealthy countries that achieve most success in sport; wealthy clubs (for example, Manchester United/Barcelona football clubs) that win more trophies; and within societies wealthy/privileged groups and individuals that saturate and achieve in the majority of sports. The wealthy and privileged, of course, also have access to the best trainers, the various dietary supplements and the best conditions and environments for success and access to the best medical services/specialists. Those without access to many of these important aspects of the modern sporting arena do not compete on an equal footing. It is also the case that cheating in many forms is rife in modern sport yet serious cheating is treated very leniently compared to PED use despite the fact that other forms of cheating may lead to much clearer and greater advantages than that obtained through PED use. The French striker Thierry Henri intentionally handballed the ball (that led to a winning goal) in a final world cup qualifying game against the Republic of Ireland in 2009. The French team went to the World Cup; the Republic of Ireland team had their hopes dashed. The penalty for Henri or the French team – nothing. If one of the squad, however, was found to have used a banned substance – even if they played badly – it would have resulted in a ban for that player. There is currently inequality in terms of judging levels of cheating and the penalties that should be applied.

DOES MAKING PEDS PROHIBITED REDUCE HEALTH HARMS/RISKS?

Confused and contradictory concerns about fair play and equality are, arguably, also echoed in the claim that prohibiting PEDs necessarily reduces health risks and harms. Currently many sports use excessive (sanctioned) medication to *enable* athletes to compete when they should not or otherwise could not – perhaps allowing longer-term damage to be caused and exposing athletes to the potentially serious health risks attached to the medications used, such as cortisone. This is another example of how those with access to privileged (but legal) medical assistance can be permitted to take drugs that might harm them to improve their performance whereas those choosing other forms of 'assistance' are persecuted. Some have argued that a level playing field would be more achievable if all athletes were allowed to take drugs but that the drugs be prescribed (meaning the drugs and what is in them would be 'known') and the effects monitored. Over time athletes would reveal – more than can be the case at the present – where the real PED health risks are and what are the safer levels and ways to use them. Such a situation would also finally allow reliable data to be collected on the efficacy of PEDs and perhaps it would show that they are not worth the trouble.

REFERENCES

Beamish, R. and Ritchie, I. (2005) 'The spectre of steroids: Nazi propaganda, cold war anxiety and patriarchal paternalism', *International Journal of the History of Sport*, 22 (5): 777–95.

Coomber, R. (1998) 'Acknowledging the contradictions and complexity of controlling drugs in sport', in N. South (ed.), *Drugs: Cultures, Controls and Everyday Life*. London: Sage. pp. 103–22.

Donohoe, T. and Johnson, N. (1988) *Foul Play*. Oxford: Basil Blackwell.

Doyle-Baker, P.K., Benson, B.W. and Meeuwisse, W.H. (1998) 'The ergogenic effects of anabolic steroids: a critical appraisal of the literature', *Medicine and Science in Sports and Exercise*, 30 (5S): S278.

Ganguly, K. (2004) 'Opium use in Rajasthan India: a socio cultural perspective', in R. Coomber and N. South (eds), *Drug Use and Cultural Contexts 'Beyond the West': Tradition, Change and Post-Colonialism*. London: Free Association Books. pp. 83–100.

32
Drug Scares and Moral Panics

> *Moral panics occur when the behaviours of certain groups of people (youthful drug takers or the urban poor) are subject to intense negative attention via media reporting of a supposedly novel and escalating 'problem' among their number. The police then deal with the problem in a repressive manner in order to protect the wider fearful public. Drug scares are specific versions of a moral panic, with a drug thought to be inherently dangerous and risky at their heart.*

Drug scares and moral panics are crucial to understanding how the **37 war on drugs** has been waged with relative impunity from critics. Illicit drug use has long been framed as a profoundly moral issue, giving rise to popular perceptions of the drug user and particularly the drug 'addict' as an immoral agent whose rational decision-making capacities and commitment to social roles and moral norms are profoundly undermined. The 'junkie' has repeatedly appeared throughout history as an abject figure; hated and feared by 'citizens' and their government and subject to medical surveillance, clinical intervention and criminal sanction. **30 International drug control history/prohibition** is littered with examples of misleading and sensationalised media coverage of drugs, drug use and drug users. In 1970s USA for example, media stories emerged of phencyclidine (PCP or angel dust) users supposedly garnering superhuman strength from the drug.

Drug scares coalesce around concerns about specific populations perceived as a threat to the established moral and social order (Reinarman, 2007). Drug scares are rarely just about the substances involved, but more about the use of a particular

key concepts in drugs and society

substance by specific groups of people (rebellious youth, the urban poor, working-class immigrant populations) who are already perceived to be a threat by powerful groups in society (the middle-classes, the clergy, politicians, medical professionals). In early Australian drug prohibition history, drug scares were driven by a fear of Chinese immigration made manifest through the spectre of 'Yellow Devils' consuming opium and corrupting the nation's morality (Manderson, 1999). In 1920s Britain, drug scares centred on the use of opium and cocaine by 'dope girls' working in London's thriving entertainment industry (Kohn, 1992). In late 1980s America, a drug scare about crack cocaine centred around the doubly deviant figure of the 'crack mum', a 'model of depravity' who supposedly symbolised all that was wrong with modern America at the time (Humphries, 1999). In more recent times 'evil ecstasy dealers' were brought to the UK public's attention through a tabloid newspaper-driven scare about the rave drug ecstasy, epitomised by the emotive 'one pill can kill' slogan of 1990s anti-E campaigners. Systematic analysis of newspaper coverage of ecstasy-related deaths has found that such deaths tend to be more newsworthy than others, particularly compared to deaths among users of diazepam and methadone (Forsyth, 2001). Over-reporting and misreporting of drug deaths may contribute to a 'moral panic' about particular substances and their usually youthful users.

During the 1960s, 1970s and early 1980s, there was much activity in academia surrounding the cultural study of visible working-class street corner (male) youth subcultures, conceptualised as being distinct from the 'straight' mainstream culture of the time. This body of work produced classic studies on moral panics, which looked at the process by which groups of young people at leisure come to the attention of the authorities. Stanley Cohen's (1972/2002) seminal work documents how the media, police and moral entrepreneurs take a real but marginal threat, amplify deviance to produce identifiable folk devils (as with 'junkies') and then promote policy measures to deal with the problem as they see it. The police and the media are understood as agents of control charged with upholding the social and moral order. The process of how (primary) deviancy may become amplified in this way is a relatively simplistic yet effective model. The classic moral panic cycle involves concern about an issue measured by extensive and sensationalised media coverage of a case or cases. Certain behaviours are labelled as deviant by the authorities, including the media. Public fear increases, exacerbated by politicians capitalising on fear for political gain. This occurred in the second 'Summer of Love' in late 1980s Britain when thousands of young people gathered in public spaces to dance or 'rave', many under the influence of ecstasy. Calls are made to control such deviants, which serves to further isolate them from mainstream culture. Justifications given for greater control over drug users deploy dualistic portrayals of (usually) young people as simultaneously vulnerable victims *and* vicious villains. Hostility towards the deviants grows, with outrage typically fuelled by a dichotomisation process whereby folk devils are distinguished from folk heroes in a morality play of good versus evil (Cohen, 1972/2002). This occurred in early 1990s Britain with the misreporting of Leah Betts' ecstasy-related death. Leah, who died from excessive water hydration following ecstasy consumption, was portrayed as an innocent victim, while the friend who supplied her was cast as an evil villain. Eventually a consensus emerges that action must be taken against the deviants. Disproportionate criminal justice responses are subsequently enacted; highly repressive drug laws may be passed and rights to privacy or peaceful assembly undermined.

Drug scares are a form of moral panic ideologically constructed to construe one or another substance as indicative of a wider social malaise, as occurred with crack cocaine in the 1980s. Hence drug scares generated by media and 'moral entrepreneurs' (Becker, 1963/1997) are specific versions of a moral panic with a substance thought to be inherently risky and dangerous at their heart. The notion of 'politico-moral entrepreneurs' (Reinarman, 2007) captures how certain social actors, typically political elites, use and generate power in order to persuade others to adhere to their moral universe. US alcohol prohibition advocates in the early 20th century, driven by the belief that temperance was the moral duty of god-fearing US citizens, are an example. However, in our contemporary risk-averse times, drug scares draw less on explicitly moralising (and religious) discourses and more on the elaboration of possible risks and harms associated with illicit drug use. Recent drug scares (for example, around emergent psychoactive substances or novel psychoactive substances such as mephedrone in the UK) have tended to focus on possible risks and harms from specific substances, with the media magnifying and dramatising drug problems through the 'routinisation of caricature' (Reinerman, 1994). The routinisation of caricature, the repetition of the abject figure of an 'out of control' drug user, involves representing worst cases (serious physical illness, psychotic episodes, death) as typical cases. Episodic drug use is reported as an impending epidemic through phrases such as 'sweeping the nation'.

CRITIQUES OF MORAL PANICS AND DRUGS SCARE CONCEPTS

It has been argued then that there are links between moral panics, drug scares and prohibition, in that contemporary illicit drug control policies are largely the result of past scares and panics (Ben-Yehuda, 1989). In opposition to this view, it might be said that national and international drug policies merely reflect the *legitimate* concerns of societies about the use of certain substances. Indeed one of the key criticisms of moral panic and drug scares is that the concepts effectively dismiss the concerns 'ordinary people' have about certain behaviours in society. However, it is often unclear just how worried 'ordinary people' actually are, despite national media and politicians' populist claims that they are addressing the concerns of the 'general public'. It should not be assumed that if something is extensively reported in the national media, the general population are all and equally concerned about the 'problem'. This links to questions about whose 'morality' is being attributed to moral panics as the concept – at least in the way in which it was originally conceived by Cohen (1972/2002) – tends to presuppose that morality is shared by all members of a given society, apart from those belonging to the deviant 'subculture' in question. As we know this is not the case – with drug taking seen as immoral by some but not by others (including abstainers) – meaning there is often little or no societal consensus around responses to drug use.

It has also been highlighted that in contemporary society there are multiple contemporary youth cultures, not one marginalised youth 'subculture'. Young people may still participate in 'mainstream' society, even if they commit deviant or even criminal acts such as binge drinking and illegal drug taking. Classic 'folk devils' such as drug-takers are now less isolated due to the **14 normalisation** of 'sensible recreational' drug use, particularly in relation to cannabis and within rave/club scenes. In relation to this point, it can be beneficial for youth (drug) cultures to be the subject of a 'moral panic' as deviant activities are widely publicised by the media while retaining their rebellious appeal to youth. This implies that 'moral panic' has become a mere rhetorical move in cultural politics, losing much of its original academic rigour and explanatory power. Another key criticism of the moral panic concept is its focus on short-term volatile media coverage of specific social (including drug) 'problems'. Instead drug scares and moral panics may be regarded as part of longer-term ideological struggles waged across all fields of public representation (Reinarman, 2007).

It is a matter of debate whether drug scares or moral panics remain useful concepts when seeking to explain contemporary relationships between the state, media, the public and drug users given contemporary media plurality in the age of the Internet, emergent understandings of media audiences as active consumers rather than passive receivers of 'misinformation', and the cultural diversity of drug users. Yet global media continues to frame what the public thinks of as 'drugs'; exaggerates relative risks and harms of drug use; perpetuates convenient stereotypes about drug takers, particularly heroin and crack users; and justifies increasingly punitive responses to drug use despite growing evidence against the efficacy, and even morality, of such responses.

REFERENCES

Becker, H. (1963/1997) *Outsiders: Studies in the Sociology of Deviance*. New York: Free Press.

Ben-Yehuda, N. (1989) *The Politics and Morality of Deviance: Moral Panics, Drug Abuse, Deviant Science and Reversed Stigmatisation*. Albany, NY: State University of New York Press.

Cohen, S. (1972/2002) *Folk Devils and Moral Panics*, 3rd edn. London: Routledge.

Forsyth, A. (2001) 'Distorted? A quantitative exploration of drug fatality reports in the popular press', *The International Journal of Drug Policy*, 12 (5): 435–53.

Humphries, D. (1999) *Crack Mothers: Pregnancy, Drugs and the Media*. Columbus, OH: State University Press.

Kohn, M. (1992) *Dope Girls: The Birth of the British Drug Underground*. London: Lawrence & Wishart.

Manderson, D. (1999) 'Symbolism and racism in drug history and policy', *Drug and Alcohol Review*, 18 (2): 179–86.

Reinarman, C. (2007) 'The social impact of drugs and the war on drugs: the social construction of drug scares', in J.A. Inciardi and K. McElrath (eds), *The American Drug Scene: An Anthology*, 5th edn. New York: Oxford University Press.

33
Drug Dealers

> Drug dealer is the term attributed to individuals involved in the illegal supply of illicit drugs to others for profit or gain. While there is a common perception that drug dealers are essentially similar in character and type – a perception that is largely reflected in most legal systems – 'the' drug dealer is in fact an unhelpful way of understanding those involved in drug supply and can lead to a weakened response by the criminal justice system and a misunderstanding of the drug problem itself.

Just as we have seen when considering *the* drug market (see also **34 drug markets**), something that is considered to be simple in character, origins and outcomes is in fact, when considered more closely, often not so simple. Stereotypes involving people relate exaggerated and over-simplified views of particular individuals or groups. In the case of so-called drug dealers, as with many negative stereotypes, conceptualisations of them have been shoe-horned into a singular highly symbolic entity – the 'evil' drug dealer inherently capable of almost any predatory and violent crime caring little for the destruction they cause to individuals and communities and seeking only their own gratification and betterment through drug sales.

HISTORICAL AND CONTEMPORARY VIEWS OF THE DRUG DEALER

How the drug dealer has been understood over time through to the present day is inextricably linked to notions of 'otherness', difference, mistrust and fear (Coomber, 2006). Most illicit (and licit) drugs are natural in origin (heroin, cocaine, cannabis, various hallucinogens, tobacco and alcohol) and most were originally native to one geographical region where they were often integrated into the lifestyle of various groups and often involved relatively non-problematic use (see also **12 cross-cultural and traditional drug use**). However, over time whether due to trade, war and/or other forms of exposure of one culture to another, substances found in one place became available to others. Sometimes these substances were treated with wonder and accepted as a useful and fruitful addition whereas at other times – especially those substances that were associated with strong psychoactive effects and with cultures or people deemed to be in some way debased or uncivilised – it was surrounded by mistrust, prohibition and serious penalty for its use or distribution. A fear of 'pollution' – by a powerful substance associated with 'lesser' culture or people – of the host culture and of individual destruction (drugs were attributed with all sorts of powers they did not have) led to various substances – even tea and coffee – being seen as a serious threat to a nation's well-being. Historically, people have been imprisoned and even killed for trading in chocolate, tea, coffee and all manner of substances. In Saudi Arabia today alcohol is illegal. The history of prohibition has been neither consistent nor predictable and how drugs and those that sell them have been understood has differed over time and space. In the West, by the end of the 19th century, opium smoking and supply was largely associated with Chinese immigrants and the so-called 'opium dens'. Stories of drug 'pushers' and 'dope peddlers' often resonated with stories of predatory activity by non-white immigrant populations or by the criminal classes. Pushers or peddlers were presented as having either the intention to drug, render impotent and seduce white women (Kohn, 1992) or to simply create new regular clients by initially providing them with free or cheap drugs of addiction – particularly the young and innocent – and then when 'hooked' having them at their (and the drug's) mercy.

DEALER MYTHS

The mainstay of how drug dealers are depicted is reliant upon what drug dealers are thought to *do*. The ways that they seek new clients and how they treat them, the things they do to the drugs they sell and the way that they *do* business. Space makes a full account of this impossible but the commonsense view (and those of much media and 'enforcement' representations) of some of the defining aspects of what dealers do will be considered.

DANGEROUS ADULTERATION (CUTTING) OF STREET DRUGS

It is a truism that you cannot know what is in street drugs as they are not subject to any formal quality control. One widely accepted belief about street drugs such as heroin and ecstasy is that they are 'cut' or adulterated with other substances down through the chain of distribution to dilute the product, make it go further and thus increase the profits. A further assumption is that desperate or evil street dealers routinely cut the drugs they sell with dangerous powders from rat poison (strychnine) to brick dust, domestic scouring agents and even ground down light-bulb glass (Coomber, 2006). As such some commentators have likened the use of street drugs to be akin to playing Russian roulette. Despite almost achieving the status of an uncontested truth – dangerous adulteration is accepted by nearly all users, non-users, drug field professionals, the media and the police – the international research evidence is clear: dangerous adulteration, the purposive cutting of drugs such as heroin with rat poison, brick dust or ground glass is neither almost never found – and is in fact improbable. Far less cutting also takes place than is often assumed and it certainly does not take place at each stage of the chain of distribution. Nearly all cutting is with substances less harmful than the main drug itself; is nearly always put there prior to importation and cuts are often with substances that either attempt to mimic the main drug's effects or even to improve on them. Overall, while street drugs have little by way of safety or quality control they are also, in practice unlikely to be laced with dangerous substances by drug dealers as is commonly believed.

PREYING ON CHILDREN AND NON-USERS BY GIVING AWAY FREE DRUGS TO 'HOOK' THEM

Another pivotal notion thought to characterise the drug dealer is that of predation: that drug dealers prey on the young and innocent, intentionally seducing them with the lure of cheap or free drugs so that once addicted they become, almost slave-like (because of their addiction), a new long-term customer of expensive drugs for the dealer that enticed them. Again, only the evil or the most heinous would undertake such an uncaring approach to others and children in particular. This particular notion, however, is more than a hundred years old, draws upon beliefs about the power of drugs to instantly (or nearly so) addict and of drug dealer activity that is essentially violent and predatory. As discussed elsewhere (see also **4 addiction**), addiction is not a simple bio-chemical reaction to a drug such as heroin, it is more complex than that. Addiction to drugs such as heroin is neither instant nor particularly quick and takes many months and sometimes years to become addicted to. Drug dealers can not afford to risk supplying drugs to children or non-users for long periods in the hope that they will become addicted *and* continue to buy their drugs from that dealer. In addition, children have less money than adults making them poor targets and are more likely to report predatory behaviour to their parents, the police or other authorities making the activity highly risky. The focus on 'drug dealers at the school gates' or 'hanging on the corner opposite playgrounds' or out off ice-cream vans smacks of hysteria and fear not reason, and as stated, because of the fact that addiction is not instant is undermined by the real bio-pharmacology of the addiction process, the fact that it takes too long to make this a real activity. Most children, in fact, get their drugs (in school and outside of school, at community playgrounds and on the street) from other schoolchildren. Other schoolchildren do not typify the stereotype of the drug dealer and by ignoring this fact the real risks of drug initiation are being ignored.

TYPES OF DRUG DEALER

Although the view of the drug dealer is largely homogenous, that is: male, violent and amoral, predatory (on the young and non-drug users), uncaring and one that routinely uses dangerous cutting agents to dilute the product they sell a brief foray into the make-up of who the drug dealer *is* confounds that image.

To begin with drug dealers are not all men and neither do female drug dealers necessarily work in the same way that male dealers do (Denton, 2001). Many that would be deemed drug dealers by the criminal justice system – such as the large numbers of young people (boys *and* girls) brokering (facilitating or acting as an intermediary) or selling, for little or no profit, recreational drugs such as cannabis or ecstasy – are not seen that way by others (Coomber and Turnbull, 2007; Parker et al. 1998) and appear not to be part of the adult market 'proper'. Such activity has been termed social supply and social suppliers are seen as distinct from drug dealers whose primary motivation is profit. A further form of 'social supply' and one that is closely related to that found in young people's networks is that of adult 'friend' dealers that 'sort out' other friends and acquaintances and who again do not conform to the dealer stereotype (Dorn et al, 1992) of committing immoral, violent and dangerous acts or being predatory in their pursuance of new customers. Many middle-class dealers may be understood – dealing apart – as non-distinct from other law-abiding citizens; addicted 'user-dealers' that deal only to other already addicted users often do so primarily to secure their own supply of drugs rather than see it as a lucrative business while some individuals are suppliers simply because they are mainly *advocates*, for example, of the hallucinogenic experience and wish to spread the word and the experience (Blum et al., 1972). As related in the chapter on drug markets (see also **34 drug markets**) this differentiation of personnel means that drug dealers as they are commonly understood or depicted do not correspond to many of those that are actually involved in dealing drugs of different types and in different ways. Social suppliers and user-dealers make up the bulk of those selling drugs and thus to see them in some way as not relevant to an understanding of drug dealing is erroneous.

There are, of course, also those that conform to a far greater degree to what is understood as the 'drug dealer'. Such individuals are full or part-time sellers looking to make meaningful profits from their sales and may operate individually or as part of a small, medium or large gang or organisation. Depending on a range of factors these individuals may use violence or the threat of it as intrinsic to the way they operate and are likely involved in other forms of crime. Even here however there are a number of different roles that those involved in drug sales play.

DIFFERENT 'ROLES'

Individual, independent sellers (freelancers) can sometimes source the drugs they sell from abroad or the point of manufacture and sell direct to the 'street'. Other freelancers will source the drugs they sell from 'wholesalers' one or more steps above them in the ladder of distribution. In both cases the level of autonomy, power, control and profit is largely in the hands of those independents. Those that belong to gangs or some other kind of criminal organisation will tend to have a role/position in the hierarchy of that organisation. Their role – and as such the level of power, autonomy and profit that goes with it – will depend on where they sit in the hierarchy. Those at the top will have lots of each and those at the bottom far less. The television programme *The Wire* depicts numerous roles related to low-level street sales and shows those that act simply as lookouts (for example, for trouble from those they sell to and/or other sellers or law enforcement), those that act as runners (who 'run' with the cash and or the drugs to the seller/buyer), those that manage 'corners' or 'houses' and those that are backups. Brokers and facilitators are usually even more marginally involved and some 'traffickers' such as 'drug mules' (often women from poor countries who have been either enticed with the promise of earning large sums of money, blackmailed or even tricked into carrying drugs abroad) can often be ignorant of their involvement or ignorant of the seriousness of the offence. Mr Big drug dealers or nasty violent street dealers may predominate in representations but they are neither typical nor particularly informative of the roles involved in drug selling/trafficking.

DEALERS AS SOCIALLY SITUATED BEINGS RATHER THAN INHERENTLY EVIL

Understanding drug dealers as essentially 'bad' or 'evil' individuals and that involvement in supply activities necessarily translates into specific dealer activities such as cutting with dangerous substances, is as we have seen, both mistaken and unhelpful. Those that sell drugs do so for varying reasons: those that do so for little or no gain 'sorting' friends because they can; those that 'drift' into dealing because that is the lifestyle they have grown up into and been exposed to; those that prefer to sell to other drug users rather than commit other crimes such as burglary to feed their drug addiction, and those that see it as an opportunity to make money, among others.

Even for this latter group, however, those thought most likely to conform to the stereotype of the drug dealer, are diverse in values and approach and some researchers, such as Bourgois (1995) have chosen, rather than to define such individuals as bad, to understand their engagement with street culture, drug dealing and a host of other activities as examples of cultural resistance whereby dealing becomes one of the means acceptable to elevate themselves above the low-status, low-employment, low-life-chance context in which they have grown up.

Thus, once we understand that dealers differ we can understand that they are 'situated' by their class, gender, ethnicity, age, values and experiences in ways that show us that the drug dealer is not simply understood and therefore not a simply definable entity.

REFERENCES

Blum, R.H. and Associates (1972) *The Dream Sellers*. London: Jossey-Bass.
Bourgois, P. (1995) *In Search of Respect: Selling Crack in El Barrio*. New York: Cambridge.
Coomber, R. (2006) *Pusher Myths: Re-Situating the Drug Dealer*. London: Free Association Books.
Coomber, R. and Turnbull, P. (2007) 'Arenas of drug transaction: adolescent cannabis transactions in England – "social supply"', *Journal of Drug Issues*, 37 (4): 845–66.
Denton, B. (2001) *Dealing: Women in the Drug Economy*. Sydney: University of New South Wales Press.
Dorn, N., Murji, K. and South, N. (1992) *Traffickers: Drug Markets and Law Enforcement*. London: Routledge.
Kohn, M. (1992) *Dope Girls: The Birth of the British Underground*. London: Lawrence & Wisehart.
Parker, H., Aldridge, J. and Measham, F. (1998) *Illegal Leisure: The Normalisation of Adolescent Recreational Drug Use*. Adolescence and Society Series. London: Routledge.

34
Drug Markets: Difference and Diversity

In relation to illicit drugs the drug market is a commonly used term that is often imprecisely used. It can be used interchangeably to mean the global market in drug production, trafficking and sales that operates internationally, across any one

continent or nation or indeed in any one city or other smaller geographical loca-
tion. It can also refer to the market in particular substances and/or groups of
individuals. This section will focus on the drug market as it is typified within
developed western nations particularly those across Europe and North America.

STEREOTYPES

Popular media imagery of the drug market in Western societies tends to suggest
something that is fairly straightforward to understand, has just a few basic characteristics and is similar in form wherever it appears. Essentially, the Western drug
market is considered to be something riddled with violence and violent characters,
to have a strong hierarchical structure whereby a few organised crime bosses, gangs
or groups (for example, Chinese Triads; Italian Mafia; Columbian cartel members)
manage the distribution of drugs throughout their territories and where street
dealers push their drugs with impunity and earn large sums of money doing so. As
we shall see this stereotype is largely unhelpful as a way of understanding how
drug markets should be understood.

DRUG MARKET ORGANISATION: STRUCTURES, VIOLENCE AND ACTIVITIES

To start with we should disabuse ourselves of the idea that there is such a thing as
the drug market; an easily defined single entity into which all drug-related activity
neatly fits. The reality is that there are numerous drug markets (many of which
overlap and co-exist alongside each other) and any one drug market in any one
location will differ over time depending on a whole variety of factors that affect
how it is organised and how it operates. These differences will also affect the
extent to which any one market conforms, or doesn't conform to the stereotypes
mentioned above (Coomber, 2010).

Let us explore an example of how this difference, overlap and coexistence can work.
Imagine an inner-city suburb that has numerous substances being sold. Some sellers
will supply a range of substances but many only supply specific ones. Some sellers are
heroin and crack cocaine suppliers while others are more 'dance drug' orientated
(ecstasy, ketamine among others) while others specialise only in cannabis. Even this
can differ over time. Today it is common in the West (but not everywhere) for sellers
of heroin to also sell cocaine but this is a fairly recent occurrence and previously the
two markets were fairly distinct. Different substances tend to be sourced in different ways: some are imported from different regions of the world where different political, economic and cultural conditions exist and this can impact on *how*
the drugs are trafficked. Sourcing ecstasy tablets or cannabis from one part of
Europe to another may involve large consignments and highly organised systems
to manage and protect them but it commonly also involves small-scale consignments with individuals or small-scale collaborators with little by way of organisation or links to cartels or organised crime of any sort and to whom violence is not
the normal way to resolve conflict or operate. Likewise once drugs are in any one
nation or geographical area, depending on who sells them the drug market will
differ in form and activity and different groups (for example, gangs; individuals;

small franchises, etc.) can sell even within any single drug market (for example, ecstasy). All of these things impact on how any one drug market will work and as such not all drug markets have the same levels of violence or predatory activity they are assumed to have. They also all operate – each often not 'touching' the other – within the same geographical areas at the same time. An example of this would be where the supply of cannabis among (and largely between) young people in the UK appears to be almost completely separate from the adult 'drug market proper' (Coomber and Turnbull, 2007) or where in New York an adult cannabis market can operate separate to that of so-called harder drugs such as heroin (Curtis et al., 2002).

ORGANISED CRIME STRUCTURES AND MARKET CONTROL

The idea that there are 'Mr Bigs'; 'King Pins' or various crime syndicates (ethnically or otherwise based) essentially controlling the drug market from the top to the bottom is not supported by the research evidence – despite regular media and law enforcement assuming this and reporting to this effect. No doubt there are individuals and groups that have significant interests and maintain significant activity within various drug markets and sometimes these activities are managed with extreme levels of actual and threatened violence. There are probably also 'moments in time' or pockets of opportunity when less mature markets are developed and controlled by a few big players – as seems to be the case with the heroin market of North America in the1970s. Even this pattern, however, is far from an inevitable one as is evident by the way that the new heroin markets that emerged in the UK in the 1980s developed in a more fragmented and looser fashion.

For the sake of ease of understanding, there is a broad structure that is often depicted as a pyramid (a few 'big-time' actors at the top; a moderate number of mid-level operators that distribute between those at the top and those who make up the bulk at the bottom – the so-called 'street dealers', essentially those that sell to users) that has some use as depicting market shape. It fails to recognise, however, where small-scale individuals/groups can often be importers as well as street or lower-level sellers, or that sellers can move up and down the hierarchy over time. Thus, drug markets in Western countries in the 21st century are in fact better understood as constituted by a numerous actors/structures at the different levels of the drug market with 'control' over the market being a rarity rather than the norm.

'OPEN' AND 'CLOSED'

The most visible of drug markets are the open or 'street' markets. In such contexts street sellers may be obvious to those who know what they are looking out for, or sellers may whisper to passers-by that they believe to be users or on the look out to buy illicit drugs. Occasionally, as happened in New York City in the mid-to-late 1980s, street markets become so visible and prevalent that they seem to be openly flouting the law and can severely disrupt neighbourhoods.

For the most part however, street markets tend to be consigned to specific streets or areas and are now, in the developed nations of the West at least, less numerous than they once were. Increased police concentration on street markets and the development of technologies such as cheap disposable, non-traceable mobile communications have meant that it is safer to sell drugs by controlling both communication and location – by becoming less visible in a 'closed' market.

If open markets are effectively open to anyone who comes looking,[8] closed markets are characterised by a concern on the part of dealer to maintain some control over those they sell to. Sellers prefer to have a regular client base that they maintain and new customers usually need some kind of recommendation from someone the seller knows to reassure that they are who they say they are. Closed markets tend to have lesser levels of violence attached to them and are often less visible to the broader community.

STRUCTURED AND FRAGMENTED MARKETS

As stated above, the idea that drug markets are a rigidly structured market controlled by a few big players (be they individuals, crime syndicates or gangs) belies the fact that a picture of any one part of the market (for example, the cannabis market) will be made up of many types of seller and organisational shapes (for example, single importers/growers; friend-only sellers; groups of collaborators with no essential hierarchy; groups of collaborators with clear hierarchy; those that control a 'patch' or local area, and/or areas where there is almost no obvious control by any one group). Research suggests that on the whole drug markets are fragmented, disjointed and the various parts often only loosely connected – if at all.

Historical and geographical context will also play a part in terms of what the organisational picture looks like. In those areas where the drug trade was initiated by a particular group or groups that held a monopoly over supply – as occasionally happens – top down control can lead to predictable patterns of supply and consistent market practices. The monopoly can also produce inflated prices and poorer quality drugs due to lack of competition. The establishment of new markets and new competition however can, initially at least, lead to 'turf wars' and elevated violence until the market reaches some equilibrium. Even here, however, the level of violence reached can be influenced by numerous factors such as the criminal justice response and the culture of violence already embedded within the practices of those in the traditional market and those fostering the new one(s). Some research on rural (village, small town) heroin and cocaine markets in the UK has shown that in such contexts there is a tendency for them to conform only

---

[8]Within reason, dealers in open markets do try to control who they sell to as they have to be wary of undercover police. This control however usually means little more than feeling that they can simply 'know' when someone is a genuine client or an existing drug user by the way they talk, act and dress – a strategy that has led to many an arrested street dealer (Jacobs, 2000).

marginally to stereotypical views of drugs markets (Few et al., 2004). Sellers were commonly known (and had been for many years) to those they sold to, heroin-based market interaction was overwhelmingly social as opposed to business-like and the use of violence or the threat of it as a means to manage transactions was largely absent. Even within such small geographical spaces the existence of market separation (that is, between substances and sellers) was evident.

While the overall picture is one of fragmentation, it is also the case that some historical patterns of supply have emerged. In the USA and some other countries, for example, Hells Angels appear to have a consistent relationship with the manu-facture and supply of amphetamines, and various ethnic groups with links from producer countries often also reproduce patterns of supply with a racial, cultural or ethnic basis. The point to be made is that while we can see some of these pat-terns it is often unhelpful to see these patterns as exclusive behaviours. Ethnic and cultural groupings often do not act exclusively (that is, supplying to their own groups only nor predictably).

Some drug markets also appear to 'sit outside' the conventional drug market. In the UK, for example, the 'social supply' of recreational (mostly cannabis) drugs among friends and acquaintances means that most young cannabis users rarely come into contact with the real drug market itself.

TYPES OF DRUG AND MARKET TYPE

Certain drugs tend to be associated with different types of market, market dangers and organisation. As is common with drug-related issues, there is a tendency to overly attribute this difference to the pharmacology of the drugs in question. Cannabis markets have therefore been understood to – on the whole – be less violent than crack cocaine markets for this reason. The crack cocaine market of the mid- to late-1980s in New York City, for example, was associated with extreme levels of drug market violence, gun crime and murder whereas a later market involving various substances in the same city has been characterised by a rejection of guns and an approach to supply which is comparatively peaceful (Curtis et al., 2002) and the emergence of crack cocaine markets in other nations did not neces-sarily produce particularly violent markets.

While it is the case that the level of violence in drug markets *overall* is much greater than its occurrence in legal markets, this is in part a result of drug market structures (illegal trading in a market comprising significant numbers of crimi-nals) and culturally based responses by those occupying the market whose day-to-day practices involve problem resolution through cultures of violence. This does not mean, however, that being involved in drug selling or supply means either being routinely exposed to violence or committing it. The personnel dif-ferences in the drug market simply mean that *some* parts of the market and *some* actors are more likely to succumb to and/or perform violent acts than others. Given this, we also have to be wary of any assumption that all that is actually attributed to drug market violence is actually that. One study in a particularly notorious suburb of Sydney, Australia, for example, suggests that even in the most violent types of drug market the 'lived' experience of it for those at the sharp end of the drug market is often far less than assumed and the attempts by the same actors to avoid violent activity much greater than assumed (Coomber and Maher, 2006).

SUMMARY

Overall, we can say that drug markets do not routinely and consistently conform to the stereotypes of them so widely presented. They differ in make-up, personnel, structure and form. Their pattern can shift over time and they are subject to historical, geographical and circumstantial contexts. Each of these will affect the types of activity that take place, the interactions therein and the level of violence found there.

REFERENCES

Coomber, R. (2010) 'Reconceptualising drug markets and drug dealers – the need for change', *Drugs and Alcohol Today*, 10 (1): 10–13.

Coomber, R. and Maher, L. (2006) 'Street-level drug market activity in Sydney's primary heroin markets: organisation, adulteration practices, pricing, marketing and violence', *Journal of Drug Issues*, 36 (3): 719–54.

Coomber, R. and Turnbull, P. (2007) 'Arenas of drug transaction: adolescent cannabis transactions in England – "social supply"', *Journal of Drug Issues*, 37 (4): 845–66.

Curtis, R., Wendel, T. and Spunt, B. (2002) *We Deliver: The Gentrification of Drug Markets on Manhattan's Lower East Side*. Final Report. NCJRS. https://www.ncjrs.gov/pdffiles1/nij/grants/197716.pdf (accessed 12 July 2011).

Few, B., Turnbull, P.J., Duffy, M. and Hough, M. (2004) 'Drug markets in rural areas', unpublished report. London: Home Office.

35
Drug Trafficking

Drug trafficking refers to the movement and supply of illicit drugs for gain. Drugs initially have to be made (plants cultivated, products produced/synthesised) and then they have to be transported to their various destinations where they will be consumed. Those that export and import drugs and transport them within and beyond nations are called drug traffickers. Those that sell drugs to consumers are more commonly understood as drug dealers (see also **33 drug dealers***).*

INTERNATIONAL TRAFFICKING ACTIVITY – THE BIG PICTURE

Most of the drugs that are trafficked originate in the poorer countries of the world and most of the consumption of trafficked substances takes place in the world's more affluent nations (77 per cent of all drug sales taking place in the USA [44 per cent] and Europe [33 per cent] in 2003). Although those that produce the crops from which drugs such as heroin and cocaine derive, for example, peasant farmers in Bolivia, Peru, Afghanistan, Myanmar (formerly Burma), do so to earn better returns than if they were to grow legal crops, they still tend to receive relatively little in return for their efforts and so mostly remain in relative poverty/ low income difficulties while in some cases they may even be coerced into growing such crops. The real money to be made is in the trafficking and distribution of drugs beyond the borders of where they were produced to where there is demand and consumption – particularly to the advanced industrial nations of the West. Because the trafficking of drugs is both illegal and hugely lucrative (in 2005 the United Nations reported the global drug trade to be worth around US$321.6 billion, a figure higher than the GDP of over 80 nations) it is often associated with high levels of violence (see also **20 drugs-related violence**) and organised crime, particularly in source countries such as Columbia and Mexico where drug cartels vie for power over the markets and where many tens of thousands have been killed, but also down through the chain of distribution to the point of final sale in countries around the world. It is also associated – owing to bribery and the large sums of money circulating – with corruption of police and government officials (particularly in the so-called narco-states of Tajikistan and Afghanistan), but even the USA has had its fair share of drug-related corruption cases.

OPIATES/HEROIN

Most of the world's opiates/heroin now originates from Afghanistan (up to 89 per cent in 2009) and Myanmar. Afghanistan and Myanmar produced around 7200 metric tons of heroin in 2009 (UNODC, 2009). Production in Myanmar, previously the world's biggest producer, has dropped in recent years by nearly one-half and this has had the effect of increasing the relative proportions produced by Afghanistan and Mexico. Mexico is currently the third largest producer followed by Columbia. Most of the opiates produced in Afghanistan are then trafficked to and consumed in nearby Republic of Iran, Pakistan, other Central Asian countries and India where the market (approximately 5 million) is three and a half times larger than that in the West and Central Europe (approximately 1.4 million). Prices, however, are much higher in Western Europe and as such these markets have acted as a huge incentive for trafficking from Afghanistan via Iran and Pakistan and then along the 'Balkan route' towards Central and Western Europe. North America receives most of its heroin from Mexico and Columbia while countries such as Australia and New Zealand see theirs arriving on a south-east trajectory from Afghanistan and Myanmar through various Asian routes.

COCAINE

Despite some worldwide reduction in production in recent years, production remains relatively high with availability affected moderately. This is evidenced by an upward creep in relation to price and downward trend relating to purity indicating a slight squeeze on availability. Production is concentrated in countries down the north-western and mid-western side of South America. In 2009 Columbia was comfortably the world's biggest producer of coca bushes followed by Peru and Bolivia, respectively. Global production of cocaine in 2008 is estimated to have been around 845 metric tons (Columbia – 430 mt; Peru – 303 mt; Bolivia – 109 mt). The proportion of cocaine seizures or interceptions to manufacture is around 40 per cent and is mainly due to more concentrated efforts in the countries of production. Seizures outside of those countries, for example, in Europe are at the same low level (around 11 per cent) found for other drugs. Trafficking can also impact upon use and some emerging data suggests that 'transit countries' in Africa – particularly those in the west and south of the continent – are experiencing growth patterns. Other growing markets are in Oceania, particularly Australia and New Zealand, where growth doubled between 2003 and 2006.

CANNABIS AND AMPHETAMINE-TYPE SUBSTANCES

Cannabis and amphetamine-type substances (ATS) production differs from heroin and cocaine production in a number of ways, such as geographical production, ethnicity/nationalities heavily involved and in terms of domestic production and the amounts produced. Cannabis is easily the most consumed drug in the world and production estimates range from between 13,300–66,100 metric tons for cannabis leaf and 2200–9900 metric tons for cannabis resin (UNODC, 2009). Cannabis is grown globally and suitable conditions for its cultivation exist in most continents. At least 172 different countries have reported some cultivation in recent years but many others no doubt also contribute to worldwide production. Somewhat surprisingly the fact that cannabis cultivation is so widespread has led to both the 2006 and the 2009 World Drug Reports relating this as the reason as to why so little is known about its cultivation in any detail. Major producing and trafficking nations for cannabis, however, are the Netherlands, South Africa, Jamaica, Paraguay, Morocco, Afghanistan, Columbia, Nigeria and Lebanon but other countries such as the USA also produce significant yields but mainly service their own and each other's populations. Many other countries could be listed but there is little other available data.

ATS production in 2007 was estimated to be roughly between 300 and 780 million tons. Of this roughly 230–640 million tons was of the amphetamines group and 72–137 million tons to be of the ecstasy group. Being product manufactured ATS can be made almost anywhere for little cost. Laboratories in which they are made can be moved around or abandoned and new ones set up with relative ease. Because of the ability for ATS to be produced anywhere most trafficking and distribution, when compared to other controlled substances, is relatively local and this abrogates the need for riskier trafficking beyond borders (other than those nearby and easily accessible). Seizure success rates – as with most substances – is relatively low between 6 per cent and 19 per cent.

DOMESTIC PRODUCTION

Although, as we have seen, a lot of trafficking has historically related to trafficking from source countries to where demand is, an increasing amount of production and distribution now takes place within the countries of consumption themselves. Cannabis in the USA is cultivated and grown in enormous quantities and is estimated to be the fourth largest cash crop behind only corn, hay and soybeans but ahead of tobacco, wheat and cotton. In nine states it is the number one cash crop – despite the fact that growing it is illegal. Much of this cultivation will be relatively organised but home cultivation (that is, grown indoors, in the loft or basement with specialist – but cheaply and easily available – hydroponic equipment) of cannabis is a growing phenomenon in many countries around the world. Given that large sections of the cannabis market already sit outside the conventional drug market (see also **34 drug market**) this trend will reinforce that and make managing trafficking harder still.

Drugs such as heroin and cocaine still need to be trafficked across borders to reach the developed nations of the West (but of course for the large numbers of domestic consumers within their own borders this is not the case). Other drugs, however, particularly those synthetically produced, are drugs potentially synthesised/produced within any nation where the materials needed to do so are available. Many ATS are produced locally and they also tend to have less of an ethnically based origin and may be associated more with localised gangs or independents. In relation to amphetamine production in Australia this has been the case for some time.

Criminal justice organisations do regularly control, and with varying success, access to the various materials needed to make such drugs, but new drugs are synthesised regularly and domestic production of various legal and illegal psychoactive substances continues to be of concern to drug control organisations.

NARCO STATES AND CORRUPTION OF FORMAL AGENCIES AND ORGANISATIONS

A 'narco state' is a nation where drug trafficking heavily influences decisions, both political and economic, to facilitate the successful trade of illicit drugs. Corruption will exist at numerous levels: central government; local government; the military; the police and will 'pollute' the systems of government to such an extent that trafficking can become integral to the support and income of large sections of the population in a narco state. When this happens it is extremely difficult – as in Tajikistan – to reverse the situation. Other countries, such as Columbia, Mexico and Peru (among others), while not being narco states have, over many years suffered from high levels of corruption at various levels of government and enforcement and as such have had effective efforts to control production and trafficking stymied and/or purposively undermined.

key concepts in
drugs and society

HOW IS TRAFFICKING ORGANISED

Just as with have seen with drug dealing and drug dealers (see also **33 drug dealers**) both trafficking and traffickers vary. Some trafficking will be the result of highly organised cartels or other forms of organised criminal syndicate. At other times drugs will be produced and distributed by small firms or groups or even individuals. Large-scale trafficking and seizures of containers holding many tons certainly grab the headlines but smaller quantities of drugs are also trafficked in lorries; cars and motorbikes; in packages sent by post (drugs have been concealed in letters, children's toys, famous bands' instrument cases, in famous and non-famous works of art – in just about anything you can imagine) or carried.

Just as trafficking profits tend not to benefit those that grow or produce drugs to the same degree as those more organised, there are many involved in the literal transportation of drugs (as opposed to those that buy and trade the drugs and organise for their transportation), the couriers and carriers that also often benefit little for their part in the activity. Just as the growers sometimes suffer disproportionately compared to the traffickers (by having their crops poisoned and their livelihoods destroyed by crop eradication, (see also **36 crop eradication, crop substitution and legal cultivation**) couriers, who are far more often caught, are severely punished as traffickers. This disparity is perhaps most exemplified by couriers, usually acting as individuals and sometimes known as 'mules' who have often either been tricked into carrying drugs abroad, have been pressurised into it or in some cases do not understand the gravity of what they are doing. Many of these couriers are women – usually from poor families in developing countries – who have swallowed 'balloons' of drugs (for example, contained in condoms and the like) and attempt to traffic by passenger travel (air and sea). There are far too many ways that drugs are trafficked to be outlined here but it is estimated that less than 20 per cent of trafficked drugs is intercepted.

SUCCESSES

The level of success in the war on drugs (see also **37 war on drugs**) to reduce trafficking or drug use is marginal at best, as has been outlined elsewhere in this book. In terms of its own criteria for success the war on drugs has failed miserably as trafficking and access to drugs has grown enormously since The Hague Convention in 1914 first attempted to prevent the traffic and sale of substances considered appropriate to come under strict control. Drugs are generally easier for users to acquire and are also much cheaper than they used to be. In recent years we can see the dual processes of some decline in drug use in developed nations and an increase in drug use in other parts of the world. The decreases, it is widely accepted, are not down to successes in the prevention of trafficking and the increases continue to coincide in part with increasing ease of access and relative drops in prices.

REFERENCE

UNODC (2009) *The World Drug Report*. Vienna: The United Nations Office on Drugs and Crime.

35 drug trafficking

Crop Eradication, Crop Substitution and Legal Cultivation

Crop eradication, crop substitution and legal cultivation are 'supply-side' policies pursued as part of the global drug prohibition regime. Supply-side policies such as crop eradication focus on 'producer countries' in an attempt to disrupt the global trade in illegal substances at its source.

CROP ERADICATION: THE HUMAN AND ENVIRONMENTAL CONSEQUENCES

Crop eradication involves burning, cutting down or spraying crops with pesticides to kill them. Crop eradication aims to make the cultivation of illegal crops, such as cannabis, coca and opium poppy, unattractive for local farmers and rural workers. It has been argued by some that crop eradication through aerial fumigation by 'spray planes' has had limited success which has come at a high price in terms of human rights violations and environmental damage alongside increasing conflict and militarisation (see below) within countries such as Bolivia, Columbia and Peru (the Andean region) and Afghanistan (Youngers and Rosin 2005). Putting such issues aside, it is hard to pinpoint the specific impact that crop eradication programmes have in reducing illegal crop cultivation and disrupting trafficking routes. In Andean region producer nations Bolivia, Columbia and Peru, which have been host to numerous crop eradication programmes, coca cultivation has remained remarkably stable between 2003 and 2011, with the share of cultivation fluctuating between the three countries as crop displacement occurs (UNODC, 2011). Cannabis, cocaine and heroin, the products of illegal crops, remain widely available and in demand around the world.

Environmentalists have consistently condemned crop eradication, particularly indiscriminate fumigation such as that carried out against coca in Columbia. Substantial ecological damage has occurred either directly as a result of eradication, such as pollution caused by long-lasting and virulent herbicides, or indirectly as a result of the displacement or 'balloon' effect of eradication efforts (Rouse and Arce, 2006). Deforestation has occurred within Peru's national parks as coca cultivation has displaced from Columbia to its neighbour, following US-funded crop eradication efforts between 2000 and 2011. Concentrating on efforts to undermine the production of coca in South America, Bastos et al. (2007) note that aggregated coca acreage has not been decreasing, but instead has been displaced to other areas, with overall acreage remaining stable. Large acreage coca farms have also been replaced with multiple small acreage coca farms, in some cases causing the deforestation of previously 'virgin' areas, as new access roads are built. It is estimated that for every acre of coca destroyed in southern Columbia, three acres of Amazon rainforest are cut down to replace them.

Given the poorest are often totally dependent on the land, damage to their local environment has devastating effects. The international harm reduction community has highlighted how crop eradication policies situated within the broader **37 war on drugs** and counter-terrorist activities of the West have also resulted in human displacement, often involving 'intrastate' population movements as seen in Columbia and more recently Afghanistan, Mexico and Pakistan. Civilians are driven from their homes by armed conflict between allied forces, state military forces, paramilitary organisations and insurgent groups, some or all of whom may be involved in the drug trade. As Barrett (2010) notes, 'internally displaced peoples' (IDP) leaving their homes as a result of crop fumigation and/or manual crop eradication are rarely entitled to social welfare, making their numbers hard to estimate, although IDPs are thought to be in the millions in Columbia alone. Aside from human displacement, human rights activists have also expressed disquiet about the tendency to disregard legal principles and local elected officials' concerns during the implementation of crop eradication (notably aerial fumigation) strategies over the past 30 years, thus undermining the rule of law, government authority and ultimately democratic processes, including the reform of weak civil institutions.

Opium crop eradication in Afghanistan can usefully be considered in the context of the war on drugs and the war on terror, given that human rights violations have been perpetrated in the service of both wars by allied forces and insurgent groups alike. There remains a tension between the USA/UK foreign policy goal of rebuilding Afghanistan as an embryonic democracy to emerge from the war on terror and the USA/UK war on drugs policy of reducing if not eradicating the production of opium poppy within the region. With Afghanistan accounting for the majority of the world's opium supply, reducing poppy cultivation has become an integral aspect of military success in the region. However, as in the Andean region, those who suffer disproportionately from such policies tend to be poor rural populations. Poor farmers and their families suffer in terms of being subject to violence and intimidation from insurgent groups if they do not or cannot produce opium poppy crops. Poor rural populations may also experience alienation in the face of destitution following crop destruction, rendering them vulnerable to militant groups offering an alternative to financial ruin.

CROP SUBSTITUTION

Crop substitution aims to make other crops such as wheat, plantains or palm hearts more attractive to farmers than cannabis, coca leaf or opium poppy. Crop substitution appears to be a less harmful policy alternative to aerial fumigation or manual crop eradication, although only if implemented sensitively. International development agencies and human rights organisations have highlighted the importance of *sequencing*, with development policies needing to be in place *prior* to crop eradication/substitution activities to support farmers and rural workers in pursuing their livelihoods through other crops or different forms of labour. Nonetheless, efforts to curb illegal crop cultivation have concentrated on funding military interventions, while social and economic development interventions in 'producer nations' such as Columbia have remained severely underfunded and largely unsupported by successive US administrations. Without broader development strategies in place such as support for education, health services, infrastructure building and enterprise support, both crop substitution and crop eradication programmes remain problematic.

For Afghanistan's rural poor, alternative development in the form of opium poppy crop substitution has not been forthcoming. Illegal crop farmers remain susceptible to market forces, which in turn can undermine crop substitution efforts. It is difficult to find crops or other rural activities that generate similar or greater incomes to those generated by illicit crops. The gross income per hectare for opium crops has plummeted since 2003, yet opium poppy cultivation remains an attractive option compared to wheat, which generates only one-third of the income produced by opium. Alternative harvests may take longer than native (illegal) harvests such as coca to mature. Hence, alternatives are available but remain unattractive to subsistence farmers. Finally, there is evidence that Afghan farmers are co-cultivating or displacing to other illegal crops such as cannabis in the face of the Western allies' focus on opium.

LEGAL CULTIVATION IN THE 'NARCO-TERRORIST' ERA

Effectively the global war on drugs has become interwoven with the war on terror in South-Central Asia, forming part of the democratic nation-building ambitions of Western liberal democracies. It is increasingly presupposed that one war cannot be successful without the other. The militarisation of drug prohibition enforcement, exemplified by the US military funding of both public and private counter-drug and counter-terror forces active within many drug producer nations, is testimony to how the two wars are often assumed to be focused on the 'same' enemy, previously the 'narcoguerilla' and more recently the 'narcoterrorist'. The war on drugs/war on terror closes down consideration of alternatives to crop eradication and crop substitution, such as a legal licensing scheme enabling Afghan's poppy yields to be turned into legal analgesics such as morphine and codeine; substances for which there is considerable demand, not least in Afghanistan itself (ICOS, 2007). Currently the production of licit opium for painkillers is concentrated in India, Turkey, Australia, France, Spain and the UK, under the watch of the International Narcotics Control Body (INCB) and to the profit of large multinational pharmaceutical companies, such as GlaxoSmithKline who supplies 25 per cent of the world's opiate from poppies grown in Australia. A move from illegal to legal production of Afghan opium is perhaps unsurprisingly contrary to the USA and indeed the UNODC's stance, both of which support indiscriminate crop spraying in the region as part of the war on drugs/war on terror. The UK is similar in its position, arguing that security needs to be brought to the region before any consideration of licit opium production can be undertaken. It has been argued that Western allies, pursuing the global prohibition regime which generates an illicit drug market regulated by violent entrepreneurs while under-investing in development policies in South-Central Asia, are effectively condemning Afghanistan (alongside Pakistan and Iran) to 'rogue nation' status, whether or not the Western allied forces are ever successful in their fight against the Taliban and Al Qaeda (Mena and Hobbs, 2010).

Crop eradication, whether via aerial fumigation or via manual eradication, has many critics. Crop substitution does seem to offer a less harmful alternative, not least to 'producer nations', their farmers and the local environment, but again is not without its detractors. Other alternatives have little support in the West; the development of an Afghan industry in legal opium production, for example, looks unlikely in the face of powerful opposition from the USA, the UNODC and International Narcotics Control Board (INCB). The current status quo is likely to continue at least in the medium term.

REFERENCES

Barrett, D. (2010) 'Security, development and human rights: normative, legal and policy challenge for the international drug control system', *International Journal of Drug Policy*, 21 (2): 140–44.

Bastos, I., Caiaffa, W., Rossi, D., Vila, M. and Malta, M. (2007) 'The children of mama coca: coca, cocaine and the fate of harm reduction in South America', *International Journal of Drug Policy*, 18 (2): 99–106.

ICOS (2007) *Poppy for Medicine: Licensing Poppy Cultivation for the Production of Essential Medicines: An Integrated Counter-Narcotics, Development and Counter-Insurgency Model for Afghanistan.* Brussels: The International Council on Security and Development.

Mena, F. and Hobbs, D. (2010) 'Narcophobia: drugs prohibition and the generation of human rights abuses', *Trends in Organised Crime*, 13: 60–74.

Rouse, S. and Arce, M. (2006) 'The drug-laden balloon: U.S. military assistance and coca production in the central Andes', *Social Science Quarterly*, 87 (3): 540–56.

UNODC (2011) *Plurinational State of Bolivia: Coca Cultivation Survey.* Vienna: United Nations Office of Drugs and Crime.

Youngers, C.A. and Rosin, E. (eds) (2005) *Drugs and Democracy in Latin America: The Impact of US Policy.* Boulder, CO: Lynne Reinner.

37
War on Drugs

The 'war on drugs' describes the controversial rhetoric used to elicit support for repressive drug prohibition policies by those for whom drug use is inherently problematic. The war on drugs has profoundly shaped national and international approaches to the cultivation, production, distribution and use of those substances deemed to be 'dangerous'.

The war on drugs is one of the defining discourses of the 20th century and beyond. In June 1971, US President Richard Nixon officially declared a war on drugs following a campaign to implement a national anti-drug strategy at state and federal levels. This declaration was the culmination of a gradual development of prohibition as the dominant drug control system over the previous 100 years (see also **30 international drug control history/prohibition**). Since then successive US administrations, including those headed by President Reagan and President George W. Bush, have pursued the war on drugs both rhetorically and practically. In the USA and the many other countries pursuing the war, we have witnessed government spending on anti-drug efforts with little or no accompanying assessment of policy impact; the creeping militarisation of anti-drug activities; ever-increasing arrest rates for drug offenders; increasingly draconian legislation to deal with drug offenders; imbalances in the racial and ethnic composition of those arrested and charged with drug offences; and the mass incarceration of drug offenders.

Critics of the war on drugs have highlighted the ways in which the term 'war' invokes a permanent state of emergency (as with the war on terror) used to justify military expenditure and paramilitary interventions which would not be deemed acceptable in 'peacetime'. Other critics have noted that the war on drugs is not simply propaganda, but amounts instead to a real war waged with a vengeance by governments predominately against their own citizens, particularly the poor, and people of colour. This point is raised in answer to hard-right conservative critics in the USA who maintain that the drug war has not been 'lost' but just has not been fought hard enough, with countries enforcing brutal drug laws, such as Iran and China, held up as examples of what should be done to drug users in the Western world. Supporters of the war on drugs argue that more resources are needed to 'win' the war, but it remains questionable as to whether increased resources would have the desired effect (in light of huge sums previously spent and currently allocated).

THE USA LEADS THE GLOBAL WAR ON DRUGS

Advocates of the war on drugs have succeeded in criminalising the cultivation, production, distribution and possession of a wide range of intoxicants, including amphetamines, cannabis, cocaine, heroin and ecstasy. A growing number of substances are being made illegal across national and international jurisdictions. Militaristic interventions, such as the use of paramilitary-style special weapons and tactics (SWAT) raids on homes of drug offence suspects in the USA have become typical of the war on drugs waged on the domestic front, where drug users are dealt with predominately as criminals. Military campaigns are also waged against drug producers and traffickers, often with financial support from the USA. In 2000 alone, for example, US President Clinton gave US$1.3 billion under Plan Columbia to the then Columbian President to fund combat helicopters and training for the Columbian military to tackle coca cultivation and cocaine production (see also **36 crop eradication, crop substitution and legal cultivation**).

The USA continues to be one of the strongest advocators and pursuers of the war on drugs on both national and international fronts. Federal investment in the war has predominately been in terms of law enforcement rather than on treatment for those dependent on illicit drugs, for example. The war on drugs has played a central role in the development of the US penal system, not least the system's highly racialised nature and increased incarceration rates. There remain significant socio-economic, racial and ethnic imbalances in terms of who is affected by the US war on drugs. Black drug users in poor areas of the USA, for example, are far more likely to be apprehended and incarcerated than white drug users in wealthier areas (Tonry and Melewski, 2008).

IS THE WAR ON DRUGS WORKING?

Much has been written on the failure of the war on drugs. It is useful to consider the principal objectives of those who advocate or support the war on drugs approach in order to access whether it may be deemed a success or failure. Underpinning the war on drugs approach is the aim to produce a 'drug-free world', supported by tough anti-drugs crusades such as US First Lady Nancy Reagan's infamous 'Just Say No' campaign launched in 1984. Hence it is often suggested that any reductions in drug use prevalence patterns across national populations point to the success of the war on drugs. However, it is difficult to pinpoint the reason for changes in drug use prevalence, with changes as likely to spring from the vagaries of drug 'fashions' than as a direct result of the war on drugs. Drug war supporters argue that prohibition reduces drug production, distribution and ultimately availability, while criminalising substances discourages initiation or provides an incentive for current users to abstain. Contrary evidence suggests, however, that production, distribution, availability and the use of **7 common illicit drugs** has for the most part remained stable or increased under global prohibition. When substances have been banned, use often continues or even increases. Such evidence is taken by drug war supporters that an escalation of the war is needed, with even stricter controls advocated.

One of the key objectives of the war on drugs is to disrupt the supply of drugs in global, national and local markets. Supply disruption, it is argued, would lead to a rise in drug prices as drugs became less available (that is, scarce commodities). A rise in price, it is assumed, leads to a lessening of demand for drugs as people struggle to afford them, although rises in street prices can simply mean higher profit margins for drug producers and drug sellers if demand does not lessen. However, generally speaking the street prices of illegal drugs have not risen or have actually fallen. Neither has demand for drugs fallen. More than 200 million people (about 5 per cent of the world's population) worldwide continue to take illegal drugs, a figure which has increased over the past decade (UNODC, 2011a). There is some evidence of demand stabilisation in the developed world. War on drugs advocates in the USA point to evidence of falling rates of illegal drug use, although this varies depending on the drug and the drug users in question, with problematic drug use continuing to rise or be maintained at high levels. In developing countries demand is rising substantially, notably for amphetamine-type substances (ATS) (UNODC, 2011b). Interdiction (law enforcement) efforts have largely failed to stem the global flow of illegal drugs. Even during a successful year of cocaine supply disruption such as that claimed by the UK's Serious Organised Crime Agency (SOCA) in 2009, street prices and demand did not fall, although there were indications that purity levels dropped dramatically. Indeed, successful supply reduction may result in greater use of cutting agents as drug dealers seek to 'bulk out' their products to maintain profitability.

What of counter arguments that the war on drugs should be replaced by a system of global drug regulation? Drug war supporters believe that any alternative form of regulation aside from complete prohibition will inevitably lead to increased availability and increased use. Campaigners against ending the war on cannabis users, for example, maintain that as a so-called gateway drug (see also **19 the gateway hypothesis/stepping stone theory**), any capitulation on cannabis would inevitably lead to increased drug use per se. However, it remains unclear whether drug policies are able to have such a profound effect on user behaviours (Reuter and Stevens, 2007). Comparative research was undertaken with cannabis users in Amsterdam, where personal cannabis use is decriminalised, and San Francisco, where personal cannabis use is criminalised (Reinarman et al., 2004). The study found little difference between cannabis users in the two cities in terms of age at onset, frequency and quantity of use over time, intensity and duration of intoxication and patterns across the drug career such as periods of desistance. However, 'other drug use' was higher in San Francisco than in Amsterdam. It remains unclear from comparative research whether national drug policies are the principal factor determining drug-user behaviour or whether there are other factors involved, such as informal social controls within drug-using cultures or the specific nature of localised drug law enforcement activities.

Despite the war efforts, producing and distributing illegal drugs remains a hugely profitable business. In this sense it has been suggested that the hardest disruption for illegal drug producers and distributors to deal with would be an end to the global war on drugs and a move towards the global regulation of drugs as legal commodities. Room and Paglia (1999) argue that while the international drug control system which pursues prohibition is seen largely as a failure, notably in terms of reducing the numbers of people using (illicit) substances, the broader rhetorical war on drugs has been a successful mechanism for rallying consensus and solidarity, for example, between the USA and Russia in the post-Cold War era. Illegal drugs and drug producers/traffickers are now considered 'suitable enemies' of nation states and international regimes, while within individual countries' criminal justice systems, drug dealers and users are often subject to levels of surveillance and control not seen in other areas of crime and punishment. In the USA, federal statutes effectively impose what are called 'collateral consequences' on drug offenders, such as loss of drivers' licenses, student loans and other educational benefits, alongside bans on access to public housing and food stamps.

SUMMARY

The hotly contested global war on drugs continues into the 21st century, although there does appear to be some appetite for a change to the current status quo. Perhaps most significantly, Latin American countries such as Mexico and Argentina have denounced the war on drugs' economic and social costs and acted to effectively decriminalise personal use of marijuana, cocaine and heroin (see also **40 decriminalisation, legalisation and legal regulation**), although they are continuing with their military-style battle with drug cartels following intense pressure from the USA to do so. This suggests a potential shift from a war on drug users to an escalation of the war on drug suppliers. Nonetheless, the various harms that result from the war on drugs to civilian populations caught in the cross-fire between drug suppliers and state authorities will continue.

Proponents, who still dominate drug debates, argue that giving up on the war would have calamitous short- and long-term effects on individuals, communities and countries. Detractors point to the harmful effects of the war on the environment and biodiversity; on nation states, specifically producer countries such as Afghanistan (opium/heroin) and Columbia (coca/cocaine); on local ethnic communities, for example US African-American inner-city dwellers; and on individuals, notably intravenous drug users who remain marginalised and stigmatised by the war. It remains questionable whether framing the 'problem' of drug use in contemporary society as a 'war' is the most humane way forward, particularly as war on drugs rhetoric and policies also typically entails a war on drug users (Buchanan and Young, 2000). Indeed, a criticism of the repressive policies against drug users characteristic of the war on drugs is that they are harm inducing rather than harm reducing, resulting in more damage to the user without satisfactorily tackling drug problems on either an individual or a societal level.

REFERENCES

Buchanan, J. and Young, L. (2000) 'The war on drugs: a war on drug users?', *Drugs: Education, Prevention and Policy*, 7 (4): 409–22.

Reinarman, C., Cohen, P. and Kaal, H. (2004) 'The limited relevance of drug policy: cannabis in Amsterdam and in San Francisco', *American Journal of Public Health*, 94 (5): 836–42.

Reuter, P. and Stevens, A. (2007) *An Analysis of UK Drug Policy: A Monograph Prepared for the UK Drug Policy Commission*. London: UK Drug Policy Commission.

Room, R. and Paglia, A. (1999) 'The international drug control system in the post-cold war era: managing markets or fighting a war?', *Drug and Alcohol Review*, 18 (3): 305–15.

Tonry, M. and Melewski, M. (2008) 'The malign effects of drug and crime control policies on Black Americans', *Crime and Justice*, 37 (1): 1–44.

UNODC (2011a) *Amphetamines and Ecstasy: 2011 Global ATS Assessment*. Vienna: United Nations Office on Drugs and Crime.

UNODC (2011b) *World Drug Report 2011*. Vienna: United Nations Office on Drugs and Crime.

Drug Testing in Schools and Workplaces

The laboratory analysis of biological markers to detect the presence of particular drugs.

Various technologies have been developed to identify individuals who have consumed drugs. These technologies involve the collection of bodily fluids or hair whereby specimens are used to test for the presence of one or more drugs. Although urinalysis remains the most common method of drug testing, drug use can also be detected through blood, oral fluids (for example, saliva), perspiration and hair. Drug tests are limited in that they cannot determine drug addiction or dependency. Nor is drug testing able to decipher the dosage (for example, amount consumed) or extent (for example, one-time versus daily use) of drug use. Additionally, urinalysis in particular is generally restricted to the detection of recent drug use, that is, consumption during the past 48–72 hours.

DRUG TESTING IN SCHOOLS

Under the threefold guise of prevention, intervention and safety, surveillance of school pupils has increased in the USA, where some schools have introduced procedures to detect drugs and weapons. These procedures include metal detectors, random searches, on-site police officers, sniffer dogs and drug testing. The last has been used to detect drug use among student athletes since 1995 when the US Supreme Court ruled that the practice was constitutional. A second high court ruling in 2002 authorised the use of drug testing among students who participate in extracurricular school activities. Testing can also occur when school officials 'reasonably suspect' (for example, by observing erratic behaviour) that a pupil has engaged in drug use. The legalities of drug testing all students enrolled in a particular school have not yet been examined by the US Supreme Court.

Outside the USA, few countries have implemented drug testing in schools. In Europe, drug testing is used to some extent in schools in Sweden, Norway and Finland, although in general the schemes are not used systematically and tests must be conducted by health care professionals. In other European countries (for example, Ireland, the UK), decisions to implement drug-testing schemes are made by individual schools, which also have the responsibility for funding the initiatives. Implementation is rare, however, a pilot drug-testing scheme in England (Kent) was introduced in 2005. The scheme was described as a success after one swab of 270 was returned as positive. However, a through evaluation was not conducted and plans to introduce a county-wide programme were cancelled when not one school agreed to participate. Elsewhere, plans are underway for a voluntary drug-testing programme in selected secondary schools in Hong Kong.

DRUG TESTING IN WORKPLACES

In the work sector, drug testing is promoted as a means of maximising productivity and offering greater safety for employees. Workplace drug testing can be traced to the 1960s when US military personnel were screened for drug use. The idea was embraced by former US President Ronald Reagan who extended the policy of drug testing to US federal employees. His 1986 Executive Order served as the foundation for the Drug-Free Workplace Act 1988. Currently the Act extends to organisations in receipt of federal monies over a minimum amount. Workplace drug testing can occur prior to employment whereby positive drug tests can be used to prevent hiring. Testing is also used after employment commences.

Within a decade of the 1988 Act, the use of drug testing in the USA had spread to private workplace settings and the vast majority of large US employers had introduced screening of job applicants or had a policy of drug testing employees. A substantial number of legal cases were put forward to challenge workplace drug testing, however the judiciary in the USA tended to side with employers. In the USA, an estimated 30 to 40 million job applicants and employees were tested for drugs in 2007 (Walsh, 2008). Advocates of the policy have argued that drug testing is important for increasing productivity among employees and securing a safe work environment.

In general, the US objective of 'drug-free workplaces' has not expanded to other countries. The strong influence of trade unions is one reason why workplace drug testing has not become widespread in Europe (Pierce, 2007). It is generally confined to the transportation industry or other safety-critical work sector, although debates have surfaced in some European countries with regard to drug testing other employees. Still, pre-employment drug testing is not permitted in some nations (for example, the Netherlands). Some reports have suggested that workplace drug testing is increasing in the UK although the availability of recent data is limited. Workplace drug testing continues to be controversial in Canada, where the issue has been addressed by courts and tribunals. The consensus to date suggests that random drug testing in workplaces is not permissible, even for safety-sensitive employment. Canadian employers must demonstrate a high standard of justification for testing, which few have been able to do.

EFFECTIVENESS OF DRUG TESTING

To date, relatively few studies have investigated the impact of drug testing on school pupils' use of drugs. Most research has been plagued with methodological difficulties. For example, in the absence of a controlled experimental design it is difficult to determine whether changes in students' drug use are linked to the introduction of drug testing. Moreover, research often relies on students' self-reported drug use, and students may under-report drug use when they are concerned that revealing drug use may result in penalty. Still, a study by Goldberg et al. (2007) found similar rates of drug use between student athletes who underwent drug testing and student athletes who were not exposed to drug testing. The US federally funded study (Koski, 2004) had earlier sparked a wave of controversy with regards to research ethics, for example, informed consent and a vulnerable sample of minors.

Although workplace drug testing might reduce employee drug use, measures of employee drug use are often limited to self-report data. In political climates where zero-tolerance is paramount and workers fear reprisal, under-reporting drug use is a rational response. Research that relies on indicators of work absenteeism, productivity and injury is limited because several factors other than employee drug testing can contribute to these outcomes. In the UK, a review by the Independent Inquiry into Drug Testing at Work found no evidence that drug testing deterred drug use among employees. In contrast to US policy, the UK review concluded that workplaces should not have the authority to 'police' people's private lives. Although recognising the concern for safety in the workplace, the Inquiry found that strategies other than drug testing can be more effective, less expensive and less likely to invade employee privacy. In Australia, workplace drug testing has been described as a 'reasonable' option only for jobs that are safety-sensitive (Roche et al., 2008).

DRAWBACKS OF DRUG TESTING

There are several limitations associated with drug testing in schools and workplaces. First, the accuracy of testing devices varies considerably. False positives occur when a test erroneously indicates that a drug has been consumed. These outcomes can result in negative stigma and labelling (for example, identifying an individual as a 'drug user'), punishment or sanction (for example, refusing to hire an individual) as well as loss of confidence (for example, being falsely accused). Estimates from Australia have suggested that an estimated 10 per cent of school pupils would falsely test positive for drugs even when the testing devices were deemed to show an acceptable standard of validity (Roche et al., 2008). In contrast, false negatives refer to test results that fail to show drug use when a drug has been consumed. A potential consequence is that people who might need help with a drug problem may not be identified. Various sources provide information and products designed to show false negatives. These sources include Internet websites, other media and 'head' shops.

Second, school pupils, job applicants and employees who are faced with drug testing may engage in drug 'switching', whereby they desist from using drugs that are tested by the organisation, and switch to other substances that are not tested. Third, the financial and social costs of drug testing are high. A policy of drug testing can alienate pupils and workers and can contribute to low morale. At some US universities, non-academic job applicants are subjected to pre-employment drug testing whereas academic applicants are exempt. Such regulatory differences were enacted because of perceived difficulties in recruiting academic staff if drug testing were a condition of their employment. Fourth, drug testing can contribute to truancy among pupils and requests for sick time among employees. Finally, some scholars and laypersons have questioned the ethics of drug testing (for example, Koski, 2004).

SUMMARY

In the mid-1980s, the drug-testing industry was estimated to generate US$2 billion annually (Hoffman and Silvers, 1987). Collectively, company profits grew by 10 per cent each year during the next decade, and to counter the growing testing enterprise, the 'detox industry' followed suit (Tunnell, 2004). Drug testing in schools and workplaces occurs primarily in the USA, where the strategy is consistent with that country's emphasis on abstinence and prohibition. In most other countries, the alleged benefits of drug testing in schools and workplaces have been reviewed more critically (for example, McWhirter, 2005) noting for example that better alternatives are available for dealing with drug use within these settings.

REFERENCES

Hoffman, A. and Silvers, J. (1987) *Steal this Urine test: Fighting Drug Hysteria in America.* New York: Penguin Books.

Koski, G. (2004) 'Drug testing research in high school students: is there a will or a way?', *American Journal of Bioethics*, 4 (1): 33–35.

McWhirter, J. (2005) 'Editorial: Just say "no" to drug testing in schools', *Health Education*, 105 (2): 85–88.

Pierce, A. (2007) 'Workplace drug testing outside the U.S.', in S.B. Karch (ed.), *Workplace Drug Testing.* Boca Raton, FL: CRC Press, Taylor & Francis. pp. 44–53.

Roche, A.M., Pidd, K., Bywood, P., Duraisingam, V., Steeson, T., Freeman, T. and Nicholas, R. (2008) *Drug Testing in Schools: Evidence, Impact and Alternatives.* Research Paper 16. Canberra: Australian National Council On Drugs.

Tunnell, K.D. (2004) *Pissing on Demand: Workplace Drug Testing and the Rise of the Detox Industry.* New York: New York University Press.

Walsh, J.M. (2008) 'New technology and new initiatives in US workplace testing', *Forensic Science International*, 174 (2–3): 120–14.

39

Drug Courts

Specialised courts which work with treatment providers to encourage drug-involved offenders to participate in drug treatment, and divert them from traditional criminal justice interventions such as prison.

Drug courts were developed in the USA in response to the rising numbers of drug-involved offenders in the criminal justice system. These specialised courts offer drug treatment to eligible offenders whose successful participation in treatment allows them to avoid certain legal sanctions. The underlying objective of drug courts is to recognise that conventional courts may not deal with drug offenders in the best way and that a more effective way to reduce drug use, and in turn, drug-related crime is through a system specifically designed deal with such issues. The first drug court was implemented in Dade County, Miami, Florida in 1989.

Huge increases in arrests for drug possession coupled with overcrowded jails and prisons contributed to the development of the drug court. Since then, their popularity has spread to various parts of the USA. As of January 2007, a total of 1662 drug courts had been established in the USA, including 431 juvenile drug courts (American University, 2007a). US drug courts operate within the federal, state and tribal judicial systems. Beginning in the late 1990s, drug courts expanded to other countries and now are offered to some extent in 10 countries worldwide. Some jurisdictions have adopted the US model of drug courts whereas others have implemented alternative forms of criminal justice-based treatment schemes (for example, the UK). The International Association of Drug Treatment Courts offers support and guidance to those jurisdictions which have an interest in developing drug courts.

The drug court model specifies that arrestees and offenders undergo assessment to identify eligibility and treatment needs. Eligibility criteria vary widely across jurisdictions. For instance, some courts accept only those individuals who have been arrested for minor offences. Others exclude potential clients who have a prior criminal record or whose current charges include violent offences.

Treatment clients are monitored (often through urine testing) once they are accepted into a treatment programme. Positive drug tests or rule violations can result in a failure to complete the programme. This outcome generally violates the court order so that individuals are then processed by conventional courts.

An important dimension of drug courts is the team of professionals who are actively involved in monitoring the treatment goals. Judges are key players and regularly attend meetings with the client, other criminal justice staff and drug treatment personnel. The length of treatment varies but usually lasts between one and five years.

Drug courts are organised at either pre- or post-conviction[9] stages. Pre-conviction drug courts are designed for arrestees who face criminal charges but who have not yet been convicted for a crime. By participating in a drug treatment programme, arrestees avoid entering a plea of guilty and do not proceed to trial. In other words, prosecution is deferred until the outcome of treatment is established. Charges are dismissed upon successful completion of the treatment programme. Post-conviction programmes are used for defendants who have pleaded or have been found guilty of a crime. In these circumstances, drug courts are used in lieu of a custodial sentence, for example, prison.

[9]Also referred to as pre- and post-adjudicatory stages.

KEY COMPONENTS OF DRUG COURTS

An expert group established by the United Nations Office on Drugs and Crime identified 12 'key principles' or key components that were deemed to be fundamental for good practice within drug courts. These principles draw on the importance of an integrated team approach involving both criminal justice and treatment personnel who manage and coordinate cases. This idea departs from the traditional approach to offenders in the criminal justice system. One key component acknowledges the importance of a continuum of care in the provision of drug treatment. Another component suggests the need for timely entry into treatment. Most US drug courts abide by at least some of the key principles, and federal funding for the courts is supposedly contingent on the degree to which the key components have been implemented.

EVALUATION OF DRUG COURTS

Evaluations of the effectiveness of drug courts tend to focus on three issues: completion rates, recidivism and subsequent drug use. In a study of 27 adult drug courts in the USA, completion rates ranged from 27 per cent to 66 per cent (GAO, 2005). Substantially lower completion rates (that is, less than 16 per cent) have been observed in parts of Canada, although Thomas (2008) argued that Canadian programmes appear to accept more offenders with histories of cocaine and heroin problems than do drug courts in the USA. Moreover, drug courts in Canada and Australia are more likely to offer substitute prescribing (for example, methadone maintenance) compared to courts in the USA. In Ireland, the number of drug participants over a 7-year period was substantially lower than anticipated. Moreover, 66% of individuals referred to the drug court failed to complete the programme (Department of Justice, Equality and Law Reform, 2010). An evaluation of Scottish drug courts found that the re-conviction rate as well as the frequency of subsequent convictions was roughly equivalent to a comparison group of offenders (Scottish Government Community Justice Services, 2009). Drug court administrators in the USA have noted higher completion rates among women offenders when child care and specialised services are offered in conjunction with drug treatment. These specialised services can focus on sexual abuse or violence, which disproportionately affect women (American University, 2007b). A small number of US drug courts cater specifically to women offenders.

In a review of 37 evaluations of US drug courts conducted between 1999 and 2001, Belenko (2001) found reductions in drug use and arrests during programme participation, however, none of the evaluations focused on clients' drug use after they had completed programmes. Belenko suggested that traditional diversion programmes may achieve similar outcomes to drug courts, but at lower cost. Several more recent evaluations have shown decreases in re-arrests or re-convictions that extend beyond programme completion.

Still, a number of drug court evaluations are limited in their methodological approach, resulting in misguided conclusions. The General Accounting Office

(2005) reviewed 117 evaluations of US adult drug courts. Each of the evaluations reported outcomes relating to recidivism, drug use, and completion rates. However, less than one-third of the evaluations ($N = 27$) were judged to be 'methodologically sound'. Some evaluations fail to compare drug court participants with control groups, that is, individuals who are eligible for the drug court treatment, similar to drug court participants in other ways (for example, age, gender, offence), but who do not participate in drug court treatment. Other evaluations use indicators of drug use that are methodologically weak, for example, drug use detected through urinalysis (see **38 drug testing in schools and workplaces**). Finally, although some evaluations have shown that drug courts can reduce recidivism, even over the long term (Weatherburn et al., 2008), it is more difficult to obtain data on individuals' drug use after they complete court-assigned treatment.

LIMITATIONS OF DRUG COURTS

Critical reviews of drug courts have focused on case processing, programme components and treatment. Several problems have been highlighted. First, some critics have argued that drug addiction should be addressed through public health rather than through the criminal justice system (National Association of Criminal Defense Lawyers, 2009). Second, the primary role of defense attorneys is to facilitate cases in the 'stated interests' of their clients. Drug courts often require defense attorneys to work with the opposition, that is, prosecutors, a requirement which might compromise this role (National Association of Criminal Defense Lawyers, 2009: 32). Third, officials in various countries (for example, the USA, Australia) have acknowledged that drug courts operate under the premise of coercion. Individual motivation is an important factor that often contributes to successful treatment outcomes, however, coercion does not necessarily contribute to individual motivation. Potential clients who do not opt for treatment are prosecuted or sentenced for criminal offences. Coercive techniques include pressure to engage with treatment, frequent urinalysis testing and subtle threats from legal sanctions.

A fourth limitation concerns the mismatch of client needs with appropriate treatment. Successful treatment outcomes depend in part on drug treatment that meets the needs and circumstances of individuals. Treatment options for drug court clients are often limited so that most or all clients are referred to a single treatment modality, regardless of individual circumstances. Fifth, although pre-adjudication drug courts are better suited to due process, post-adjudication courts have been criticised because the conviction remains even with successful treatment outcomes (National Association of Criminal Defense Lawyers, 2009). Sixth, although some jurisdictions require the involvement of certified treatment agencies, others rely on self-help groups, for example, Narcotics Anonymous, Alcoholics Anonymous. Moreover, unlike criminal justice treatment programmes in the UK, physicians are rarely involved in the treatment of offenders who are processed through drug courts in the USA. Finally, drug courts require frequent monitoring and court appearances which may adversely affect people from low-income backgrounds who must cover transport costs to/from proceedings (National Association of Criminal Defense Lawyers, 2009).

SUMMARY

Drug courts have the potential for benefiting drug-involved offenders, the criminal justice system as well as the wider community. Programme policies vary widely in terms of eligibility, stage at which they operate (pre- or post-conviction), and a host of other factors. Many courts follow the recommended key components, although in some jurisdictions these principles are not implemented appropriately. Diversion and the provision of drug treatment are important, yet drug courts are limited in several ways. Some evaluations suggest that drug court participants have lower rates of recidivism compared to controls, although it is sometimes difficult to determine which programme factors contribute to reduced recidivism. Considerably less is known about the long-term impact of drug courts on participants' drug use.

REFERENCES

American University (2007a) *Drug Court Activity Update. Bureau of Justice Assistance Drug Court Clearinghouse*. Washington, DC: American University.

American University (2007b) *Information Relevant to Female Participants in Drug Courts: Summary Overview. Bureau of Justice Assistance Drug Court Clearinghouse*. Washington, DC: American University.

Belenko, S. (2001) *Research on Drug Courts: A Critical Review, 2001 Update*. New York: National Center on Addiction and Substance Use, Columbia University.

Department of Justice, Equality and Law Reform (2010) *Review of the Drug Treatment Court*. Dublin: Author.

General Accounting Office (2005) *Adult Drug Courts: Evidence Indicates Recidivism Reductions and Mixed Results for Other Outcomes*. Washington, DC: United States Government Accountability Office.

National Association of Criminal Defense Lawyers (2009) *America's Problem-Solving Courts: The Criminal Costs of Treatment and the Case for Reform*. Washington, DC: National Association of Criminal Defense Lawyers.

Scottish Government Community Justice Services (2009) *Review of the Glasgow and Fife Drug Courts*. Edinburgh: Scottish Government Community Justice Services.

Thomas, G. (2008) 'A frank analysis of Canada's newest drug policy approach', *Canada's Journal of Ideas*, 3: 1–6.

Weatherburn, D., Jones, C., Snowball, L., and Hua, J. (2008) *The NSW Drug Court: A Re-evaluation of its Effectiveness. Crime and Justice Bulletin, Number 121*. Sydney: New South Wales Bureau of Crime Statistics and Research.

40

Decriminalisation, Legalisation and Legal Regulation

> *Decriminalisation, legalisation and legal regulation are alternative approaches to prohibition as the principal response to drug use.*

DRUG POLICY REFORM: THE PROHIBITION CONTEXT

Proponents of alternative approaches to drug use typically start from a position of opposition to the current status quo. Despite differences between the ways in which drug use is dealt with country to country, the current international drug control system, with its global conventions, international strategies, national laws and domestic policies is largely 'strict' prohibitionist and can be placed at the far end of a continuum of possible responses to drug use. Strict prohibitionists argue for the continued necessity of severe penalties (including imprisonment and capital punishment) on those who consume, possess, supply and produce substances deemed illicit. Anything less than the continuation of strict prohibition is represented as conceding ground to the 'evil' of drugs in the ongoing **37 war on drugs**. Prohibitionists argue that drug use is immoral; undermines the individual's potential to be a responsible and productive citizen; destroys families; exacerbates the risk of infection from blood-borne viruses; and increases criminal activity as drug addicts seek to fund their habits. Problematically, however, it is hard to identify causality in relation to prohibitionists' claims. Indeed, many argue that prohibition results in much of the damage that prohibitionists attribute to drugs per se. Most drug users do not use excessively, do not come to harm, nor do they become addicted; indeed in some countries for example, the UK, it has been argued that 'sensible recreational' drug use is closer to the norm.

In contrast to those who propose decriminalisation or legal regulation/legalisation, strict prohibitionists tend to argue for tougher penalties and more consistent application of punitive measures with a view to completely eliminating all illegal drug use from societies (excluding alcohol, tobacco, caffeine, prescription drugs and so on). Moderate prohibitionists in contrast acknowledge that the complete elimination of drugs from society is unobtainable. Instead they argue for stricter law enforcement on the supply (trafficker/dealer) side rather than demand (user) side of drug markets. Prohibitionists advocate the continued use of national and international criminal justice systems in tackling drug use. Calls for greater cooperation between European member states, particularly in terms of intelligence sharing about drug production and trafficking activities, is one example of prohibitionist tendencies in supranational efforts to eliminate the illegal drug trade. Critics of such positions point to the failure of prohibition to stop drug use so far. In contrast supporters of prohibition point to falls in the prevalence rates of certain drugs among young people in the USA and relatively stable or falling drug use rates among young people in the UK in recent years. Others highlight the paucity of evidence that drug laws, however configured, have much impact upon drug consumption patterns (Reuter and Stevens, 2007). Those arguing for drug policy reform tend to argue that prohibition entails little or no market regulation as illegal drug suppliers operate with near impunity; reformists see this as akin to the unregulated free drug markets advocated by libertarian proponents of decriminalisation, ostensibly the opposite end of the drug policy continuum (Transform Drug Policy Foundation, 2009).

DECRIMINALISATION: REDUCING THE ROLE OF THE STATE

Perhaps the most radical drug reform position taken is that of libertarian decriminalisation. Again starting from a critique of the current prohibitionist drug control system, those advocating this form of decriminalisation want laws prohibiting or even regulating the manufacture and distribution of current illegal drugs to be eliminated. 'Full' or libertarian decriminalisers want to contract rather than expand the role of the state in personal behaviour such as drug consumption (McBride et al., 1999). Perhaps the best known advocate of this position is the anti-psychiatry movement's founder, Thomas Szasz. Arguing from a classic liberal position of freedom from the state, Szasz (1992) maintains that the government has no legitimate authority to tell us what we can and cannot ingest. He calls for a return to the consumerist position of the 19th century, with 'illicit drugs' becoming just like other freely traded commodities across international markets (see also Trebach and Inciardi, 1993). Libertarian decriminalisers (alongside some harm reductionists) tend to frame (drug) consumers as intelligent, rational and educated individuals 'capable of exercising self-control and good citizenship without the paternalistic intrusiveness of government as overseer' (McBride et al., 1999: 37). Contrary to advocates of legal regulation/legalisation and harm reduction approaches, full decriminalisers do not envisage a greater role for the state in providing information on drugs and certainly do not advocate that governments should play a role in the distribution of legalised substances. Szasz (1992) for example maintains that drug education has primarily consisted of drug *mis*information enlisted to service the **war on drugs**. The state has a vested interest in shaping citizens' drug choices – legal or otherwise – and therefore cannot be trusted to deploy a rational, scientific basis in the event of illicit drug policy reform. Finally, libertarian decriminalisation may be the only way to stop the erosion of civil rights related to drug prohibition and user criminalisation, as the criminal justice system would concentrate on serious (including drug-related) violent crimes rather than personal behaviours.

There remain considerable limitations to this 'supermarket model'. Libertarian decriminalisers place considerable faith in capitalist free markets which have proved to have pernicious effects on individuals, families and societies, with critics arguing that markets are in need of *more* rather than *less* regulation. Governments remain responsible at least in part for the health and well-being of their citizens (in some countries such as the UK, Australia, Italy and Germany and many others publicly funded health systems still exist, for example). Further, those working with people 'addicted' to drugs and alcohol point to how the very nature of dependent use can limit supposed 'free choice'. With dependent use of often harmful substances concentrated in the poorest and most disadvantaged groups in society, libertarians have little to say about the likelihood that full decriminalisation would result in aggressive marketing of substances by private companies in a free market, particularly to potential (young) and existing (potentially 'addicted') customers.

DRUG REGULATION: INCREASING THE ROLE OF THE STATE

Between these two extremes of the continuum of possible responses to drug use (that is, strict prohibition and libertarian decriminalisation) sits legal regulation/ legalisation and forms of partial decriminalisation. The less radical position of partial decriminalisation, often centred on cannabis, has occurred in some European countries, including the Netherlands, the Czech Republic and Portugal. Examining the experience of Portugal, a European Union member state, is helpful here. In 2001, following the introduction of Law 30/2000, Portugal effectively ended the application of penal sanctions for the possession and acquisition of all illicit drugs for personal use, with 'personal' defined as being up to 10 days' supply. In this sense Portugal has partially decriminalised (but not legalised) illicit drugs; possession remains prohibited under Portuguese law and is dealt with as an administrative offence, with criminal sanctions remaining for drug growers, dealers and traffickers. Crucially in the case of Portugal, partial decriminalisation occurred in parallel with a greater emphasis on drug use as a public health issue. To this end, Commissions for the Dissuasion of Drug Addiction (Comissões para a Dissuasão da Toxicodependência [CDTs]) were established to deal with those referred by the police for drug possession. A range of responses are available to CDTs including community service and fines, both more traditionally considered to be tools of criminal justice systems. CDTs have been charged with persuading dependent drug users to enter treatment and dissuading new and non-dependent drug takers from continuing their use. Investments have been made in extending drug prevention and treatment, particularly school-based drugs education and greater support for heroin users whom the CDTs deal with disproportionately compared to their numbers in the general population. Lifetime prevalence rates of all drugs have decreased in Portugal since the reform despite an initial rise in cannabis and ecstasy use, thought to be linked to people being more likely to reveal their drug use in self-report surveys post-decriminalisation (Greenwald, 2009). Portugal has also experienced significant reductions in drug-related deaths and drug-related cases of HIV/AIDS, hepatitis C and hepatitis B, despite the large increases of users in treatment; a reduction in the number of prisoners sentenced for drug offences; and a subsequent reduction in prison overcrowding alongside an increase in charges for trafficking, possibly related to the Portuguese police refocusing their efforts on large-scale drug operations rather than small-scale street deals.

The key criticism of partial decriminalisation of personal possession is that it still operates within the much maligned prohibitionist framework. Most worryingly the production and distribution of potentially dangerous substances remains in the hands of criminals. In contrast supporters of legal regulation argue that the state is best placed to control production and regulate consumption of illicit drugs within a legal framework, much as it does with regards alcohol and tobacco. Legal regulation consists of various options that again sit between the two extremes of strict prohibition and libertarian decriminalisation. There are various overlapping models of legal regulation for drugs which are currently illegal, all of which already exist in the sense that medical, quasi-medical and non-medical psychoactive drugs are distributed in the ways described. These include drugs on medical prescription only; over-the-counter, lower-risk medical drugs distributed by pharmacies; licensed sales, such as alcohol sales in off-licences and supermarkets; licensed premises, such as restaurants, pubs, bars and clubs, with entry and sales subject to restriction based on age, time of day and levels of intoxication; and finally unlicensed sales of lowest risk substances, such as tea or coffee (Transform Drug Policy Foundation, 2009). Each of these models involve a varying degree of regulatory legislation that relevant agencies could oversee within a broader enforcement infrastructure, with penalties for distribution through non-legal channels such as selling drugs to those without prescriptions. Supporters of illicit drug regulation usually also call for increased government regulation of those substances which are already legal. This answers critics of legal regulation, who point to some governments' failures to control alcohol and tobacco consumption, particularly among minors (McBride et al., 1999).

Key issues remain regarding drug policy reform, not least the social, cultural, economic and political barriers to change. There remain vested interests in retaining the status quo with regards drug control, not least among the criminal networks that currently profit from the illegal drug trade. While some countries such as Portugal have decriminalised personal possession of illicit drugs, other countries, such as the UK, continue to criminalise possession of novel psychoactive substances such as ketamine, benzylpiperazine (BZP), cannabinoids ('spice'), gamma butyrolactone (GBL) and mephedrone ('M-cat'). Drug prohibition remains the framework within which nearly all governments and political parties work in liberal democratic countries around the world, owing partially to political elites' perception that drug prohibition is popular among citizens/voters. However, research across US metropolitan areas suggests that public support for spending on criminal justice approaches to drug use is waning, while support for spending on public health responses (such as prevention and treatment) remains robust (Lock et al., 2002). Processes of **41 liberalisation** have been documented in Europe and beyond, although it remains to be seen where exactly our future global drug control system will sit on the continuum of possible responses to drug use.

REFERENCES

Greenwald, G. (2009) *Drug Decriminalisation in Portugal: Lessons for Creating Fair and Successful Policies*. Washington, DC: Cato Institute.

Lock, E.D. and Timberlake, J.M. (2002) 'Battle fatigue: is public support waning for "war"-centered drug control strategies?' *Crime and Delinquency*, 48 (3): 380–98.

McBride, D.C., Terry, Y.M. and Inciardi, J.A. (1999) 'Alternative perspectives on the drug policy debate', in J.A. Inciardi (ed.), *The Drug Legalisation Debate*. London: Sage. pp. 9–54.

Reuter, P. and Stevens, A. (2007) *An Analysis of UK Drug Policy: A monograph prepared for the UK Drug Policy Commission*. London: UK Drug Policy Commission.

Szasz, T.S. (1992) *Our Right to Drugs: The Case for a Free Market*. New York: Praeger.

Transform Drug Policy Foundation (2009) *After the War on Drugs: Blueprint for Regulation*. Bristol: TDPF.

Trebach, A.S. and Inciardi, J.A. (1993) *Legalize it? Debating American Drug Policy*. Washington DC: American University Press.

41
Liberalisation

Liberalisation of drug policy involves the relaxation or the complete removal of restrictions (including legal sanctions) on the consumption, possession, production and supply of currently controlled drugs.

Classical liberalism maintains that individuals should be free to pursue their own self-interest and that individual rights (to free speech, for example) have primacy over collectives, such as the state. Advocates of liberalisation argue that the state does not have the political legitimacy to prevent competent adults from choosing to undertake certain activities, even if they are potentially harmful. It is not the state's role to 'interfere' in an individual's choice. Taking the pursuit of intoxication as an inalienable human 'right' is the basis for liberalisation arguments regarding drugs (Szasz, 1992). In relation to the international drug control system, supporters of liberalisation argue that the state is unreasonably criminalising people for individual acts about which it has no mandate to interfere, not least because in such matters the state tends towards an overly moralistic and reactionary approach, epitomised by the **37 war on drugs**.

Complete legalisation may be characterised as one form of liberalisation, involving the decriminalisation of most if not all activities related to illegal drugs, including consumption, possession, production and supply, and the creation of a 'free market' in intoxicating substances (Bean, 2010). Those advocating economic liberalisation or a 'free market' solution to the drug 'problem' argue that the desire for intoxicating substances is so great that prohibition (or even state regulation) is doomed to failure, as supply 'naturally' attempts to meet the demands of individuals. However, liberalisation usually involves more piecemeal, tentative drug policy changes to those advocated by 'free marketeers', such as a gradual move away from a prohibitionist position involving criminal sanctions for illegal drug possession (see **40 decriminalisation, legalisation and legal regulation**).

Cautious liberalisation of drug laws may entail the use of scientific evidence to rank substances in terms of relative harms and risks (from high to low) with lesser or no legal penalties attached to the possession of those deemed least harmful. Liberalisation within a harm reduction framework may lead to retaining the illegal status of drugs, but working to identify 'addicts' in order to legally prescribe them a controlled amount. This occurs in Switzerland. Elsewhere, notably in the UK, Australia and some parts of the USA, those dependent on heroin are typically treated via methadone maintenance programmes. This approach, tackling drug use within health rather than criminal frameworks, could be interpreted as drug policy liberalisation. It is problematic, however, to interpret potential coercion into such treatment programmes via the use of criminal sanctions as the 'liberalisation' of responses to 'problematic' drug use.

Opponents to liberalisation argue any move away from strict prohibition 'sends the wrong message' to current and potential users and hence that liberalisation would likely result in an increase in drug use. Yet repressive (illiberal) laws may exist in a social and cultural context in which drug use is 'normalised' (see also **14 normalisation**). This means that possession of small amounts of illegal drugs for personal use may rarely be dealt with by a country's criminal justice system. This is known as 'de facto decriminalisation', illustrated by the low risk of detection for most UK cannabis users (Pudney, 2010), different approaches towards cannabis possession between UK police forces and the discretion police officers have with regards to cannabis possession.

LIBERALISATION IN A GLOBAL CONTEXT

International drug policies remain within the dominant prohibitionist framework although there is some acknowledgment that liberalisation may be needed to reduce drug risks and harms, particularly from supporters of harm reduction and human rights approaches. It must be remembered that remaining in accordance with United Nations (UN) drug conventions precludes the complete liberalisation of signatory states' drug laws. Yet in Europe and beyond, nation states do vary considerably in their stance towards illicit drugs, with moves towards drug policy liberalisation often occurring 'under the radar'.

Changes in laws regarding the possession of cannabis provide an example of the subtle liberalisation of drug laws. In Australia, for example, while it is illegal to possess, grow or sell cannabis, penalties vary from state to state, Western Australia (WA) has a 'prohibition with civil penalties' policy towards the possession and cultivation of 25 grams or less of cannabis, enacted under the WA Cannabis Control Act 2003.

Those caught are given a formal caution and required to attend a drug re-education programme. Crucially, to ease this reform through WA parliament in the face of opposition from anti-drug campaigners, the policy was presented by state legislators as a merely a change in police enforcement practices rather than a liberalisation or 'softening' of drug laws (Lenton and Allsop, 2010).

The USA remains one of the staunchest supporters of drug prohibition, although many of the most vocal supporters of liberalisation, including Thomas Szasz (1992), live and work there. As in Australia, there are important differences between states in the USA in terms of their approach to possession of illicit substances, notably cannabis/marijuana. This is particularly relevant in relation to debates in the US regarding 'medicinal marijuana'. Despite cannabis/marijuana being a Schedule I drug in the USA at a federal level (the highest classification on a par with heroin), numerous states permit the registered use of the drug for 'medicinal purposes', although not for 'recreational purposes'. However in 2012, several US states moved to liberalise laws around possession of cannabis for personal use.

In other countries around the world there appear to be little or no signs of liberalisation emerging within their national borders. China, for example, has illiberal drug laws with sanctions including in some cases capital punishment (death penalty) for drug trafficking. Chinese drug addicts undergo enforced rehabilitation at police-run facilities or labour camps. Other countries including Iran, Indonesia, Saudi Arabia, Singapore, Malaysia, Thailand and United Arab Emirates remain fiercely anti-drugs, with severe criminal sanctions attached to all drug offences.

LIBERALISATION WITHIN THE EUROPEAN UNION

There is no wholly uniform drug policy across European Union (EU) member states, meaning that drug policy liberalisation may take a number of diverse forms, varying across time and place. Individual EU member states may be placed on a continuum of responses to illegal drugs, from the relatively liberal approaches of the Czech Republic and Portugal, to the illiberal approaches of Sweden. However, generalisations on the level of nation state disguise differences in terms of responses to different drugs, user groups such as minors and use contexts such as workplaces.

While EU member states differ in their approaches to illicit drug use, they are increasingly bound to principles of cross-border cooperation, coordination and intelligence sharing with respect to drug trafficking and organised crime (Chatwin, 2007). Any discussion regarding trends of liberalisation within Europe, evidenced by the Czech Republic's move in 2009 to decriminalise possession of up to 15 grams of cannabis and 1.5 grams of heroin, must be situated within the broader context of the EU Drugs Strategy 2005–2012 which supports prohibition.

When considering drug policy liberalisation in Europe, the counter-trend of pursuing ever more illiberal drug policies acts as a reminder that criminalisation of drug use and drug users remains the norm. Although a member of the EU, Sweden's drug policies differ to other member states. Sweden disrupted the embryonic trend towards drug policy liberalisation within the EU when it joined in 1995. As youth and drug counter-cultures emerged in Sweden in the late 1970s, the country moved away from its previously moderately liberal drug regime. By 1980 every incidence of possession of any illegal drugs (including cannabis) was brought before a Swedish court of law. Almost all forms of involvement with drugs are prohibited via the Narcotic Drugs Criminal Act, which includes possession for personal use, supply and manufacture. Drug consumption (the act of adding a drug to the human body) has been prohibited since 1988 and the Swedish police are authorised to conduct urine or blood tests on people suspected of using illegal substances. The Swedish authorities publically pursue the goal of a 'drug-free Sweden' and frame illicit drugs and their users as a negative outside threat which is contrary to good Swedish identity and citizenship (Tham, 1995). All drug *use* is viewed as *abuse*, with no room for social-recreational and/or experimental use among Swedish young adults.

In sum, liberalisation entails a move away from the prohibition of those intoxicating substances currently controlled by national and international laws, although such moves rarely if ever involve the complete legalisation of drugs. Instead, contemporary liberalisation trends have seen the partial reduction in criminal sanctions against drug users and the implementation of policies that frame drug use as a problem to be dealt with by public health professionals rather than law enforcement officials.

REFERENCES

Bean, P. (2010) *Legalising Drugs: Debates and Dilemmas*. Bristol: Policy Press.

Chatwin, C. (2007) 'Multi-level governance: the way forward for European illicit drug policy', *International Journal of Drug Policy*, 18 (6): 494–502.

Lenton, S. and Allsop, S. (2010) 'A tale of CIN – the cannabis infringement notice scheme in Western Australia', *Addiction*, 105 (5): 808–16.

Pudney, S. (2010) 'Drugs policy: what should we do about cannabis?', *Economic Policy*, 25 (61): 165–211.

Szasz, T. (1992) *Our Right to Drugs: The Case for a Free Market*. New York: Praeger.

Tham, T. (1995) 'Drug control as a national project: the case of Sweden', *Journal of Drug Issues*, 25 (1): 113–28.

41 liberalisation